Digitalization and Control of Industrial Cyber-Physical Systems

SCIENCES

Computer Science, Field Directors –
Valérie Berthé and Jean-Charles Pomerol

Information Systems, Subject Heads – Florence Sèdes,
Camille Rosenthal-Sabroux and Damien Trentesaux

Digitalization and Control of Industrial Cyber-Physical Systems

Concepts, Technologies and Applications

Coordinated by
Olivier Cardin
William Derigent
Damien Trentesaux

WILEY

First published 2022 in Great Britain and the United States by ISTE Ltd and John Wiley & Sons, Inc.

ISTE Ltd
27-37 St George's Road
London SW19 4EU
UK

www.iste.co.uk

John Wiley & Sons, Inc.
111 River Street
Hoboken, NJ 07030
USA

www.wiley.com

Library of Congress Control Number: 2022931036

British Library Cataloguing-in-Publication Data
A CIP record for this book is available from the British Library
ISBN 978-1-78945-085-9

ERC code:
PE6 Computer Science and Informatics
  PE6_2 Computer systems, parallel/distributed systems, sensor networks, embedded systems, cyber-physical systems
  PE6_9 Human computer interaction and interface, visualisation and natural language processing

Contents

Chapter 8. Holonic Control Architectures.   135

Olivier CARDIN, William DERIGENT and Damien TRENTESAUX

Part 5. Learning and Interacting with Industrial Cyber-Physical Systems   149

Chapter 9. Big Data Analytics and Machine Learning for Industrial Cyber-Physical Systems.   151

Yasamin ESLAMI, Mario LEZOCHE and Philippe THOMAS

Chapter 10. Human–Industrial Cyber-Physical System Integration: Design and Evaluation Methods.   171

Marie-Pierre PACAUX-LEMOINE and Frank FLEMISCH

Part 6. Transforming Industries with Industrial Cyber-Physical Systems . . . .

Chapter 11. Impact of Industrial Cyber-Physical Systems on Reconfigurable Manufacturing Systems . . . .

Catherine DA CUNHA and Nathalie KLEMENT

Chapter 12. Impact of Industrial Cyber-Physical Systems on Global and Interconnected Logistics . . . .

Shenle PAN, Mariam LAFKIHI and Eric BALLOT

Chapter 13. Impact of Industrial Cyber-Physical Systems on Transportation 225

John MBULI and Damien TRENTESAUX

Chapter 14. Impacts of Industrial Cyber-Physical Systems on the Building Trades 243

William DERIGENT and Laurent JOBLOT

Conclusion . . . .

William DERIGENT, Olivier CARDIN and Damien TRENTESAUX

Foreword

André THOMAS

Retired

History has shown that the development of knowledge and science is not at all linear. These last decades have seen many scientists questioning ideas that are accepted by all (as Galileo had already done). Some physicists (including a Nobel Prize winner[1]) have questioned the principle of what the universe is, taxing it with a "phantasmagoria of spiritual essence". But how does it matter? What we must remember is that, on the path of our evolution, there are always milestones, high points either marked by resounding breakthrough innovations such as the birth of certain major theories, or by works of synthesis based on analyses and long-standing work. This book, which introduces our industrial future, falls, I think, into this category. However, we are not at the end of the road; ICPS (industrial cyber-physical systems) – since that is what we are talking about here – will have to be integrated into an alternative and symbiotic economy (in the sense of Delannoy[2]), where living beings, natural elements, and communicating and smart devices will live in harmony and, moreover, they will still be, I am convinced, called into question and redesigned when our community has assimilated all of the fundamentals of modern physics and its applications more fully.

It is commonly accepted that in order to project oneself into the future, it is necessary, on the one hand, to rely on and understand one's **past** and its evolution, and on the other hand, to adopt **innovative** approaches that leave room for evolution and breakthroughs. Let us quickly outline their main features.

---

1. Discovery by R. Penrose.
2. Delannoy, I. (2017). *L'économie symbiotique*. Editions Actes Sud Nature, Arles.

Digitalization and Control of Industrial Cyber-Physical Systems,
coordinated by Olivier CARDIN, William DERIGENT and Damien TRENTESAUX.
© ISTE Ltd 2022.

The past: after more than a century of industry, we went from intelligence in the head and hands of the craftsman to (to caricature) intelligence in the head in offices and the specialized hands of operators, then finally to the intelligence in the head in computers and the hands of human beings and cyber-physical objects (robots, cobots, etc.) for the same objective of providing customers with quality products at controlled costs and deadlines. The idea was and remains good, but its first implementation in huge industries "crowded with players" was less so. The big change came in the 1980s after the discovery that finally, and no matter what was done, problems appeared all along the flow of components and products, so it was necessary to "follow" it more closely in order to make decisions and thus bring intelligence to it. The first solution was obviously the human being as an actor of this decentralized intelligence. If we only look at the future of our industries (and not life in general), we can see that many attempts have been made to develop functional specifications for such systems. What are we trying to do in the end? What is the ideal functioning of a company? Let us go back to the question posed by Goldratt and Cox[3] in the mid-1980s, "What is the purpose of a company?" The answer was "to make money from the sales resulting from its activity". There are two obvious ways to achieve this goal: to maximize the financial income generated by sales, on the one hand, and to limit to the maximum necessary expenses, on the other hand. Thus, limiting what others have called "waste". The search for these wastes and their origins has led us to highlight the importance of "control of physical flows and the activities inherent in them", in particular by relying on Plossl's demonstration of the impact[4] of the desynchronization of these physical flows with the flows of information necessary for their control. Moreover, the experience also validated the proposals initially made by the creators of our decision support systems (Orlicky, Plossl), namely that the management and steering of a factory or a supply chain must be performed with several levels of horizon and granularity to ensure good anticipation and good decisions. Thus, hierarchical systems (the only ones that could be implemented in the 1960s) were born, followed by increasingly heterarchical and distributed systems (as soon as technology and IT made it possible to implement them). As a result, it was first a human being who constituted the vector of intelligence in physical systems and, little by little, mechatronic systems helped to do so, and even supplanted the human being. Today, technology, software robots, physical robots, AGVs[5] and sensors are becoming increasingly numerous and covering more and more functionalities, so that we are thinking about how not to exclude humans from these systems! The experience of

---

3. Goldratt, E. and Cox, J. (1984). *Le but*. AFNOR Gestion, Paris.

4. Plossl, G.W. (1993). *Les nouvelles donnes de la gestion de production*. AFNOR Gestion, Paris.

5. Automatic guided vehicle.

the 1980s with the CIM[6] was "unfortunate" and yet many so-called visionaries of that time assured that the future would be made of factories without humans. There have been such factories – I myself have had the opportunity to visit them – but they quickly showed their limits! As always in these cases of extreme "rationalization", these solutions have proven themselves only in a stabilized and "ideal" mode of operation; any malfunction or any "degraded mode" induced big problems and additional costs, which finally killed the dream. Today, we are asking ourselves many more questions about the future of human actors in these new "cyber-x societies and industries": what will be their roles, what are the underlying ethical problems (even if, to date, the existing studies on these subjects are limited, or rather only refer to our "Western way of thinking").

There are **two paths to innovation**: *evolutionary innovation*, a more or less coherent extension of the path taken from the past to the present, and *disruptive innovation*, which must certainly be based on the weaknesses and shortcomings of existing solutions, but which starts from scratch to propose new "functionally reasonable" approaches and tools.

People who invent by means of a technological or conceptual leap in a field unknown to them are rare. During all of these years of transition, computer science was still poorly known; so, it was the evolution and especially the speed of evolution of computer systems that regulated the development of solutions for the "modernization" of life and industries in particular. The innovations of automatic and computer systems in the industry have followed those of electronic technologies and algorithms, and it is often step by step and by "trial and error" that these innovations have seen the light of day (let us keep in mind, for example, the case of the Minitel).

However, some innovations have been very significant and have allowed considerable "leaps forward". Let us mention, of course, the Internet (who remembers today what TRANSPAC was?). Let us also mention the RFID type systems[7] and especially their miniaturization. Note that these two examples of innovation are related to the field of communication. Making more use of "field

---

6. Koren, Y. (1983). *Computer Control of Manufacturing Systems*. McGraw Hill, Inc., New York; Waldner, J.-B. (1990). *CIM, les nouvelles perspectives de la production*. DUNOD-BORDAS, Paris; Dorf, R.C. and Kusiak, A. (1994). *Handbook of Design, Manufacturing, and Automation*. Wiley-Interscience, New York; Vernadat, F. (1996). *Enterprise Modeling and Integration*. Chapman and Hall, London.

7. Radio-frequency identification; Stockman, H. (1948). Communication by means of reflected power. *Proc. IRE*, 36(10); Hunt, V.D., Puglia, A., Puglia, M. (2007). *RFID – A Guide to Radio Frequency Identification*. John Wiley & Sons, New York.

data", distributing intelligence as close as possible to where it is useful (in time and space) can only be envisaged by new generation communication systems, wireless of course, in real time and with high data rates.

Sophisticated methods have therefore emerged and been developed to help and support these innovation processes. The most important ones in the last decades have undoubtedly been the approaches of "value management" and "systems engineering".

This book shows the evolution, describes the point of view of researchers and finally "sets the scene" for the current ICPS, without focusing on the inherent technology and its developments. It shows us the future of our industries and the various innovations that have been, are being and will be made in the near future. It first introduces us to the concept of cyber-physical systems from a historical perspective on the evolution of our society and industries. The question to be debated is why does our society need it? Various answers come to mind, such as the increase in the speed of execution of the activities and the necessary decision-making, or the increase in the dimension of the systems, as well as their complexity, or the increase in the globalization of the problems, etc.; and finally the will to leave human beings as important actors; then, to describe this crucial field that is the data; how to capture and distribute "field information". Indeed, without recent and relevant data, no analysis, measurement, modeling or decision can be envisaged. It will then deal with the evolution of "smart products", the digitalization of information and these systems. Then, the equally crucial problem of their piloting, control and interaction (or integration) with humans. The very essence of intelligence shared with the part relating to their learning; the current artificial intelligence solutions are based on two pillars, which are learning and algorithms. Their potential contributions to our companies and logistic systems, as well as their probable future and evolutions will also be looked at. The last parts of this book deal with the consequences and impacts of such systems on the industry, as well as the ethical and legal issues and aspects related to ICPS. This book is structured into chapters and sections, which are described in Chapter 1.

Thus, this book coordinated by O. Cardin, W. Derigent and D. Trentesaux comes at the right time and, based on the results of a think tank that began its work several decades ago, it offers us an informed look at these systems (ICPS) that have already left their mark and will continue to do so in the years to come.

January 2022

Introduction

Olivier CARDIN[1], William DERIGENT[2] and Damien TRENTESAUX[3]

[1] *LS2N UMR CNRS 6004, Nantes University, IUT de Nantes, France*
[2] *CRAN CNRS UMR 7039, University of Lorraine, Nancy, France*
[3] *LAMIH UMR CNRS 8201, Université Polytechnique Hauts-de-France, Valenciennes, France*

Due to their characteristics of adaptability and robustness, cyber-physical systems (CPS) are becoming increasingly important as a future path for industrial evolution and are gaining more and more credibility, both with academics and industry. However, it must be noted that at present, this concept is often misunderstood, misinterpreted or applied too restrictively. The purpose of this book is to clarify, in an educational manner, the gray areas that may surround this concept and provide the main keys to understanding and illustrating it to readers who wish to deepen their knowledge in the field. Six major reasons can be described to explain this lack of understanding – reasons that will structure the reading of this book.

The first reason for which this book attempts to provide keys to understanding can be summed up in a problem of terminology, which is as vast as the notion itself. In this book, we have chosen to speak of *industrial cyber-physical systems* (ICPS) when referring to the application of CPS in the industrial domain, in order to simplify the reading. Throughout this book, new terminologies (CPES, CPLS, CPPS, etc.), which allow us to specify the field of application within the industrial field, appear from time to time, in order to provide the reader with the broadest possible vision of the concepts handled by each field of activity. However, we only mention very little about the other classic names (among which, Industry 4.0 or

Industry of the Future are probably the most emblematic) that often represent a more global objective, which is less focused on the applicative notion proposed by the ICPS.

The second reason is probably the disruptive nature of this concept, which profoundly changes the way industrial systems should be perceived. Chapter 1 therefore begins with a clear definition of the concept, which serves as the basis for all of the following developments. In particular, we insist on the boundaries between the physical and cyber worlds, which crystallize the differences between classical systems and ICPS. This new point of view is accompanied by renewed objectives and constraints, truly moving towards a pragmatic and efficient sustainable development that Chapter 2 takes the time to explain in detail.

The third reason is probably that this concept is taking full advantage of the new technologies appearing on the market, which allow it to be implemented effectively in the field. These new technologies are bringing about a number of breaks in the way industrial systems are designed:

– in terms of information flows between different decision-makers in the system (Chapter 3), and throughout the lifecycle of the industrial product (Chapter 4);

– in terms of the virtualization of the system's elements and its information system (Chapter 5), with all of the associated cybersecurity issues (Chapter 6);

– in terms of the autonomy of decision left to the control systems, via multi-agent systems (Chapter 7), which support control architectures that enable the adaptability sought within the ICPS (Chapter 8);

– in terms of decision-making, notably through the integration of artificial intelligence tools in the decision loops (Chapter 9).

In addition to technology, the human factor, which is essential to this type of vision, also participates in industrial evolution, taking over the place where its characteristics are most effective. Chapter 10 presents an often forgotten point of view of industrial transformation, which will allow operators to better distribute the skills and responsibilities within their industrial apparatus.

The fourth reason often lies in the difficulty of projecting these concepts onto our own field of activity, and thus projecting the evolutionary trajectory to follow in order to transform our own system. In its first parts, this book has been deliberately written to be as generic as possible, in order to speak to as many people as possible. In a second step, Chapters 11 to 15 highlight some of the business sectors in which the application of ICPS has already or will soon propose major evolutions. The purpose of these chapters is to allow students to discover these different fields of application and understand their specificities, as well as their similarities. They are entry points to these fields of application of ICPS, providing the keys to understanding the ins and outs and illustrating the potential gains with concrete examples.

The fifth reason is usually self-censorship due to a lack of knowledge about the ethical or liability issues involved in using such disruptive concepts. Chapter 16 aims to present a multidisciplinary reflection on the direction of work on these two aspects. This chapter will be of particular interest in the context of direct application in industry, by showing the range of ethical and regulatory facets that need to be addressed.

The final reason that is generally identified concerns the training of staff. Implementing an ICPS generally requires a wide range of skills, usually multidisciplinary. At present, it is not only very difficult to recruit staff with this profile, but it is also true that new graduates very rarely have the required range of skills. Chapter 17 provides feedback and a set of best practices for the creation of training courses, both at bachelor and master levels.

In order to enrich and renew the reading of this work, we invite readers to consult the website of this work:

                    https://industrial-cps.net

Readers will have access to additional information on each of the chapters and will be able to contribute to their enrichment in a community.

A large majority of the chapters in this book represent the culmination of more than 10 years of study by the IMS[2] (Intelligent Manufacturing Systems and Services) working group of the CNRS French Research Group MACS (*Modélisation, Analyse et Commande des Systèmes Dynamiques*). Since 2018, the group's response to these issues has also materialized in the organization of an annual winter school, which has gradually gained an international following. As an extension of this training, it seemed appropriate to propose, to PhD and master students, a reference book focused on the application of CPS to the industrial world. By extension, this book will also prove invaluable for engineers who wish to deepen their proficiency of the concept in order to determine the best implementation on their case of application, for experienced researchers who seek to broaden their field of expertise by opening up to this new field of application, or for training managers who seek to expand their training offer on the theme of industrial evolution. Whether you fall into one of these categories, or have simply opened this book out of scientific curiosity, we hope that you will find it both enjoyable and instructive.

PART 1

Conceptualizing Industrial Cyber-Physical Systems

1

General Concepts

Olivier Cardin[1] and Damien Trentesaux[2]

[1] *LS2N UMR CNRS 6004, Nantes University, IUT de Nantes, France*
[2] *LAMIH UMR CNRS 8201, Université Polytechnique Hauts-de-France,*
Valenciennes, France

1.1. Industry at the heart of society

Based on the many concepts resulting from the development of new information and communication technologies (networks, artificial intelligence, etc.), a new model of society is taking shape for the years to come. In this model, all areas of daily life are impacted, through vectors such as housing, transport, energy supply and the work world. The relevance of implementing these technologies is obviously at the heart of the concerns of many research themes, discernible through concepts such as BIM (building information modeling), the autonomous vehicle and smart grids, for example.

Nevertheless, it is crucial to note that it will indeed be the interconnection between these technologies that will enable a smooth implementation in society. Lau *et al.* (2019), for example, propose an analysis of the relevance of data fusion for 21 application domains (illustrated in Figure 1.1). The generalization of the term "smart" to all of these domains reflects the desire to move towards less siloed management, more cooperative and with decision-making mechanisms that may be more complex, particularly due to the volume and diversity of information it processes.

For a color version of all figures in this book, see www.iste.co.uk/cardin/digitalization.zip.

Digitalization and Control of Industrial Cyber-Physical Systems,
coordinated by Olivier Cardin, William Derigent and Damien Trentesaux.
© ISTE Ltd 2022.

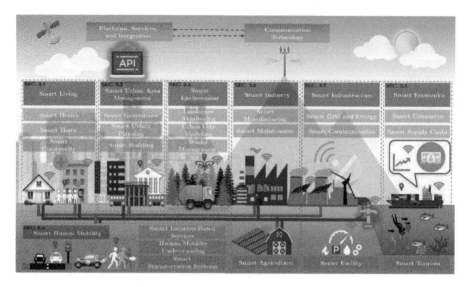

Figure 1.1. *Interconnection of smart concepts (Lau* et al. *2019)*

At the heart of these concerns, industry holds a central role due to its impact on both everyday life and the implementation of most of the other application domains (Mazali 2018). As such, the issues related to the industry of the future (Cardin *et al.* 2017) and its evolution (or revolution) are fundamental, and the study of new concepts related to the evolution of industrial systems brings its share of perspectives, hopes, questionings and even concerns that it is imperative to raise.

1.2. Industrial world in search of a new model

Industrial organizations have been in constant evolution for several centuries, and are regularly undergoing profound upheavals, linked as much to technological perspectives as to societal implications. As such, the reading grid of these organizations must be established in light of the major technological evolutions of the different eras and the important societal ruptures at the global level.

If the first model considered refers to the beginning of the 19th century, the industrial organization was still in its infancy. The flow was totally driven by the customer's order, with a strong customization of the products offered. The major lever of added value was then the competence of the various craftspeople who marked out the still stammering logistic chain. Thus, in the production phase, these craftsmen were specialists in the products manufactured, and were able to intervene in the entire manufacturing cycle of an instance. The flexibility of this type of organization was therefore very important, because we are talking about almost unique products, which depended heavily on the know-how of the workforce. Productivity was relatively low, as little mechanical assistance was offered to the craftspeople, so the target market was not very large around the production site, which implied a very factory-centered industrial system and very rudimentary logistics. Water- and steam-powered machines were developed to assist the workers. As the production capacity increased, the business also grew from individual owners looking after their own needs to organizations with owners, managers and employees serving customers.

At the beginning of the 20th century, electricity and mechanization were introduced in a major way to production sites. As a result of higher investment costs, the target market expanded and the productivity required for profitability increased. The flow then shifted to a push model, favorable to the management of large batches of identical products (see the famous quote from H. Ford in 1909, talking about the Model T: *Any customer can have a car painted any colour that he wants, so long as it is black*). The major lever of added value was then focused on volume, to the detriment of variety. The industrial organization therefore adapted to the massive standardization of products by deploying larger logistic structures and specialized workstations for each production operator. The impact of the world wars on the population and the world economy made this model last for almost half a century, enabling the reconstruction and massive reindustrialization of a world in difficulty. As technology improved, markets expanded to include the entire world and industrial organizations were able to handle the associated volumes.

It was only after this reconstruction that a different model was born. Due to the increasingly varied demands of consumers, and therefore the greater variety of products to be supplied, industrial organizations had to evolve towards a less unbalanced compromise between productivity and flexibility, with mass customization being the lever most frequently used. At the same time, the energy crises highlighted the need to rationalize the use of energy resources, which had been little considered until then. For half a century, organizations have gradually moved towards a modular design of the industrial tool, making it possible to ensure the continuity of supply and production of increasingly complex and changing products. The appearance of the industrial programmable logic controller, and its ability to perform different tasks according to the parameters associated with it, is a strong technological vector of implementing these systems on the production aspect. The human factor has also evolved, and its versatility has been put to good use in order to best support the flexibility of the new processes. Production and the associated organization were increasingly refocused on increased regionalization, driven by the marketing objective of reducing the time between order and delivery, while seeking to reduce costs and increase the efficiency of systems. It was at this time that the lean manufacturing tools popularized by Toyota became widespread.

The aim of this book is to deal with the evolution observed since the beginning of the 21st century or so. A new industrial model is once again taking shape, but this time it cannot be described solely through the prism of industrial organization. Indeed, one of the catalysts of this evolution, the development of new computing, information and communication capacities, is spreading to many other sectors such as transport and health. The interconnection demanded by these other sectors with industry brings new requirements, which are added to the purely industrial objectives: complete control of the impact on its environment (energy, waste, pollutants, greenhouse gases, etc.), relocation of activity and creation of short circuits, resilience of activity, working conditions, to name only the most emblematic. The common factor in the parallel development of all these initiatives is that of an ever-increasing convergence and integration of the informational and physical worlds, which makes the previously clear boundaries between these two worlds increasingly blurred: digital technology is "burrowing" into matter, everything is becoming communicative, consuming and generating data; physical systems that previously ignored each other are now becoming smart, interconnecting and interacting with or without human control, whether they are mobile or immobile. This fundamental trend is irreversible; this latest revolution is that of "cyber-physical systems".

1.3. Cyber-physical systems

The first definition of cyber-physical systems (CPS) can be found in 2006 (Lee 2006), at a workshop with the American National Science Foundation (NSF). The extension of cybernetics to CPS has been explicitly discussed in the literature since 2006–2007 and is growing in popularity. Throughout their development, increasingly synthetic definitions have been proposed, such as those of Rajkumar *et al.* (2010), Baheti and Gill (2011) and Schuh *et al.* (2014), which define CPS as *"cooperative systems, having decentralized control, resulting from the fusion between the real and virtual world, having autonomous and context-dependent behaviors in which they are located, being able to constitute themselves into systems of systems with other CPSs and conducting deep collaboration with humans"*. As for the definition by Monostori (2014), he proposed a clear synthesis of the different aspects of this broad concept, highlighting the strong connectivity of CPS and relegating the human to the rank of one of the elements of this environment: *"CPSs are systems of collaborative informational entities that are intensively connected to the surrounding physical world and its ongoing processes, providing and using, at the same time, data access, and data processing services available on the internet"*. To achieve this, the software embedded in CPS uses sensors and actuators, connect with each other and with human operators by communicating via interfaces, and has the capacity to store and process data from the sensors or the network (Strang and Anderl 2014). This interconnection of systems, as stated by Gengarle *et al.* (2013), stems from the fact that a CPS encompasses control, computational as well as communication devices (Klimeš 2014).

The model proposed by Putnik *et al.* (2019) focuses on the control function commonly implemented by CPS. In particular, it makes it possible to specify and clearly illustrate the real paradigm shift proposed by the concept of CPS. Whatever the system considered (see Figure 1.2a), classical control systems enable (generally in a closed loop) the system to reach the desired performance indicators by absorbing disturbances from the external environment. A basic CPS (see Figure 1.2b) uses its cyber part to evaluate and eventually evolve the control system, notably through simulation techniques. It is this evaluation loop, ideally carried out in real time and automatically, that differentiates a CPS from a conventional system.

It should be noted that, contrary to what the term CPS might imply, the cyber/physical decoupling does not simply oppose the digital to the physical. Indeed, within the physical part, a set of digital tools allows for the control of physical elements in real time. This control system could, for example, materialize in a position control loop of a drone, a thermal regulation of a building, an industrial program automaton of assembly lines, a couple (human, cobot) carrying out an assembly or even a remote surgical operation on a distant patient. It is the integration of a cyber part to these loops that defines a CPS in an original way.

The concept of CPS is thus very broad and encompasses an extremely wide class of systems and potential application areas. As a result, many research areas are also affected by this notion. This is probably a huge opportunity, as it gives the possibility to create a coherent ecosystem in many application domains: from autonomous vehicles (Fink *et al.* 2012) to healthcare devices (Santos *et al.* 2015), from power grid management (Al-Hammouri 2012) to HVAC control of buildings (Wang *et al.* 2011).

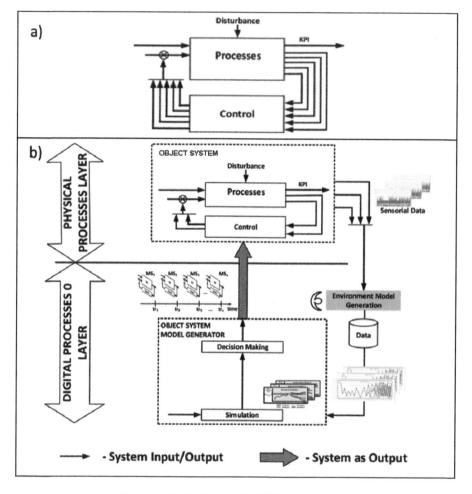

Figure 1.2. *Modeling of a CPS proposed by Putnik* et al. *(2019). a) conventional system, b) level 0 CPS*

1.4. From cyber-physical systems to industrial cyber-physical systems

The industrial sector has naturally taken an interest in this concept. The development of industrial CPS (ICPS – industrial cyber-physical systems) should contribute to the expected transformation of the industry. Returning to the definition of the potential application domains of CPS from Lau *et al.* (2019), illustrated in Figure 1.1, ICPS aim to offer developments in the fields of production (smart manufacturing), maintenance (smart maintenance) and the associated supply chain (smart supply chain).

Building on the definitions proposed by Monostori (2014) and Cardin (2019), we can generalize the definition of CPS and CPPS (cyber-physical production systems) by defining an ICPS as:

> Industrial cyber-physical systems (ICPS) consist of physical elements with their control systems, offering and consuming services along a value chain, integrated with digital systems with means of analysis and online reconfiguration of these elements. These elements have various degrees of autonomy, connect and cooperate with each other and with humans according to the situation, via information systems, in order to improve actions and decision-making processes in real time, react to unforeseen conditions and facilitate the integration of industrial system changes over time.

It is important to note that in this definition, humans are present (in the literature, we speak of cyber-physical and human system to explicitly refer to the presence of humans; see, for example, the eponymous IFAC workshop series). Depending on their involvement in the control function assigned to the ICPS, they may appear either in the physical part or in the cyber part, or both. Figure 1.3 presents a relatively generic modeling of such an ICPS, inspired by the representation by Putnik *et al.* (2019). In this representation, the physical part and the cyber part are clearly decoupled, and their functionalities and objectives largely differentiated: real-time control of the activity on the one side (physical part) and dynamic evaluation of the system's relevance on the other side (cyber part). The action lever of this cyber part is more extensive on an industrial system than it can be on a classical CPS. Indeed, a reconfiguration decided by the cyber part can be proposed to both the control system (e.g. dynamic reconfiguration of a multi-agent control architecture (Barbosa *et al.* 2015)) or the physical elements (see, for example, the works on system reconfigurability (Beauville dit Eynaud *et al.* 2019)).

Within the physical part, the main focus is obviously at the level of the elements that must be controlled in fine. At the same time, these elements contain assets (machines, transport, etc.), products (manufacturers, drugs, building materials, etc.) and human beings (operator, user, etc.) considered, at this level, as contributing elements to the operational management of the physical part. These operators have different roles and impacts on the physical part according to the type of application, sometimes performing activities within the system, making decisions or even generating disturbances or, on the contrary, preserving the situation or the safety of the ICPS. From these elements, data are sent to a control system through sensors or computer inputs, for example. This control system sends a set of decisions to the physical elements in order to reach the desired objectives for the ICPS. An interaction with human supervisors is generally established. Through this interaction, and based on various performance indicators observed on the physical elements, a supervisor can impose or modify decisions through the control system.

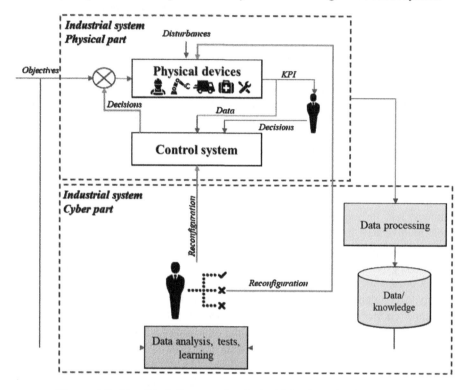

Figure 1.3. *Simplified diagram of an industrial cyber-physical system*

From this physical part, a set of data goes up to the cyber part. After processing, generally corresponding to a knowledge extraction, the data and/or knowledge are made available to an analysis process, which can generally involve human expertise. The purpose of this analysis process is to assess whether the control or configuration, both physical and digital, of the physical part is adequate for the situation encountered. If this is not the case, a decision to reconfigure all or part of the physical part (physical elements or control system) can be transmitted.

Figure 1.4 positions this same representation of an ICPS in a collaborative environment, where several ICPS are connected to meet different local or global objectives. This case is very common in the case of a complex and sectorized organization (e.g. drug distribution in a hospital), or an organization where several actors collaborate without disseminating all of their information (e.g. different competing suppliers within a supply chain). In this case, the composition of all of the ICPS can be considered as the physical part of a global ICPS, to which a global cyber part is then attached, making it possible for the configuration of the lower-level ICPS to be evaluated and evolved in real time. Obviously, it is possible to create several hierarchical levels within the ICPS in order to adapt to the complexity of the system of interest.

1.5. Perspectives on the study of industrial cyber-physical systems

In order to study the design and transformations induced by ICPS, several perspectives must be studied simultaneously. Figure 1.5 illustrates these different perspectives of the study on the simplified representation of an ICPS. All of these perspectives are correlated with the development of new technological means that allow for the evolution of uses described in this work, the comments made thus dealing with ICPS from a "digitalization" and "control" angle which are more related to the design of ICPS "architectures". The technological developments themselves (electronics, embedded systems, robotics, artificial intelligence, etc.) are, however, outside the scope of this book. The notion of control as used here covers functions ranging from the control of physical elements within the physical part to reconfiguration decisions taken in the cyber part. Digitalization corresponds to the mechanisms and technologies implemented for the creation of this cyber part, the feedback of data coming from the physical part from sensors, the processing of the associated knowledge, and the transformation of decisions and information transmitted to the actuators at the interface with the physical elements.

The first perspective of study concerns the problem of capturing and distributing information within ICPS. Indeed, new technologies such as the Industrial Internet of Things (IIoT) allow for an actual physical distribution of information and some computing resources at the heart of industrial systems. Thus, not only industrial means (machines, handling, etc.) can actively participate in the global decision-making of ICPS, but also the processed products themselves. From this idea, the concept of Intelligent Products was born in the early 2000s (Kärkkäinen *et al.* 2003), which has been one of the catalysts of the current systems transformation. Part 2 of this book aims to present these developments in detail and show how these concepts form the basis for the design of today's ICPS, with the concept of the intelligent product being without doubt the starting point, or even the precursor, of the ICPS.

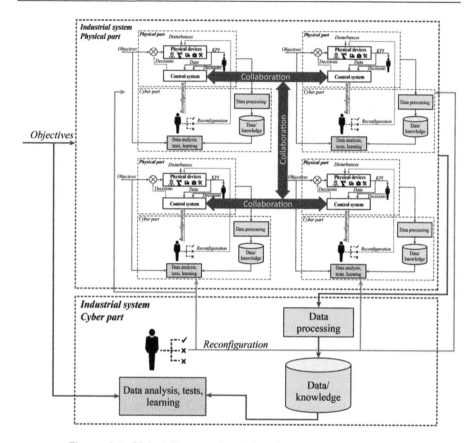

Figure 1.4. *Global diagram of an industrial cyber-physical system*

The second perspective of study concerns the digitalization of information within ICPS. Driven by the revolution in computer networks and the massive development of high-performance and affordable (technically and financially) solutions such as edge, cloud and 5G technologies, for example, it has become possible to integrate a complete digitalization of system components and thus improve the performance of data processing and, ultimately, decision-making on these systems. The downside of this opportunity is obviously the security aspects, especially cybersecurity. Both the data and the decision-making mechanisms are more vulnerable to a potential attack from outside of the system, or even from within (sabotage). It is therefore necessary to design the ICPS by integrating cybersecurity as a system performance objective, and not as a constraint. The purpose of Part 3 is to address the digitalization of ICPS under these two objectives, both in terms of improving decision-making and in terms of improving the security of data and decisions.

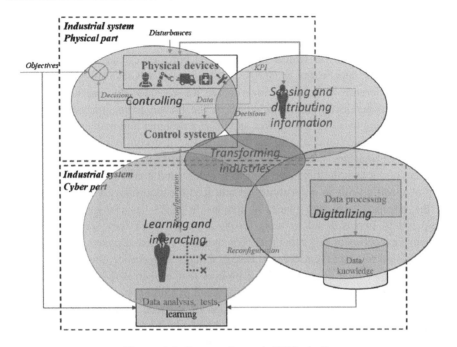

Figure 1.5. *Perspectives on ICPS studies*

The third perspective of study concerns the control function implemented by ICPS. In order to establish the feedback loop typical of ICPS between the cyber part and the physical part, it is indeed necessary to have control mechanisms that allow for a very strong adaptability to the changing conditions and reconfigurations proposed by the cyber part. To this end, since the mid-1990s, many works have contributed to the use of the multi-agent paradigm in industrial environments. The natural distribution of the action on the products and the environment of industrial systems, coupled with the distribution of the information mentioned above, made it possible to identify the physical organization of the systems very early on, with that of the classical multi-agent systems. The relevance of generalized multi-agent architectures within holarchies led to the development of numerous reference control architectures during the 2000s. In particular, the holonic paradigm is another precursor of the ICPS concept insofar, as from its creation by A. Koestler and its reuse in the framework of the intelligent manufacturing system (IMS) concept, there has been talk of bringing matter and information together, of integrating them into a "whole", a holon, which is also "part" of a larger whole, a holarchy. Part 4 of this book aims to trace these developments through the presentation of the agent and holonic paradigms and then the main control architectures presented during the years 2000–2020.

The fourth perspective of study concerns the interaction that humans can have with ICPS. The role of humans can be at different levels; they can be the physical system itself on which an ICPS acts, but they can also be responsible, decision-makers, supervisors or simple observers of this ICPS. This perspective is projected differently depending on whether we consider the interaction at the physical or cyber level. At the cyber level, the human is an integral part of the decision-making as a decision-maker and/or as a designer and manager of a digital tool (e.g. artificial intelligence) to improve the decision-making process. The evolution of machine learning or big data processing tools thus made major advances possible in the field of ICPS around 2020, and it is necessary to implement a set of specific skills in order to design and feed the algorithms with relevant data. At the physical level, the place of humans in ICPS has changed significantly compared to conventional systems. From a place where they were the almost exclusive executors of tasks that had been assigned to them *a priori*, and for which they were left to adapt themselves in case of a major disturbance, they are becoming an integral part of a decision-making process that is increasingly real time, with algorithms that have evolving behaviors. Part 5 of this book deals with these two aspects: on the one hand, the implementation of artificial intelligence tools within the cyber part of ICPS, and on the other hand via the study of the cooperation between humans and the two parts (physical and cyber) of ICPS.

A unique feature of this book is that its various chapters deal with different aspects of ICPS in general. For this reason, Part 6 focuses on the impact that these new developments have had on different industrial sectors. These sectors are characterized by different objectives, timeframes and technological maturities, but all benefit from the use of ICPS to improve their behavior. This part therefore focuses successively on several different sectors of activity, from manufacturing to logistics, from maintenance to construction, and including health systems.

Finally, the last part of this book proposes a slightly different vision of the development of ICPS, allowing for a step back and/or awareness of the assets that ICPS have for the future, as well as the pitfalls that these developments must overcome. Among these, three major themes are discussed in Part 7. First, the notions of ethics, which are not given much consideration in the work on ICPS, are of vital importance both for the relevance of the proposed solutions and for their acceptance by the humans who will be working with them on a daily basis. Similarly, the notions of legal responsibilities related to the use of ICPS are addressed because they concern all of the actors involved in the development and operation of ICPS. Similar to what can be found in the case of autonomous vehicles, for example, the modification of safety and accident management protocols induced by decision-making integrating artificial intelligence, constitutes a very vast and important field for the generalization of this type of model. Finally, the theme of ICPS training is addressed, via feedback from two European universities. The specific pedagogy to be developed in view of the interdisciplinarity inherent to ICPS leads to the consideration of a set of good practices, presented for both bachelor and master level courses.

1.6. References

Al-Hammouri, A.T. (2012). A comprehensive co-simulation platform for cyber-physical systems. *Computer Communications*, 36(1), 8–19.

Baheti, R. and Gill, H. (2011). Cyber-physical systems. *The Impact of Control Technology*, 12, 161–166.

Barbosa, J., Leitão, P., Adam, E., Trentesaux, D. (2015). Dynamic self-organization in holonic multi-agent manufacturing systems: The ADACOR evolution. *Computers in Industry*, 66, 99–111.

Beauville dit Eynaud, A., Klement, N., Gibaru, O., Roucoules, L., Durville, L. (2019). Identification of reconfigurability enablers and weighting of reconfigurability characteristics based on a case study. *Procedia Manufacturing*, 28, 96–101.

Cardin, O. (2019). Classification of cyber-physical production systems applications: Proposition of an analysis framework. *Computers in Industry*, 104, 11–21.

Cardin, O., Ounnar, F., Thomas, A., Trentesaux, D. (2017). Future industrial systems: Best practices of the intelligent manufacturing and services systems (IMS2) French research group. *IEEE Transactions on Industrial Informatics*, 13(2), 704–713.

Fink, J., Ribeiro, A., Kumar, V. (2012). Robust control for mobility and wireless communication in cyber–physical systems with application to robot teams. *Proceedings of the IEEE*, 100(1), 164–178.

Gengarle, M.V., Bensalem, S., McDermid, J., Sangiovanni–Vincentelli, A., Törngre, M. (2013). Characteristics, capabilities, potential applications of cyber–physical systems: A preliminary analysis. Deliverable D2.1, CyPhERS FP7 Project.

Kärkkäinen, M., Ala-Risku, T., Främling, K. (2003). The product centric approach: A solution to supply network information management problems? *Computers in Industry*, 52(2), 147–159.

Klimeš, J. (2014). Using formal concept analysis for control in cyber-physical systems. *Procedia Engineering*, 69, 1518–1522.

Lau, B.P.L., Marakkalage, S.H., Zhou, Y., Hassan, N.U., Yuen, C., Zhang, M., Tan, U.-X. (2019). A survey of data fusion in smart city applications. *Information Fusion*, 52, 357–374.

Lee, E.A. (2006). Cyber-physical systems – Are computing foundations adequate? *Position Paper for NSF Workshop on Cyber-Physical Systems*, Austin, Texas [Online]. Available at: http://ptolemy.eecs.berkeley.edu/publications/papers/06/CPSPositionPaper/.

Mazali, T. (2018). From industry 4.0 to society 4.0, there and back. *AI & SOCIETY*, 33(3), 405–411.

Monostori, L. (2014). Cyber-physical production systems: Roots, expectations and R&D challenges. *Procedia CIRP*, 17, 9–13.

Putnik, G.D., Ferreira, L., Lopes, N., Putnik, Z. (2019). What is a cyber-physical system: Definitions and models spectrum. *FME Transactions*, 47(4), 663–674.

Rajkumar, R., Lee, I., Sha, L., Stankovic, J. (2010). Cyber-physical systems: The next computing revolution. *2010 47th ACM/IEEE Design Automation Conference (DAC)*, 731–736.

Santos, D.F., Almeida, H.O., Perkusich, A. (2015). A personal connected health system for the internet of things based on the constrained application protocol. *Computers & Electrical Engineering*, 44, 122–136 [Online]. Available at: http://www.sciencedirect.com/science/article/pii/S0045790615000683.

Schuh, G., Potente, T., Varandani, R., Hausberg, C., Fränken, B. (2014). Collaboration moves productivity to the next level. *Procedia CIRP*, 17, 3–8.

Strang, D. and Anderl, R. (2014). Assembly process driven component data model in cyber-physical production systems. *Proceedings of the World Congress on Engineering and Computer Science* [Online]. Available at: http://www.iaeng.org/publication/WCECS2014/WCECS2014_pp947-952.pdf.

Wang, S., Zhang, G., Shen, B., Xie, X. (2011). An integrated scheme for cyber-physical building energy management system. *Procedia Engineering*, 15, 3616–3620.

2

Moving Towards a Sustainable Model: Societal, Economic and Environmental

Patrick MARTIN[1], Maroua NOUIRI[2] and Ali SIADAT[1]
*[1] Arts et Métiers Institute of Technology, University of Lorraine,
HESAM University, LCFC, Metz, France
[2] LS2N UMR CNRS 6004, Nantes University, IUT de Nantes, France*

2.1. Industry of the future and sustainable development

The industrial transition mentioned in Chapter 1 is accompanied by the consideration of sustainable development constraints (Nouiri *et al.* 2019a). Indeed, environmental issues, such as the reduction of pollution, carbon dioxide (CO_2) emissions, the reduction of raw material resources, biodiversity as well as the control of climate change, are becoming increasingly important. Some authors have even started to build a new paradigm (Industry 5.0), greatly emphasizing ecology and humans (Nahavandi 2019; Région Grand-Est 2020; EU Horizon 2020). Whatever the name, achieving a balance between production of goods, ecological aspects and human factors is a major challenge in the transition to the industry of the future.

Sustainable development is a concept of development that meets the needs of the present without compromising the ability to meet the needs of future generations (WCED 1987). A sustainable model must therefore ensure a balance between

For a color version of all figures in this book, see www.iste.co.uk/cardin/digitalization.zip.

Digitalization and Control of Industrial Cyber-Physical Systems,
coordinated by Olivier CARDIN, William DERIGENT and Damien TRENTESAUX.
© ISTE Ltd 2022.

economic, environmental and social impacts. Figure 2.1 illustrates the three working dimensions, leading to a model consistent with sustainable development. The objective of this chapter is to show how industrial cyber-physical systems (ICPS) have characteristics that contribute to solving the sustainable development challenges presented above. Our approach is thus positioned within the framework of sustainable engineering, defined in recent works as the combination of three interacting environmental, societal and economic dimensions (see Figure 2.1). Therefore, these three aspects applied to ICPS will be addressed consecutively, starting with the societal aspect, and more particularly, focusing on the role and integration of humans in ICPS.

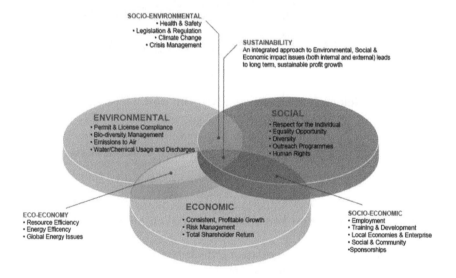

Figure 2.1. *The three dimensions of sustainable development (Mann 2009)*

2.2. Contribution of ICPS to the social dimension

2.2.1. *Background*

Humans have always been present in the industrial environment, but their scalability and versatility have not improved productivity and profitability in the face of an exponential increase in demands. Cost reduction and system efficiency optimization are among the main objectives of most industrialists, often to the detriment of a relevant integration of the human in these systems. Numerous studies (FUTURPROD 2013; Veltz and Weil 2015; EFFRA 2019; Neumann *et al.* 2021) thus underline the importance of taking into account the humans in the new challenges related to the industry of the future. New and crucial objectives are emerging, for which human expertise is relevant (Nouiri *et al.* 2019a): improving system resilience, adapting to disturbances (physical, economic, societal, etc.), taking into account environmental and social constraints, etc.

Figure 2.2 repositions the different dimensions of sustainable development presented previously on the impacting elements of an ICPS, as defined in Chapter 2. At the level of social objectives, the presence of humans is plural: observer, supervisor, operator and decision-maker, at the level of the workstation, as well as at the level of design or industrialization managers, in the physical as well as the cyber layer. The constraints specific to humans concern safety (accidents), physical health (musculoskeletal disorders, fatigue, vibrations, dangerous environments, etc.), psychological health (psycho-social risks, stress, cognitive fatigue) and, more generally, well-being at work.

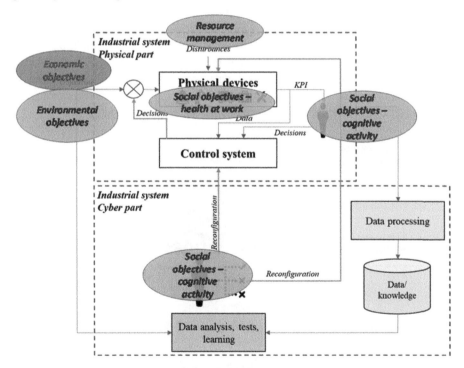

Figure 2.2. *Positioning of humans within the ICPS*

In the context of ICPS, technological developments, identified as levers for the deployment of the industry of the future with regard to work flexibility, show an evolution of equipment, manufacturing processes and procedures, and functional and even organizational constraints. Tasks can indeed be performed alternatively by a human, automated equipment, several operators or human–robot cooperation (Krüger *et al.* 2009; Murashov *et al.* 2016; Kousi *et al.* 2019), depending on the use. Automated industrial systems have made it possible, since the third industrial revolution, to ensure the repetitiveness of tasks, the rate and the constant quality of the manufactured product. Thus, humans can be relieved of tedious, repetitive tasks (physical or decisional), and with their global and contextual vision, adaptability, experience and non-formalized skills, can adapt to various tasks, make decisions adapted to complex situations and face the unknown. Nevertheless, some tasks are difficult to automate: flexible products of small dimensions, fragile, difficult to access. Thus, the interaction, cooperation, and permanent and dynamic coordination between the human and the automated system constitute the paths to be developed within the ICPS (see Figure 2.3) at the level of equipment (mechanics, sensors, communication networks, fixed or mobile robots, exoskeletons), interfaces, decision-making and organization (implementation, planning). Five levels of integration have been identified, from local solutions to the optimization of sustainable production involving humans (see Figure 2.4, EU Horizon (2020)): paper documents, software and siloed data, connectivity, offline optimization, real-time optimization. Within this process of evolution of tools and technologies, ICPS is part of the connectivity between equipment, planning and logistics.

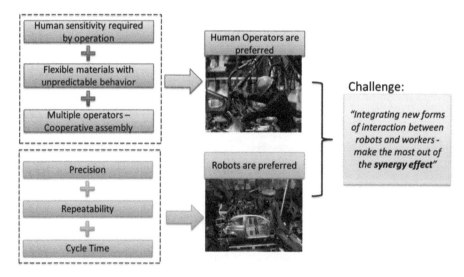

Figure 2.3. *Respective human–robot advantages (Thomas Project 2014)*

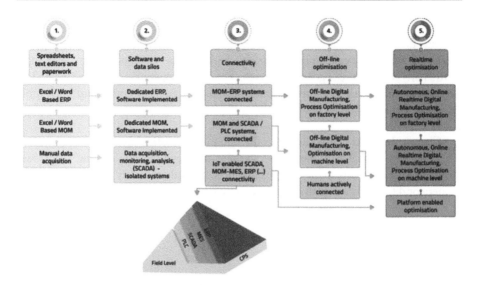

Figure 2.4. *Different stages of digitalization of production (EU Horizon 2020)*

The advantages of ICPS in favor of humans will thus be found in the different categories of aspects: the cognitive aspects, where ICPS collaborate with humans for better decision-making or to relieve humans who may be victims of mental overload, and the OHS aspects (occupational health and safety), where the adaptation capacity of ICPS will make it possible to physically relieve humans, while providing them with more advanced interaction conditions and guaranteeing their safety. The rest of this section is dedicated to the description of these two families of aspects.

2.2.2. Cognitive aspects

One of the major interests of ICPS is their ability to adapt to the context and diversity, both in terms of external elements (constraints, objectives, disturbances) and within themselves. Thus, it is expected that the ICPS can adapt to the presence of the human during various decision-making processes. The collaboration between the operator and the ICPS is positioned at the level of decision-making within the physical system (assistance for the accomplishment of a task, individualized training, etc.), at the level of the organization and planning of tasks within this same physical part with the objective of optimizing and eliminating unproductive time, or at the level of monitoring within the cyber part. Flow tension, reconfiguration and sharing the task with artificial intelligence are all parameters that should not be neglected in the evaluation of psycho-social risks engendered in operators, particularly via the stress generated by change. This cooperation leads to the need to identify characteristic parameters and develop new models combining structural, organizational and human points of view.

Chapter 10 of this book discusses the opportunities offered by ICPS to establish a fruitful relationship with the human in these different decision-making processes, in more detail. In this context, the human is then alternatively considered as an "Operator 4.0", or as a constituent part of a cyber-physical human system.

2.2.3. *Health and safety aspects at work*

The adaptation of ICPS to humans is also at the purely physical level: gender, origin, age, disability and culture are all factors that characterize the operator, which must be taken into account to optimize this relationship and offer assistance adapted to each user, in order to reduce health and safety risks (adaptation in space and in the planning of tasks, identification of weak warning signals).

Several projects have been carried out on work organization, monitoring of muscle fatigue and ergonomics (posture, vibrations, environment: temperature, humidity, noise, etc.), which are aimed at improving working conditions and reducing the workload. Mobile industrial robots are used to reduce the difficulty of tasks and the physical effort required by operators when transferring heavy products, etc. Collaborative robots, "cobots", are increasingly integrated in the industrial environment (Julien and Martin 2018). Several modes of cooperation thus exist, depending on the types of interactions possible:

– common working area when the robot is stopped (control, finishing operation, etc.);

– physical assistance (exoskeleton, third hand);

– physical and cognitive cooperation (effort, trajectory, etc.) to meet product quality and precision in the repetitiveness of the task;

– presence of the operator in the working area of the robot with stop associated with proximity or contact sensors.

These different types of robots make it possible for the humans to be relieved of heavy loads or very precise tasks, but their use is associated with the acceptability of the operator (permanent presence, physical or psychological constraint). The interfacing between the human and the robot is declined according to two major aspects:

– Sensors: in the industry, presence sensors (light barriers, pressure detection mats, cameras, distance or contact sensors, etc.), effort sensors, fatigue or vigilance sensors are increasingly being developed. In addition, measurements of environmental parameters (brightness, noise, temperature, radiation, dust, etc.) are necessary to prevent harmful effects on health.

– Interaction: this is based on interfaces that enable operators to interact with their environment (touch screens, keyboards, tablets, joysticks, etc.), to have assistance interfaces for a better knowledge of their environment (virtual and augmented reality, haptic interfaces, visualization of the state of the product, the process, the production to which they cannot have access, simulation of an operation to help its realization, etc.) and to receive real-time feedback on processing and decision-making (connected watch, tablets, etc.). However, this can only be achieved if the integration of the human in the ICPS is made in such a way that the problems related to the exchange of information between the digital and human worlds are handled in an intelligent way, taking into account the specificities and constraints of both worlds. The "shell administration" concept of the BASE architecture clearly illustrates this aspect (Sparrow *et al.* 2021). Finally, it should be noted that interaction is the basis for the cooperation mechanisms in ICPS, which are specifically studied in Chapter 10 of this book.

If many hopes are placed in the technological offer to improve working conditions, it is essential for designers to make a precise assessment of the risks they present, by endeavoring to identify those that are new, accentuated or more difficult to control. Particular attention must be paid to technologies that aim to "increase" the physical or cognitive capacities of operators (exoskeletons, physical assistance robots, augmented reality, artificial intelligence). The boundary is indeed imprecise and subject to discussion between a use that makes it possible to preserve health and safety at work and one that would, on the contrary, have negative effects because it would be primarily aimed at working faster, carrying more loads, standardizing work, etc. The opening of industrial equipment control systems to the Internet can also, in the presence of viruses, affect the operation of installations and consequently be more or less directly a cause of accidents for employees (see Chapter 6).

2.2.3.1. *Safety at work*

The accident is directly associated with the simultaneous presence of the operator and a potentially dangerous object at the workstation. The identification of dangerous situations, and thus prevention, therefore requires investigation of:

– scheduling of tasks, including those of the operator;

– identification of characteristic design parameters related to risk qualification;

– quantification of risks and their exploitation in order to help the designer in their activities of safe design of work situations.

In this sense, the concept of Design for Safety recommends the improvement of knowledge sharing between the different trades, with a strong involvement of the health and safety expert as early as possible in the design process. This has been the subject of numerous works (Fadier and De la Garza 2006; Shahrokhi and Bernard 2009; Houssin and Coulibaly 2011). The analysis of all of these methods, techniques and design tools made it possible to produce the findings synthesized by de Galvez *et al.* (2017) and Jafari-Sadeghi *et al.* (2019). In order to identify hazardous phenomena as early as possible during the design process, it is first necessary to identify the different functional elements constituting a production system. The significant parameters (energy and volume of influence) related to potential risks can be associated with each element. In these definitions, the operator is at the same level as functional modules and can perform most of these operations. The association of functional elements able to perform a task constitutes a workstation. A production cell is a set of workstations. Figure 2.5 illustrates the typology of the different elements making up a production cell in the manufacturing field.

Each module has mechanical, physical, electronic or software elements that ensure physical, quality and functionality control, and decision actions. The operator also has the same functionalities. The interaction, at a given moment between the modules and the operator(s), generates actions that can lead to dangerous phenomena. The granulometry is chosen by the designer, taking into account their objective (organization link, space management, use, etc.), knowledge of the system state and accuracy of analysis sought. It thus plays a decisive role in monitoring hazardous phenomena and their level of severity according to the modifications made to the production system.

The strong assumption for the analysis of the production system to identify and quantify the hazardous elements for health and safety is that the hazardous phenomena are related to the presence of energy. These energy flow parameters can be divided into two families: the main energy parameters that characterize a generalized energy flow (technological description of the way in which this flow circulates: mechanical, electrical, thermal, chemical/biological, radiation) and the complementary parameters (shape, material, surface condition, trajectory).

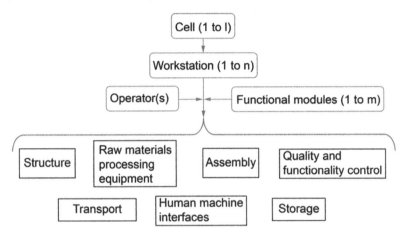

Figure 2.5. *Typology of elements constituting production cell (Gomez Echeverri et al. 2019)*

The accident is linked to the presence of the operator in the space occupied at a given moment by the dangerous object. This dangerous object can potentially appear at the level of the task carried out (cutting tool, etc.) or in the machine, released at the time of the task in a voluntary way or not (potential mechanical energy, fluid under pressure, pollutant, etc.). The hazardous area (geometry) is defined by the spaces occupied at each stage studied (sequence of static images) by the zones of influence of the equipment and the operator (simplified modeling) (see Figure 2.6).

The quantification of the severity is carried out by analyzing the standards associated (INRS 2006; ISO 2016; INRS 2017; INRS 2021) with each type of energy identified. From this information, the maximum energy value to which the worker is exposed is usually classified on a severity level scale (Gomez Echeverri *et al.* 2019). This information allows the designer to choose a technical or organizational solution so as to eliminate severe and very severe cases.

In the framework of ICPS, advanced strategies of collaboration within the physical parts, in particular through a relevant use of multi-agent or holonic systems (see Chapters 7 and 8), can propose, for example, a set of cooperative solutions, making it possible to complete the design solutions by a dynamic management of the working areas between the various controlled elements and the humans.

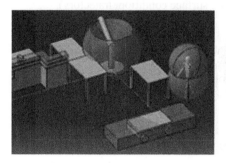 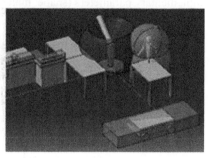

Figure 2.6. *CAD modeling of influence volumes (Gomez Echeverri et al. 2019)*

2.2.3.2. Health at work

Occupational health is an important aspect of a company's sustainable development. There are many standards, structures and committees that ensure this aspect. Beyond these regulatory aspects, there are possible actions to be carried out within the ICPS itself that contribute to guaranteeing it: scheduling of tasks under ergonomic constraints, taking fatigue into account in activities, optimizing preventive maintenance operations, etc. The study of the margins of maneuver illustrates the first action. For several years now, the ergonomics community has considered the margins of maneuver as a means of preventing musculoskeletal disorders (MSDs) and psychosocial risks, as well as a condition for keeping senior or disabled operators at work. Designing a system with room for maneuver therefore means giving it a certain "plasticity", to enable operators to manage variability without jeopardizing their health, by developing new practices and reinventing their uses, and to enable a dynamic work activity. Thus, Lean Manufacturing (operational excellence), whose objective is to eliminate non-value-added activities in order to improve the company's performance, is becoming the subject of questioning, particularly in terms of employees' working conditions. It is necessary to develop tools for the "monitoring" or "surveillance" of operator solicitations during the production phase, in order to predict "drifts" that lead to work situations or states that will cause disorders or fatigue. The margins of maneuver (see Figure 2.7) is defined as the possibility or freedom available to a worker to develop different ways of working, in order to meet production requirements, without adverse effects on their health.

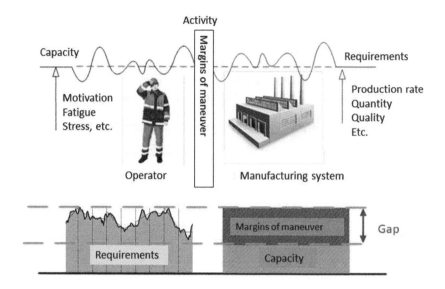

Figure 2.7. *Margins of maneuver (Lanfranchi and Duveau 2008)*

We consider that it is possible to reduce the organizational and spatial margins of maneuver to temporal margins. Thus, thanks to simulation, the effects of variability disrupting production, as well as the effects of these temporal margins left to the operator, could then be studied from the dual point of view of occupational health and safety and system performance: beyond a certain threshold of "flow tension" or "organizational rigidity", it is likely that the system is no longer capable of absorbing variability, and that the operators are no longer able to operate the regulations necessary to maintain performance under good conditions. As an illustration, this point has been studied for an ICPS purpose by El Mouayni *et al.* (2017) and focused on the simulation of "operator" variability implemented in a multi-agent model (see Figure 2.8) by studying the following points:

– parameterization of the fatigue model;

– parameterization of the learning model;

– error model parameterization: HEART (human error assessment and reduction technique) method.

2.3. Contribution of ICPS to the environmental dimension

2.3.1. *Objectives and expectations*

The consideration of the environmental impact must be ensured from the design phase and throughout the lifecycle of systems. A typical approach is to carry out a lifecycle assessment (LCA) of the production systems and products made within the ICPS (Ballarino *et al.* 2017) and verify the sustainability of the ICPS themselves, due to the intensive use of digital technologies in particular.

Table 2. Processed and rejected parts numbers

Results	Experiment	AEN-PRO	Error
Throughputs	217	200	7.8%
Rejected parts	19	17	10.5%

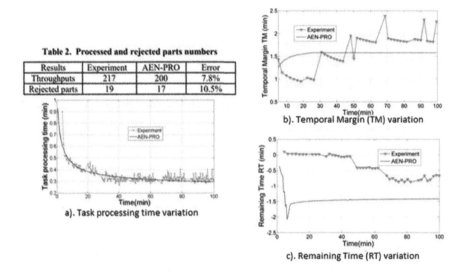

a). Task processing time variation

b). Temporal Margin (TM) variation

c). Remaining Time (RT) variation

Figure 2.8. *Simulation of the times of maneuvering margins (El Mouayni et al. 2017)*

This type of study typically leads to the use of bio-sourced materials as raw materials or recycled materials with less environmental impact (Kovarik *et al.* 2020; Carrodeguas *et al.* 2020). Reverse logistics is also developing. It is based on the use of reusable materials and packaging to reduce the environmental footprint (Ruel *et al.* 2021). Sustainable production strategies are also being developed, such as mass customization. This type of strategy aims to produce goods and services to meet the needs of each customer while ensuring effective and efficient productivity. Thus, the customer is involved in the design phase of the product. Product customization implies a specified production that best satisfies the customer's needs, thus guaranteeing an increase in the product's lifespan.

State organizations can also participate in the sustainable transition by imposing certain binding regional policies (variation of the cost of carbon, taxes, penalties for exceeding an energy or pollution threshold).

Thanks to the use of information and communication technologies (ICTs), everything within the ICPS becomes communicative: consumers, logistics operators, goods producers, energy producers, etc. This communication encourages interaction and negotiation for the local benefit of each ICPS and thus optimizes the global gain.

The concept of ICPS is relevant to reduce environmental impacts within the industrial environment (subject to its LCA, as mentioned previously). Indeed, the cyber layer makes it possible to retrieve data in real time and extract useful information in the environmental component. For example, a major advantage of ICPS is that they can be designed to use real-time information to reduce local energy consumption, manage waste or collaborate with other ICPS to optimize global energy and raw material consumption. The intelligence built into ICPS also allows them to react dynamically to internal energy constraints (exceeding an expected energy threshold) or external constraints (variation in the availability of renewable energy).

The ICPS management system can thus integrate new performance indicators relating to environmental effectiveness and efficiency. These indicators will be used to quantify an estimate of the impact on the environment (energy, waste, pollutants, greenhouse gases, etc.) during the predictive phase and monitor their evolution in real time.

2.3.2. Example of application

Mazumder *et al.* (2021) presented research books related to power electronic innovations in cyber-physical systems (CPS), more precisely new energy distribution architectures, protection techniques taking into account a wide integration of renewable energies in smart grids, simultaneous transmission of energy and information, etc. Nouiri *et al.* (2019b) proposed a multi-agent architecture named EasySched, based on the collaboration between goods producers (energy consumers) and renewable energy producers. Two types of ICPS are considered in this example: cyber-physical production systems (CPPS) and cyber-physical energy supply systems (CPES). As illustrated in Figure 2.9, the Industrial Internet of Things (IIoT) enables communication between CPPS and CPES. External communication enables the coordination and control of the energy consumption of the connected plants and the availability of renewable energy.

Renewable energy production is difficult to predict, as it is highly dependent on uncontrollable conditions (e.g. weather conditions). A disturbance related to the decrease in renewable energy availability is communicated and broadcasted to the connected plants, which then cooperate with the CPPS in order to respect this constraint. Rescheduling techniques are then executed to react quickly to this disturbance. The originality of this architecture lies in the fact that the scheduling is performed taking into account the production needs and the dynamic level of available renewable energy.

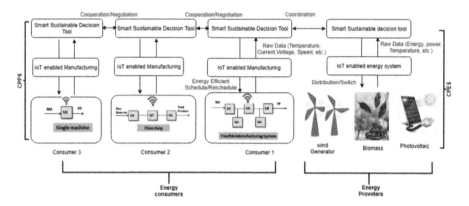

Figure 2.9. *EasySched: a multi-agent architecture for predictive and reactive scheduling of goods production systems based on available renewable energy in an Industry 4.0 context (Nouiri et al. 2019b)*

2.4. Contribution of ICPS to the economic dimension

Because of their ability to adapt quickly (to markets, hazards, urgent requests, etc.), optimize (scheduling, planning) and integrate the various information systems, ICPS clearly contribute to the economic dimension of companies. Because of their ability to process large masses of data at the cyber level, they also allow for the implementation of mechanisms to optimize the various "assets" of companies, in particular by optimizing maintenance processes (predictive, opportunistic, etc.), and to monitor the life of the various fleets of equipment, machines, tools, etc. via IIoT technologies, for example.

However, the transition to a sustainable model also implies optimizing the overall economic gain, in the longer term, beyond compliance with classic short-term financial constraints (turnover, market share, profit, margin, etc.). Typically, taking into account environmental constraints, *a priori* restrictive, can then be a source of long-term gain. For example, the use of recycled materials aims to reduce production costs, the impact on the use of non-renewable resources and the generation of non-valuable waste. In this context, the ICPS, capable of fine and global control of a production, can help to monitor the impact of the integration of these elements in the products and processes.

Reverse logistics or the implementation of dismantling channels is also an illustrative example of this global vision and is a major issue for the future (Tolio *et al.* 2017). In particular, dismantling aims to break down a product into homogeneous components, parts and materials, thus making it possible to meet the requirements of reuse or treatment at the end of life. It includes different phases: disassembly and size reduction, sorting and separation, recycling, inspection, cleaning, repackaging and logistics (see Figure 2.10). Within these phases, digital technologies associated with the Industry of the Future are present, particularly in terms of online and offline data collection, knowledge capitalization and feedback to the operator (AR headset, haptic interface). With the cyber dimension, ICPS can thus facilitate the interconnection between the various logistics chains and the information systems of the players to contribute to this global financial optimization.

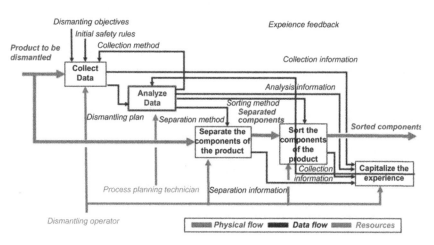

Figure 2.10. *Modeling the dismantling process (Hu 2021)*

In another area, the reduction of internal transport costs thanks to ICPS would be possible by setting up horizontal collaboration between ICPS, for example, thanks to fleets of mobile transport robots. Just-in-time or just-in-sequence delivery of components would reduce the cost of storage in warehouses, both intra- and inter-site, which is often variable. Smart management of logistics within ICPS makes it possible to not only react to disruptions (increased demands, closure of a distribution platform, etc.) but also reduce expenses related to internal and external transport and storage costs. Optimizing the filling of trucks and efficient communication within the fleet would help to minimize the overall transport costs (see Chapter 12).

The benefits in terms of health and safety and well-being at work also have a significant economic impact, only if the production resource capacity is available, through their day-to-day efficiency or the reduction of costs incurred by accidents or illnesses at work. Here again, the ICPS can contribute through their ability to capitalize on the events that have occurred and link them together to analyze the root events that cause incidents, accidents, work stoppages, etc.

2.5. Conclusion

In this chapter, the main challenges of the industrial transition towards a sustainable model were presented. The three pillars of sustainable development (environmental, social, economic) were put into perspective with the evolutions brought by ICPS, which make it possible to respond to these new challenges efficiently. A particular focus was given to the importance of the cyber layer to collect and process data from the physical layer, in order to make decisions that are increasingly in line with sustainable development. This decision-making is generally performed in the framework of a collaboration between the ICPS and the human decision-maker.

However, the digitalization of the industry is still handicapped by factors related to the adaptability of the human to accept these changes, train technologically (increase in skills, use of digital technologies) without forgetting the risk of quality degradation due to the diversification of human tasks, and the challenges of cybersecurity.

2.6. References

Ballarino, A., Brondi, C., Brusaferri, A., Chizzoli, G. (2017). The CPS and LCA modelling: An integrated approach in the environmental sustainability perspective. In *Collaboration in a Data-Rich World*, Camarinha-Matos, L.M., Afsarmanesh, H., Fornasiero, R. (eds). IFIP Advances in Information and Communication Technology, Springer International Publishing, Cham.

Carrodeguas, L.P., Chen, T.T., Gregory, G.L., Sulley, G.S., Williams, C.K. (2020). High elasticity, chemically recyclable, thermoplastics from bio-based monomers: Carbon dioxide, limonene oxide and ε-decalactone. *Green Chemistry*, 22(23), 8298–8307.

EFFRA (2019). European factory of the future association, Effra vision for a manufacturing partnership in Horizon Europe [Online]. Available at: www.effra.eu.

El Mouayni, I., Etienne, A., Siadat, A., Dantan, J.-Y., Lux, A. (2017). AEN-PRO: Agent-based simulation tool for performance and working conditions assessment in production systems using workers' margins of manoeuver. *IFAC-PapersOnLine*, 50(1), 14236–14241.

EU Horizon (2020). The ConnectedFactories project. EU Horizon 2020 grant no. 723777 [Online]. Available at: https://www.connectedfactories.eu/pathways-digitalisation-manufacturing.

Fadier, E. and De la Garza, C. (2006). Safety design: Towards a new philosophy. *Safety Science*, 44(1), 55–73.

FUTURPROD (2013). Les systèmes de production du futur, atelier de réflexion prospective de l'ANR [Online]. Available at: www.cluster-gospi.fr.

de Galvez, N., Marsot, J., Martin, P., Siadat, A., Etienne, A. (2017). EZID: A new approach to hazard identification during the design process by analysing energy transfers. *Safety Science*, 95, 1–14.

Gomez Echeverri, J.C., Martin, P., Daille-Lefevre, B., Godot, X., Marsot, J. (2019). Prise en compte dans la conception et l'exploitation des postes de travail de l'usine du futur des aspects sante – securité. *16ème colloque national S-mart*, Les Karellis, 73.

Houssin, R. and Coulibaly, A. (2011). An approach to solve contradiction problems for the safety integration in innovative design process. *Computers in Industry*, 62(4), 398–406.

Hu, H., Godot, X., Daille-Lefevre, B., Martin, P. (2021). Analyse des aspects santé-sécurité lors du démantèlement/de-manufacturing. *Proceedings of the S-mart National Conference*, 189–196.

INRS (2006). Les rayonnements ionisants. Prévention et maitrise des risques. Booklet, ED 958.

INRS (2017). Interventions à proximité des réseaux électriques aériens. Place des détecteurs de lignes électriques dans la démarche de prévention, ED6292 [Online]. Available at: https://www.inrs.fr/media.html?refINRS=ED%206292.

INRS (2021). Valeurs limites d'exposition au bruit et port de protecteurs individuels. Information pack, Fiche pratique de sécurité, ED 133.

ISO (2016). Robots and robotic devices – Collaborative robots, 1st edition. Technical specification ISO/TS 15066.

Jafari-Sadeghi, V., Kimiagari, S., Biancone, P.P. (2019). Level of education and knowledge, foresight competency and international entrepreneurship: A study of human capital determinants in the European countries. *European Business Review*, 32(1), 46–68.

Julien, N. and Martin, É. (2018). *L'usine du futur – Stratégies et déploiement : Industrie 4.0, de l'IoT aux jumeaux numériques*. Dunod, Malakoff.

Kousi, N., Stoubos, C., Gkournelos, C., Michalos, G., Makris, S. (2019). Enabling human robot interaction in flexible robotic assembly lines: An augmented reality based software suite. *Procedia CIRP*, 81, 1429–1434.

Kovarik, J.-B., Villarreal, A., Ramos, E.A., Alferaiheedi, Y., Modiselle, K.G. (2020). Carbon neutral buildings and recycled materials: How cities want to solve the challenge. Royal commission for Riyadh city in the Kingdom of Saudi Arabia, Urban 20 Mayors Summit – U20.

Krüger, J., Lien, T.K., Verl, A. (2009). Cooperation of human and machines in assembly lines. *CIRP Annals*, 58(2), 628–646.

Lanfranchi, J.-B. and Duveau, A. (2008). Explicative models of musculoskeletal disorders (MSD): From biomechanical and psychosocial factors to clinical analysis of ergonomics. *European Review of Applied Psychology*, 58(4), 201–213.

Mann, S. (2009). Visualising sustainability. *Computing for Sustainability* [Online]. Available at: https://computingforsustainability.com/2009/03/15/visualising-sustainability/.

Mazumder, S.K., Kulkarni, A., Sahoo, S., Blaabjerg, F., Mantooth, A., Balda, J., Zhao, Y., Ramos-Ruiz, J., Enjeti, P., Kumar, P.R. *et al.* (2021). A review of current research trends in power-electronic innovations in cyber-physical systems. *IEEE Journal of Emerging and Selected Topics in Power Electronics*, 1–1.

Murashov, V., Hearl, F., Howard, J. (2016). Working safely with robot workers: Recommendations for the new workplace. *Journal of Occupational and Environmental Hygiene*, 13(3), D61–D71.

Nahavandi, S. (2019). Industry 5.0 – A human-centric solution. *Sustainability*, 11(16), 4371.

Neumann, W.P., Winkelhaus, S., Grosse, E.H., Glock, C.H. (2021). Industry 4.0 and the human factor – A systems framework and analysis methodology for successful development. *International Journal of Production Economics*, 233, 107992.

Nouiri, M., Trentesaux, D., Bekrar, A. (2019a). EasySched : une architecture multi-agent pour l'ordonnancement prédictif et réactif de systèmes de production de biens en fonction de l'énergie renouvelable disponible dans un contexte industrie 4.0. *Génie industriel et productique*, 2(1).

Nouiri, M., Trentesaux, D., Bekrar, A. (2019b). Towards energy efficient scheduling of manufacturing systems through collaboration between cyber physical production and energy systems. *Energies*, 12(23), 4448.

Région Grand-Est (2020). Région Grand-Est Business act Grand Est [Online]. Available at: https://www.grandest-ba.fr/.

Ruel, S., Bourcier-Bequaert, B., Domont, S. (2021). Pratiques de logistique inverse au sein d'une coopérative : une motivation environnementale ? *Logistique & Management*, 1–14.

Shahrokhi, M. and Bernard, A. (2009). A framework to develop an analysis agent for evaluating human performance in manufacturing systems. *CIRP Journal of Manufacturing Science and Technology*, 2(1), 55–60.

Sparrow, D.E., Kruger, K., Basson, A.H. (2021). An architecture to facilitate the integration of human workers in Industry 4.0 environments. *International Journal of Production Research*, 1–19.

Thomas Project (2014). Mobile dual arm robotic workers with embedded cognition for hybrid and dynamically reconfigurable manufacturing systems. Grant no. 723616 [Online]. Available at: http://www.thomas-project.eu.

Tolio, T., Bernard, A., Colledani, M., Kara, S., Seliger, G., Duflou, J., Battaia, O., Takata, S. (2017). Design, management and control of demanufacturing and remanufacturing systems. *CIRP Annals*, 66(2), 585–609.

Veltz, P. and Weil, T. (2015). L'industrie, notre avenir. Report, Post-Print, hal-01111151 [Online]. Available at: https://ideas.repec.org/p/hal/journl/hal-01111151.html.

WCED, S.W.S. (1987). World commission on environment and development. *Our Common Future*, 17(1), 1–91.

PART 2

Sensing and Distributing Information Within Industrial Cyber-Physical Systems

3

Information Flow in Industrial Cyber-Physical Systems

Thierry BERGER and Yves SALLEZ

LAMIH UMR CNRS 8201, Université Polytechnique Hauts-de-France, Valenciennes, France

3.1. Introduction

An industrial cyber-physical system (ICPS), regardless of the field of application (e.g. manufacturing or other), is first and foremost a system, which is the seat of cyber loops (see Figure 2.3, Chapter 2) according to Wiener (1948). A loop exists from the moment that a stakeholder has a concern (objective) about a component, a property of the system. Within an ICPS (which may be recursively composed of ICPS; see Figure 2.4, Chapter 2), these cybernetic loops are supported by technologies and/or humans (see Chapter 11).

There are many loops, implemented in both the physical and cyber parts. Within the physical part, these loops are related to the control of the system and are widely studied and generally well mastered. This chapter focuses on the implementation of information flows within the cyber part of the ICPS, taking into account the evolution of the system in its lifecycle.

3.2. Information and decision loops when using an ICPS

Any system, *a fortiori* an ICPS, has a lifecycle that can be broken down into three main phases (Stark 2015):

For a color version of all figures in this book, see www.iste.co.uk/cardin/digitalization.zip.

Digitalization and Control of Industrial Cyber-Physical Systems,
coordinated by Olivier CARDIN, William DERIGENT and Damien TRENTESAUX.
© ISTE Ltd 2022.

– Beginning Of Life (BOL), gathering the stages of design and production (manufacturing);

– Middle Of Life (MOL), comprising the distribution/logistics and usage stages (including maintenance activities);

– End Of Life (EOL), including reverse logistics (collection), reconditioning (disassembly and other treatments) and recycling.

Figure 3.1 shows the major types of informational loops during the MOL of an ICPS.

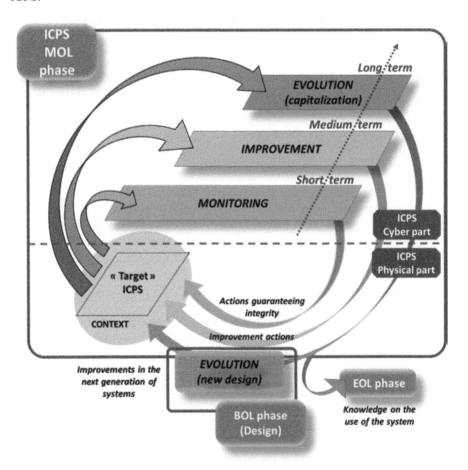

Figure 3.1. *Information flow within the loops in the MOL phase*

The use phase in the MOL of an ICPS is central and usually the longest phase of the lifecycle. These loops are organized according to different time horizons but all belong to the cyber part of the ICPS:

– in the short term, the "Monitoring" loops track and detect usage anomalies to ensure the integrity of the ICPS;

– in the medium term, the "Improvement" loops maintain the homeostasis of the ICPS (i.e. prevent degradation) and improve its performance (e.g. reduce its energy consumption) according to a principle of continuous improvement. This improvement can sometimes result in an adaptation of the associated context (e.g. modification of the operating procedure, training actions for users);

– in the long term, the loops of the "Evolution" category capitalize all of the information and knowledge useful for the other phases of the lifecycle (i.e. BOL and EOL).

The following section generically discusses the nature of the decision-making processes involved in the above loops.

3.3. Decision-making processes within the loops of an ICPS

The decision-making process within the loops of an ICPS involves various treatments (performed by algorithms or humans), corresponding to different levels of cognitive complexity. The model associated with this decision-making process must support:

– the very diverse nature (e.g. for maintenance, traceability, recycling, etc.) of the treatments related to the different categories of loops (i.e. monitoring, improvement and evolution; see Figure 3.1);

– the fact that these treatments can be supported by a human, machine or both in a mixed team.

3.3.1. *Nature of decision-making processes*

Rasmussen's model (1983) characterizes the behavior of a cognitive system (which can be human or artificial) that has to follow, supervise and monitor a system seen as a "target" for which there is/are concern(s). In the context of ICPS, this model is structuring and can usefully serve as a reference. Three levels of cognitive complexity are distinguished:

– at a lower level (i.e. "Skills/Reactive-based"), instinctive or reactive behavior, exploiting basic data, can generate alarms. For example, during an instance of use of an ICPS, an embedded system equipped with sensors detects a misuse (e.g. an applied force is too high) and generates an alarm;

– at the intermediate level (i.e. "Rules-based"), rules-based behavior can refine information from different sources. For example, in a maintenance context, diagnostic processing can run a set of rules to generate a list of suspected components;

– at a higher level (i.e. "Knowledge-based"), information processing exploits knowledge (e.g. relationships between: ICPS, users, environment, etc.) to improve the understanding of use situations. For example, a detailed context analysis for several use cases can lead to a more accurate diagnosis of a failure (Basselot *et al.* 2019).

3.3.2. *Nature of information*

The nature of the information used within an ICPS loop, in line with Rasmussen's model of cognitive complexity description, can be characterized by a DIK model, directly inspired by the DIKW hierarchy (Ackoff 1989). The DIK model highlights three "informational" types, with the following designations:

– D, "Data", are raw facts without a strong meaning. They come from real measurements (weight, temperature, current, for example). The data are obtained from sensors (embedded in the physical part of the ICPS or in the entities constituting the context) through a traditional process called "measurement".

– I, "Information", is obtained by "contextualization", which consists of adding tags to the data providing information such as "when", "where", "who", "how", "what", etc. Tags are informative and add meaning to the data (e.g. in the context of tracking a rail vehicle, the door (what) currently in a vehicle (where) and, at a specific date and time (when)).

– K, "Knowledge", can be considered as a group of information linked by relations providing semantics. These relations can be considered as metadata providing meaning (e.g. in railways, the door P_111 used in the vehicle P_11 when opening it in an operational context where the weight of passengers near the door is 520 kg). Knowledge is obtained from relations linking groups of information through a process called "semantification" that is usually associated with an "ontology", which is an explicit specification of a conceptualization (Gruber 1993).

It should be noted that with regard to Rasmussen's model (involving "signal", "sign", and "Knowledge" for each "Skills-based", "Rules-based" and "Knowledge-based" level respectively), there is a very strong coherence and similarity between "signal"/"Data", "sign"/"Information" and "symbol"/"Knowledge". The DIK and Rasmussen models provide an operational clarification on the nature of the informative elements and the processing associated with them. These two models should be considered as references, making it possible to study each loop within an ICPS. On this basis, the study of the loops (see Figure 3.1) of an ICPS can be considered according to the generic approach of the following section.

3.3.3. *Approach to studying the informational loops of the cyber part of an ICPS*

The approach, shown in Figure 3.2, involves the following five steps:

1) *Identification of the targeted system*: this involves defining what is being targeted. It is the ICPS or a subsystem, without which the interest of setting up an information and decision loop would be null and void. In connection with the examples in section 3.5, the targeted ICPS is, for example, a door (i.e. passenger access) of a train car or a robot.

2) *Identification of stakeholders and their needs*: a stakeholder, on the basis of an objective to be achieved, must make decisions in relation to a problem associated with the targeted system and the information needs to be satisfied. By finding out who has a concern with regard to the targeted system, it is possible to identify the various stakeholders (e.g. maintenance, operations, production managers, etc.).

3) *Identification of the nature of the cognitive activity*: the aim here is to determine to what extent this cognitive activity can be supported by a machine, a human (i.e. expert) or a mixed human–machine team. To do this, the category to which the loop belongs (i.e. Monitoring, Improvement, Evolution) and the stakeholder's informational needs are investigated and considered so that a result is provided in line with their expectations. Rasmussen's model is a reference to help position and investigate the decision-making aspect of the loop (e.g. skill-based monitoring activity) generally supported by technology (e.g. monitoring of stresses, vibrations, wear and tear of the physical part of an ICPS); knowledge-based diagnostic activity is supported by a human expert in the field (e.g. maintenance of the ICPS).

4) *Identification of the nature of the informational elements*: in the field of use of the ICPS, and in correspondence with the previous step, it is necessary to specify the necessary informational elements. This starts with the data to be collected and

measured. Most of the time, these measurements are related to physical phenomena. It is generally necessary to define the desired precision, interval of evolution, frequency of sampling, etc. for each measurement. The marking (i.e. "Tagging") of the Data makes it possible to transform them into "Information" (e.g. temperatures and production time of a robot identified (what), in a precise place (where)). If the decision process concerns the "Knowledge-based" level of Rasmussen's model, a modeling using an ontology may be necessary (e.g. ontology of using a machine linking information about the machine and its context of use (e.g. which operators use the machine, environmental conditions, machine in which there is a manufacturing site, etc.).

5) *Identification of interventions*: this involves determining what should be done in the event of an intervention. This concerns possible actions or action plans, to loop directly back to the targeted system (see Figure 3.2, e.g. launch of an intervention plan by the stakeholder responsible for maintenance, automatic shutdown of a robot in the event of an abnormal rise in temperature gradient).

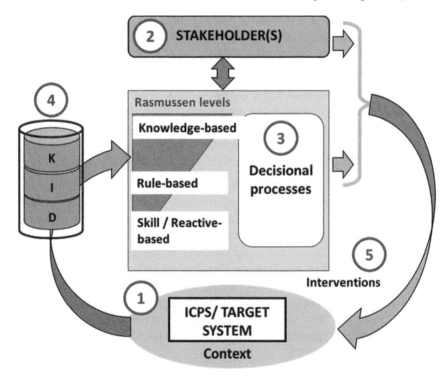

Figure 3.2. *Approach to studying the loops of an ICPS*

Having given explanatory elements to clarify the nature of the cognitive processes and the nature of the information within a loop, or several loops, the following section presents different elements of implementation.

3.4. Elements for the implementation of loops

The implementation of loops within a CPS requires the ability to transfer and process information. This corresponds to a need that is widely covered by the Internet of Things (IoT). The latter affects all sectors, whether related to industry, health, agriculture, buildings, etc. (Chen *et al.* 2014).

The IoT can be defined as an infrastructure of interconnected physical entities, systems and information resources, as well as intelligent services, capable of processing and reacting to information from the physical and virtual world and influencing activities in the physical world (ISO/IEC 2016). The declination of the IoT in industrial environments gives rise to the IIoT (Industrial Internet of Things). In the context of this book, a physical entity is any "thing", or "object" with respect to which a concern exists, such as an ICPS of type machine, automated system, robot, flexible cell, etc.

The major medium of communication is the Internet. This is not inevitable, but it is the result of the widespread use of the Internet and its protocols (especially IPv4/IPv6). The boundary between the CPS and the IoT, *a fortiori* between the ICPS and the IIoT, is tenuous; it is difficult to distinguish them very clearly (Nunes *et al.* 2015).

3.4.1. *Generic architecture*

The implementation of ICPS loops via the IoT/IIoT relies on an architecture consisting of several layers: from the field data acquisition layer (bottom) to the application layer (top). Figure 3.3 shows a generic layered architecture (Bandyopadhyay and Sen 2011). Other variants exist (e.g. Trappey *et al.* 2017), with more or fewer layers, but are broadly similar to that detailed in this chapter.

The layered architecture presented is broken down into two distinct parts that have the Internet communication layer (based on the IP protocol) in common. The two lower layers (i.e. "Edge Technology" and "Access Gateway") contribute to data capture, while the two upper layers (i.e. "Middleware" and "Application") enable data exploitation. The functionalities of these layers are as follows:

– "Edge Technology Layer": this layer consists of, for example, sensor networks, embedded systems, RFID tags and readers – in fact all of the devices that make it possible to collect data from machines, robots/cobots, AGVs, etc., and by extension (adhering to ethical rules), also from human operators, to observe the real physical world. These devices are deployed in the field, each associated with a physical object (e.g. cobots, machines) and make it possible to digitize the physical world. Generally, they include all or part of the processing, storage, interfacing with the physical world and communication capabilities. For example, an RFID tag can frequently identify an object and store data about it. However, reading or writing data on the tag very often requires that the latter be in the immediate vicinity of a dedicated reader. In this example, the tag only allows for the storage of information. Another example could be that of an embedded system measuring the temperature of a place, for example, by storing statistical data for each day, and sending an alert if a threshold or a gradient of the current measurement is exceeded. In this last example, the system must be able to measure (e.g. temperature sensor on I2C bus), memorize (e.g. Ram, Flash memories), process (e.g. M cortex processor), analyze (e.g. appropriate statistical algorithm) and communicate (e.g. Bluetooth, ZigBee) to warn and send information back to the upper layers. An energy source must be added to the different equipment, allowing the whole system to be powered.

– "Access Gateway Layer": this layer allows for the routing and publication of data from objects to the Middleware Layer, generally using the Internet as a means of communication. This layer also frequently allows for the adaptation between the specific communication protocols of the "Edge" layer and those used during the use of the Internet (e.g. the Bluetooth protocol (at the "Edge" level) to publish data via the IP network, passing through the Internet, to, for example, an MQTT broker (e.g. Mosquitto), which will redirect them to all of the software clients subscribed (at the "Middleware" level) to the reception of these data). Other protocols can of course be considered, such as OPC-UA, HTTP, etc.

– "Middleware Layer": this is an important layer that provides the link between the lower layers (i.e. Edge and Gateway), directly concerned with the physical world, and the application layer immediately above. This "Middleware" layer enables data storage, distribution, pre-processing, filtering, aggregation, semantic transformation, etc., as well as the management and control of connected objects (e.g. activation/deactivation of a flow from a connected object).

– "Application Layer": this layer, located at the highest level, is responsible for interfacing and interacting with the business applications of the various stakeholders. These applications, depending on the case, concern, for example, the fields of production, maintenance, logistics, environment, health, food industry, etc.

Network – supported services

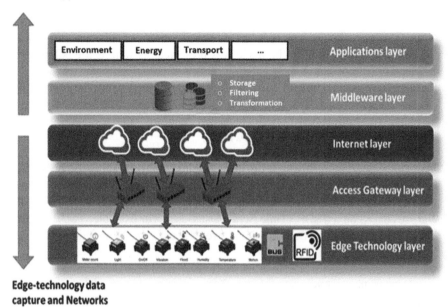

**Edge-technology data
capture and Networks**

Figure 3.3. *Layered architecture adapted from Bandyopadhyay and Sen (2011)*

It should be noted that everything suggests that only information feedback has been considered. However, it is quite possible, and frequent, from the "Application Layer" to act on a connected object (which will have been designed for this purpose) by "sending" commands via an appropriate communication protocol (often it is the object that will consult the state of a variable at the "Middleware" layer to determine whether or not it should act on the real via an appropriate actuator). Moreover, if necessary, secure communication protocols must be considered for both data feedback and control, in order to keep confidentiality and security (Zhao and Ge 2013).

Given the importance of IoT/IIoT applications, many operational architectures have been developed. For example, Trab (2018) mentions more than a dozen of them in her thesis according to the application domain: transportation (e.g. EMAR), industry (e.g. IoT@Work, FITMAN, SMART ACTION), city (e.g. RERUM, City Pulse, Clout, ALMANAC, Smartie), energy (e.g. E-PRICE, Nobel), health (e.g. CONFIDENCE) and logistics (e.g. iCargo).

3.4.2. *Link to decision-making processes and the nature of the information*

In sections 3.3.1 and 3.3.2, a classification of the nature of the processing/decisions that can be made was presented, as well as a typology of the information. From an implementation and technological point of view, the decisional aspects are located on the "Application Layer", while the informational aspects are located on the "Middleware Layer", which favors the storage and provision of information. Two categories appear: "metrics" for Data and Information, and "semantics" for Knowledge:

– The supporting technologies of the "metrics" category are based on solutions specialized in the collection of time series (i.e. time-stamped data series). Most of the time, these solutions are presented in the form of a software platform (e.g. TICK, Warp10) based on a TSDB (Time Series DataBase). For example, TSDB Graphite, OpenTSDB, TimescaleDB, InfluxDB, LevelDB, etc., can be mentioned (Basselot 2019).

– Supporting technologies of the "semantics" category, when linked, for example, to an ontology, exploit specialized databases for the storage of the application ontology used and the instances that refer to it. There are many ontology-oriented databases or software tools for developing them. For example, RDF4J, Stardog, Virtuoso, Jena, Neo4J, AllegroGraph, etc., can be mentioned (Basselot 2019).

Concerning the "Application" layer and the decision-making aspects, depending on the level of cognitive complexity, the decision is taken in charge by the human, the machine or even both as a team (especially on the "Knowledge-based Behavior" level). Any information processing technique can be used (when relevant). These techniques are generally based on threshold detection, gradient detection, signal processing, machine/deep learning, AI, visual analysis, statistical methods and generally those from "Analytics".

The following section illustrates the implementation of loops within ICPS.

3.5. Illustrative examples

Two examples are presented; the first one is related to equipment diagnosis in the railway industry, and is inspired by previous works (Le Mortellec *et al.* 2013; Basselot *et al.* 2019). The second one is related to the monitoring of a robot in a manufacturing context.

3.5.1. *Example from rail transport*

As illustrated in Figure 3.4, in this first example, the focus is on the diagnosis of a target "door" system and its context. This information loop is set up for the benefit of different stakeholders (e.g. fleet manager, maintenance manager) who need to know the status of the railway equipment. The decision-making process related to this diagnostic activity is knowledge-based according to Rasmussen's classification, and needs to be supported by a railway expert.

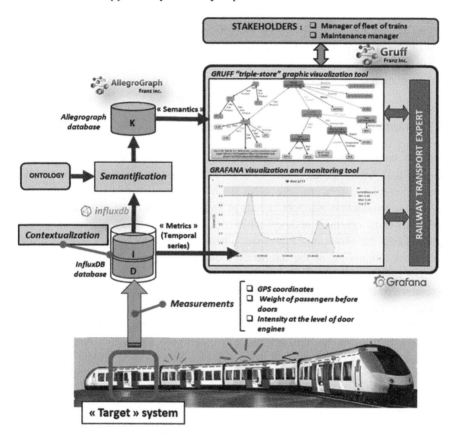

Figure 3.4. *Implementation architecture*

The lower part of Figure 3.4 shows the different measurements directly collected on the door (taken as an example) and others, related to the context, collected at the train level. The measurements are then transformed into information following a contextualization process. All of the data and information are stored in an InfluxDB database (InfluxDB 2021). A semantification process then exploits this data and information and elaborates a set of knowledge by creating links between these information through an ontology. This knowledge, stored in a triple-store AllegroGraph knowledge base (AllegroGraph 2021), is accessible by the expert using visualization tools such as Gruff (2021). The expert also has the time series stored in InfluxDB and accessible via the visualization tool Grafana (2021) at their disposal. For example, if a maximum current threshold is exceeded on a door motor, they can analyze the current curve via Grafana and examine the operating conditions and context via Gruff. By context analysis, it can, for example, explain this current overrun by the excessive weight of the passengers in front of the door, which has led to a deformation of the floor and mechanical friction at the door opening.

3.5.2. *Example from the manufacturing sector*

In this second example, the targeted ICPS is a UR5 collaborative robot from Universal Robot (2021) (see Figure 3.5). Two stakeholders are involved: one with a maintenance-related concern, the other with a production-related concern. The stakeholder "production manager" needs to know the production times of the robot in order to carry out their activity, while the stakeholder "maintenance manager" needs to know the evolution of the robot's health status. The robot's state of health requires the monitoring of the temperature evolution of each of its six axes. The cognitive level involved corresponds to Rasmussen's "skill-based" level. If the temperature of an axis exceeds a high threshold, or if there is a period of inactivity, an alert message is sent to the stakeholder concerned. The latter can consult the temperature evolution (stakeholder "maintenance manager"), the production time evolution (stakeholder "production manager") and plan a possible intervention on the robot. The nature of the informational elements is data ("Data"), such as temperatures and times, contextualized to make it "Information" (here, temperatures and production times over time (when), for a particular robot (what), in a particular place (where)).

In terms of implementation architecture, this example is implemented using the Ubidots platform (Ubidots 2021). This platform allows the storage of measurements over time (i.e. temperatures, time), monitoring, sending of alarms and visualization of measurements. The latter are collected at the robot level using Node-RED (2021). Node-RED is located at the "Access Gateway Layer" (see Figure 3.3) and, after collecting the measurements, allows them to be "injected" into Ubidots. The collection is carried out via the modbus/Tcp protocol, while the injection into

Ubidots is carried out via the https protocol and the Ubidots API (application programming interface) Rest (representational state transfer). In this example, only the "metrics" aspect is necessary. Two loops (one related to production, the other to maintenance) are involved. They concern the "monitoring" aspect highlighted in Figure 3.1. It should be noted that these loops, for the part relating to the feedback and   processing   of   information,   are   fully   supported   by   machines (i.e. "gateway" computer running Node-RED and cloud servers running the Ubidots platform). The part related to the planning of an intervention is supported by humans (i.e. stakeholder "production manager" and stakeholder "maintenance manager").

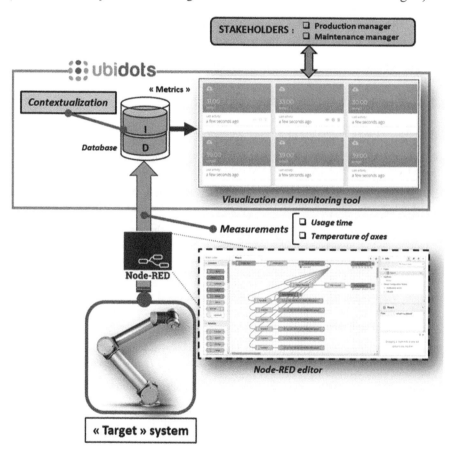

Figure 3.5. *Implementation architecture of the robot monitoring loops*

3.6. Conclusion

This chapter has shown the importance of the informational and decision-making loops associated with an ICPS. The IoT/IIoT concepts presented are valuable because they prefigure the architectures needed to support the different informational flows within the loops. The focus was on a model to characterize the information chain starting from the ICPS (target system) and its context, and leading to one or more stakeholders, before looping back to the ICPS during an intervention. This model is based on a Data, Information, Knowledge characterization of the information flows, and a "Skill/Reactive-based", "Rules-based" and "Knowledge-based" characterization of the nature of the decision-making processes. A general methodological framework for the analysis of informational and decision-making loops was also presented. Finally, two examples illustrated the framework.

3.7. References

Ackoff, R.L. (1989). From data to wisdom. *Journal of Applied Systems Analysis*, 16(1), 3–9.

AllegroGraph (2021). Software website [Online]. Available at: https://allegrograph.com/products/allegrograph [Accessed 15 March].

Bandyopadhyay, D. and Sen, J. (2011). Internet of things: Applications challenges in technology and standardization. *Wireless Personal Communications*, 58(1), 49–69.

Basselot, V. (2019). Contribution à la modélisation des chaînes informationnelles et des processus décisionnels associés à un produit intelligent : application à un connecteur de test industriel. Doctoral Dissertation, Université Polytechnique des Hauts-de-France, Valenciennes.

Basselot, V., Berger, T., Sallez, Y. (2019). Information chain modeling from product to stakeholder in the use phase – Application to diagnoses in railway transportation. *Manufacturing Letters*, 20, 22–26.

Chen, S., Xu, H., Liu, D., Hu, B., Wang, H. (2014). A vision of IoT: Applications, challenges, and opportunities with China perspective. *IEEE Internet of Things Journal*, 1(4), 349–359.

Grafana (2021). Software website [Online]. Available at: https://grafana.com/grafana [Accessed 15 March].

Gruber, T.R. (1993). A translation approach to portable ontology specifications. *Knowledge Acquisition*, 5(2), 199–220.

Gruff (2021). Software website [Online]. Available at: https://allegrograph.com/products/gruff [Accessed 15 March].

InfluDB (2021). Software website [Online]. Available at: https://www.influxdata.com/products/influxdb [Accessed 15 March].

ISO/IEC (2016). Information technology – Internet of things reference architecture (IoT RA). 20160910.

Le Mortellec, A., Clarhaut, J., Sallez, Y., Berger, T., Trentesaux, D. (2013). Embedded holonic fault diagnosis of complex transportation systems. *Engineering Applications of Artificial Intelligence*, 26(1), 227–240.

Node-RED (2021). Software website [Online]. Available at: https://nodered.org [Accessed 15 March].

Nunes, D.S., Zhang, P., Silva, J.S. (2015). A survey on human-in-the-loop applications towards an internet of all. *IEEE Communications Surveys & Tutorials*, 17(2), 944–965.

Rasmussen, J. (1983). Skills, rules, and knowledge; signals, signs, and symbols, and other distinctions in human performance models. *IEEE Transactions on Systems, Man, and Cybernetics*, 3, 257–66.

Stark, J. (2015). *Product Lifecycle Management (Volume 1)*. Springer, Cham.

Trab, S. (2018). Définition d'un modèle d'aide à la décision logistique et à la sécurité exploitant une communauté d'objets communicants. PhD Thesis, Ecole Nationale d'Ingénieurs de Gabès, Tunisia.

Trappey, A.J., Trappey, C.V., Govindarajan, U.H., Chuang, A.C., Sun, J.J. (2017). A review of essential standards and patent landscapes for the IoT: A key enabler for Industry 4.0. *Advanced Engineering Informatics*, 33, 208–229.

Ubidots (2021). Software website [Online]. Available at: https://ubidots.com [Accessed 15 March].

Universal Robot (2021). Company website [Online]. Available at: https://www.universal-robots.com [Accessed 15 March].

Wiener, N. (1948). *Cybernetics or Control and Communication in the Animal and the Machine*. Hermann & Cie, Paris, The Technology Press, Cambridge and John Wiley & Sons, New York.

Zhao, K. and Ge, L. (2013). A survey on the internet of things security. *9th International Conference on Computational Intelligence and Security*, IEEE, 663–667.

4

The Intelligent Product Concept

William Derigent

CRAN CNRS UMR 7039, University of Lorraine, Nancy, France

4.1. The intelligent product, a leading-edge concept in industrial cyber-physical systems

The previous chapter detailed the new technologies resulting from the Industrial Internet of Things applicable within industrial cyber-physical systems (ICPS). These technologies, which have become mature and economically accessible, allow for industrial resources (machines, handling, etc.) and the products themselves to be equipped with the decision-making, data collection and processing capabilities required for the deployment of ICPS. These industrial entities, augmented with these new functions, are then called "intelligent" and can be used as elementary elements of the physical part of the ICPS, as shown in Figure 1.5 of Chapter 1.

Among all these industrial entities, the product is a particular entity, due to its importance in industrial systems, since it is often the main objective and therefore a determining performance indicator. This certainly explains why, long before the advent of CPS and ICPS, the intelligent product has been a widely-studied concept for over two decades, starting in the 2000s, when several authors separately presented several definitions of the notion of product intelligence. The objective of this section is therefore to introduce the intelligent product concept and to produce a history of the work done in this field.

For a color version of all figures in this book, see www.iste.co.uk/cardin/digitalization.zip.

Digitalization and Control of Industrial Cyber-Physical Systems,
coordinated by Olivier Cardin, William Derigent and Damien Trentesaux.
© ISTE Ltd 2022.

Section 4.2 presents the different definitions of intelligent product and provides a comparison. The introduction of this new concept has led to the proposal of alternative, product-centric ways in which supply chains and automated manufacturing might operate. These new models describe production environments and supply chains in which products monitor and potentially influence their own progress within their environment. They have been the starting point for many developments that will be detailed in section 4.3.

4.2. Definitions of the intelligent product concept

There are many definitions of the notion of intelligent product, which differ according to the point of view adopted (computer science/production management, conceptual/technological, etc.). In the field of industrial cyber-physical systems, we can retain three major ones. The first, that of McFarlane and Sheffi (2003), defined the intelligent product as "*a physical and information-based representation of a product*". It has the following characteristics:

1) it has a unique identification;

2) it is able to effectively communicate with its environment;

3) it may store or retain data about itself;

4) it can deploy a language to describe its characteristics and production constraints;

5) it is able to participate in/make important decisions for its future.

Based on this definition, two types of intelligence are then defined by Wong *et al.* (2002). So-called type 1 intelligence essentially covers points 1–3, where the product is able to communicate its state (form, location, composition, etc.), while type 2 intelligence covers points 1–5, enabling the product to evaluate and influence the course of its life. It thus becomes proactive in addition to being able to communicate its states. Kärkkäinen *et al.* (2003) defended the idea that the intelligent product is a means of the input–output control of products on the supply chain. In other words, individual products in the supply chain control their destination as well as their route. For this, the authors explain that the product must have the following characteristics:

1) it has a unique identification;

2) it is a means of accessing the information that concerns it in the organization, whether through the identification code or through other mechanisms;

3) it can communicate.

Ventä (2007) provided another definition of product or system intelligence, which essentially refers to products capable of making decisions, i.e. an extension of point five of the first definition and point three of the second definition. Intelligence is defined as:

1) continuous monitoring of its status and environment;

2) reactivity and adaptation to operational and environmental conditions;

3) maintenance of optimal performance under all circumstances (even in unforeseen situations);

4) active communication with the user, the environment or other systems/products.

This definition mostly focuses on products with sufficient processing and communication capabilities to interact with external systems. This point highlights a significant difference from previous definitions, in which products only have identifiers used to access information and decision agents offloaded onto the network.

Meyer *et al.* (2009) proposed a three-dimensional classification of the works dealing with the intelligent product, which takes up the aspects introduced in the previous definitions, adding a dimension related to the level of aggregation of the intelligence (described below). This classification is illustrated in Figure 4.1, where we also show the different criteria related to the previous definitions in order to highlight the points of overlap. The three dimensions of the classification are the *level of intelligence*, the *location of intelligence* and the *aggregation of intelligence*. The level of intelligence includes three levels:

– *information processing*: the product must at least be able to manage its own information (from sensors, RFID readers, etc.). Without this capability, it would be difficult to talk about an intelligent product;

– *problem notification*: in addition to the ability to carry information, the product can also notify/warn its owner when an anomaly or any other event occurs. At this stage, the product is not yet capable of managing its behavior or of modifying its fate;

– *decision-making*: the most intelligent product is one that is completely autonomous, capable of making decisions about its future without external intervention.

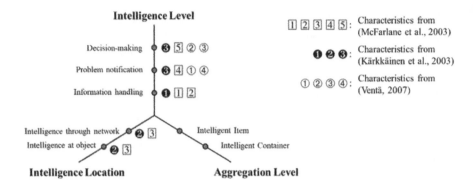

Figure 4.1. *Classification of intelligent products, according to Meyer* et al. *(2009)*

The localization of intelligence includes two levels:

– *Intelligence through the network*: the intelligence of the product is accessible remotely, from an identifier carried by the product. The example of the spaghetti can, proposed in Wong *et al.* (2002), describes this organization (Figure 4.2). The can is a physical object whose information is stored in a remote database, and the intelligence is provided by the decision-making agent. The connection between the physical product and the appropriate information representation is made via an RFID tag reader.

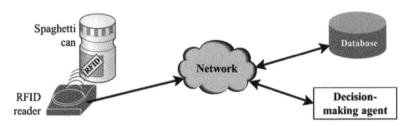

Figure 4.2. *Spaghetti can, adapted from Wong* et al. *(2002)*

– *Embedded intelligence in the object*: all the intelligence takes place in the object. This requires equipping the product with embedded systems capable of performing data storage and decision-making functions. These functions are often secondary to the main functions of the product.

The latter level is the form of aggregation of intelligence that transcribes the fact that a product can be made of more elementary components. The analysis of this dimension leads to the following structuring:

– *Intelligent item*: the object only handles information, notifications and/or decisions about itself. If it is composed of several components (parts), they will not be distinguishable as individual objects.

– *Intelligent container*: the intelligent container not only manages its own information, notifications and/or decision-making, it is also aware of the components that form it. If the container is disassembled or parts are removed, the parts are able to continue to function as intelligent items (previous point). An example would be a car engine that is removed or renovated, and new components such as an alternator, radiator, etc. are added.

The intelligent product is therefore a concept that can take several forms depending on the context of the applications. The rest of this chapter presents a classification of works from the literature with examples of contributions for each category identified.

4.3. Developments in the concept of intelligent products

Derigent *et al.* (2020) proposed a representation of the works related to the intelligent product and their relations, in the form of a co-occurrence network, built from keywords resulting from the bibliographical analysis of the SOHOMA workshop series proceedings[1] (Figure 4.3). It is composed of nodes representing the different keywords and of links representing the relations between these nodes. The shorter the links, the more the keywords are used in the same bibliographic references. It is then possible to define groups of keywords, according to their co-occurrence distance, which can be interpreted here as research domains. The network thus shows a total of six clusters: 1) product-driven systems (PDS), 2) product lifecycle information management (PLIM), 3) Physical Internet (PI), 4) multi-agent systems (MAS), 5) Internet of Things (IoT) and 6) digital twin (DT).

This classification, initially built for SOHOMA, is exhaustive enough to be extended to all existing works in the field. Among these groups, we distinguish between a "necessary tools" category (MAS and IoT), and a "scientific

---

1. The SOHOMA (Service Oriented, Holonic and Multi-Agent Manufacturing Systems for Industry of the Future) workshop series, which has been held for more than 10 years, brings together world experts in intelligent manufacturing systems and holonic manufacturing systems. Their work on the intelligent product is very popular.

contributions" category (PDS, PLIM, PI and DT). In the rest of this section, we only develop the PDS and PLIM groups associated with the latter category, since the notions of digital twin and Physical Internet will be addressed in Chapters 6, 10 and 13.

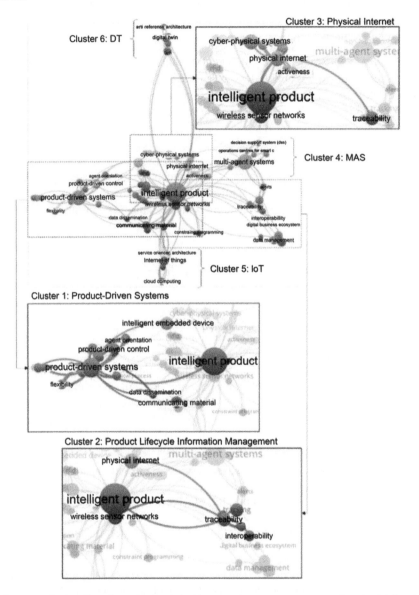

Figure 4.3. *Intelligent product-related keywords co-occurrence network obtained from SOHOMA workshop series proceedings (Derigent et al. 2020)*

4.3.1. *Group 1: product-driven systems (PDS)*

This concept, formalized by Morel *et al.* (2003) on the foundations of holonic systems[2], proposes a more flexible combination of centralized and distributed control modes, taking into account the product's ability to play an active role in synchronizing exchanges between different centralized business systems (enterprise resource planning (ERP), product lifecycle management (PLM), manufacturing execution systems (MES)) and systems distributed in the physical system (PLCs, CNC machines, self-guided pallet trucks, etc.). In this context, the product becomes capable of making decisions, while at the same time, it constitutes an interoperable medium for intra- and inter-company communication, which must ensure the dissemination of the information associated with it (Figure 4.4).

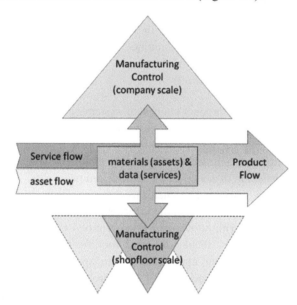

Figure 4.4. *Product-centric decision architecture (Pannequin 2007)*

The design of a PDS is a challenge that requires the joint consideration of three essential and complementary dimensions: the functions of the PDS, the architecture of the PDS and the interactions (or collaborative mechanisms) of the PDS. The functional characteristics are more closely related to the work of Group 2 and will therefore be described below.

---

2. Chapter 8 presents the concept of holonic manufacturing systems (HMS) in detail and presents several holonic control architectures (HCA).

The architecture of a PDS can be approached using isoarchy (absence of hierarchy between the elements of the production system), which is the organization most commonly used for product control approaches: at the same decision-making level, all the decision-making centers have the same decision-making capacity. Thus, the product evolves in its environment, making reservation requests to the resources it needs and collaborating with the other elements of the production system, without any hierarchical relationship between products. PROSIS (Pujo *et al.* 2009) is an example of this type of isoarchic architecture inspired by PROSA, where the Holon Staff is replaced by a Simulation Holon. However, other structures are also possible. Thus, guided by the idea that all distributed intelligent approaches can mimic human nature and behavior, several researchers have also explored bio-inspiration to organize PDSs. For example, Herrera *et al.* (2012) define a control architecture based on the viable system model called VSM_SCP, exhibiting interesting recursive properties, just like the natural structures of living organisms, and making it possible to combine centralized systems (long-term vision/strategic-tactical levels) with distributed systems (short-term vision, fast reaction capabilities/operational level).

The interactions within product-controlled systems are a final aspect that has been studied extensively. Three types of approaches can be distinguished (Mezgebe 2020): bio-inspired approaches, physics-based approaches and socially-inspired approaches. Bio-inspired approaches are widely used in PDSs. They consist of reproducing the behavior of social or non-social animals (ants, bats, fireflies) in order to benefit from distributed mechanisms that are simple and robust (but not necessarily always optimal). For example, Valckenaers and Van Brussel (2005) and Pannequin (2007) work with stigmergy, where entities of the production system indirectly exchange signals, thanks to local modifications of the environment (pheromone deposition). Other approaches try to apply physical phenomena to model the interactions. Thus, Pach *et al.* (2012) propose a mechanism based on a potential field approach, where resources will be able to attract or repel products, which will then choose the most attractive resource. Regarding the last category, negotiation approaches are, for example, studied in Mezgebe *et al.* (2018). They propose a negotiation heuristic based on the notion of critical ratio ((Due_date - current_date)/total time left in the store). By exchanging this value, the products negotiate their orders to pass between them. The collaboration mechanism between intelligent products can also be formalized using multi-criteria decision-making (MCDM) techniques. For example, in Dubromelle *et al.* (2012) and Pujo and Ounnar (2018), the collaboration mechanism is based on AHP/ANP (analytic hierarchy process/analytic network process).

PDSs have the advantage of being very agile and responsive, and they allow for potentially greater end-customer involvement. However, they are not widely accepted in industries due to the lack of performance evidence, mainly because of their myopic behavior, allowing them to make locally effective decisions but ones that are not in line with the overall goal. However, this is highly dependent on the use case and the working conditions. Indeed, in certain conditions, the performance of a distributed architecture can be as good as with a centralized control solution. This myopia can be corrected via data centralization mechanisms, where a discrete event observer can help to make better decisions (Cardin and Castagna 2012). This notion of a "discrete event observer" is an online simulation model running in parallel to the observed manufacturing system. It may be noted that this notion is fairly close to the notion of digital twin that appeared years later.

In conclusion, PDSs are advanced manufacturing systems that can lead to greater agility and responsiveness, with better end-customer integration. The exploration of this area has made many contributions to the proof of concept of useful implementations in industry and generic framework architectures (PDS architectures, interactions between products, coupling of centralized and decentralized decision-making, machine learning, etc.).

4.3.2. *Group 2: product lifecycle information management (PLIM)*

As previously explained, the intelligence (and therefore *a fortiori* the information) associated with the product can be located remotely or embedded on the product itself. Sallez (2012) introduced the notion of a product "augmentation" system, which supports the product (called the "target" system) temporarily or permanently, in order to equip it with secondary functions (i.e. communicating, triggering, memorizing, deciding, etc.). This augmentation system can be integrated in the target system as well as be available online (there can be coexistence of online and embedded parts), with the secondary functions following the product throughout its lifecycle, from manufacturing to recycling. These functions can be added or removed, moved into the target system or online, depending on the requirements of the phase. For example, the work of Basselot *et al.* (2019) applies the augmentation concept to the use phase, to give products increased monitoring and analysis functions.

This work on the functional aspect of the intelligent product shows that the management of data associated with the product is a complex process, distributed between all actors and phases of its lifecycle, often called product lifecycle information management (PLIM[3]). For example, when the implementation of the intelligent product is carried out via a unique identifier stored on an RFID tag (thus a type 1 product[4]), the PLIM system is the architecture that will allow this identification to be used as a network pointer to access a linked database. If the product is type 2, the information can be stored directly in a memory carried by the product itself, and the PLIM system will be in charge of maintaining the coherence between the different versions of the information, with the reference version on the product and its copies hosted on the information systems of the actors who handle it. These different mechanisms make it possible to obtain information that is available throughout the supply chain, and even throughout the product lifecycle. This availability of data makes it possible to offer new services during the various phases of the lifecycle, obviously in the manufacturing or logistics phase, but not limited to it. Therefore, PLIM systems make it possible for information to be available anywhere, at any time, and give concrete form to new paradigms supporting the circular economy, like CL2M (closed-loop lifecycle management) (Kiritsis 2011) detailed in Chapter 3. For type 1 products, PLIM systems are therefore essentially distributed data management systems and different architectures, protocols and message formats have been proposed in the literature. The EPCIS architecture is one of the best known, standardized by GS1 and specifically adapted to track products in the supply chain (Ranasinghe *et al.* 2011). DIALOG is another architecture proposed by the IMS community, based on a multi-agent system distributed between each actor of a given supply chain. Figure 4.5 shows a comparison of the two architectures: in Figure 4.5(a), each company has an EPCIS database. When the product is presented to the RFID reader, the latter retrieves its identifier. There are two cases: either the identifier is known to the local EPCIS database, in which case the data associated with the product is immediately retrieved, or it is unknown locally and the local EPCIS node uses an ONS/DS service to retrieve the remote database(s) hosting data related to the same identifier. Figure 4.5(b) shows the DIALOG architecture, using the agent paradigm. Each physical product is associated with a product agent, remotely accessible via a predefined identifier. When the tag is read, the retrieved identifier is used to contact the remote agent to request product information. In this architecture, a specific messaging protocol, initially called PMI (Product Messaging Interface), and later called QLM (Quantum Lifecycle Management) is used. Like EPCIS, QLM is now a standard called O-MI (Object Message Interface).

---

3. PLIM differs from PLM in that it is concerned with both the data exchange formats and the (high-level) communication protocols for making these exchanges.

4. A type 1 product, equipped with a passive RFID chip, can also carry information, but in a much more limited way.

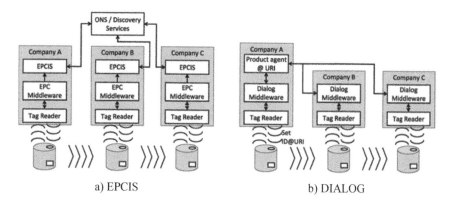

a) EPCIS   b) DIALOG

Figure 4.5. *Comparison between EPCIS and DIALOG*

PLIM systems are systems composed of multiple entities exchanging messages carrying content that must be understood by all actors in the product lifecycle. In order to ensure this semantic interoperability, many authors have proposed reference ontologies adapted to one or more lifecycle stages (Fortineau *et al.* 2013). The work carried out by Baïna (2006), Auzelle (2009) and Tursi *et al.* (2009) is specifically focused on semantic interoperability, centered on the product, leading to the Onto-PDM ontology.

To store intelligence directly on the product, many different devices can be used, not only RFID, but also microcomputers or wireless sensor nodes. Since they have more computing power and memory than conventional RFID tags, they can perform some or all of the secondary functions of the product. Many research platforms have implemented this type of product. For example, Quintanilla *et al.* (2013) shows an example of the evolution of communicating products (products equipped with RFID tags) to autonomous products. The authors provide a case study of a flexible manufacturing system where transport pallets, initially equipped with RFID tags, receive a miniaturized electronic device consisting of a CPU, an RFID reader, some steering actuators, a sensor and an HMI. They are then able to make decisions and move autonomously. These miniaturized devices have also been used to design communicating materials, which are materials equipped with either RFID tags (Kubler *et al.* 2015) or self-powered sensor networks embedded in the material (Mekki 2016). These materials are able to store their information and keep it even if they are assembled together or cut out. This is achieved by fragmenting the information and disseminating it throughout the material. The first works dealing with communicating materials focus on the problems of data distribution and reproduction in this type of material (Figure 4.6).

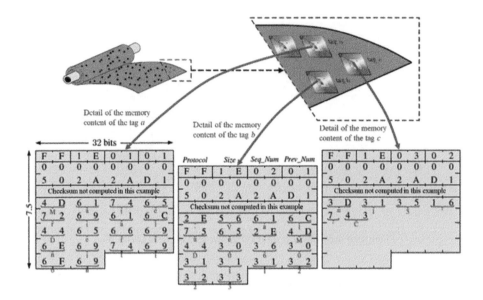

Figure 4.6. *Distribution of data on communicating material*

Recently, the work of Wan *et al.* (2020) aims to explore the monitoring capability of communicating materials by developing concrete beams equipped with sensor networks (application detailed in Chapter 15). This work shows that intelligent products can exhibit monitoring functions and can be aggregated to build a global architecture, capable of monitoring the performance of an entire system. This is another aspect of the intelligent product that has attracted the attention of researchers such as Le Mortellec *et al.* (2013), whose work focuses on the development of data management systems for train fleets, capable of gathering, storing, manipulating and communicating data from the equipment. They are developing the data management architecture of the SURFER project applied to rail transport.

4.4. Conclusions and perspectives on the intelligent product

Over the past 20 years, much varied work has been done in the world of intelligent products. This chapter has traced the evolution of related topics that have revolved around this concept for decades, reflecting the fact that intelligent products are a broader concept than just a specific industrial solution. Here we show that this notion is a rich concept for industrial management, both for production control and for data management. Members of communities such as IMS or SOHOMA have contributed to intelligent product research in a number of different areas (referred to here as "clusters"). Four main clusters have been identified, as the most representative contributions, through a literature review: PDS, PLIM, PI and DT. The first two have been described here, as the other two will be described elsewhere in this book.

In the past, the advent of technologies such as RFID tags and WSN helped prove the feasibility of the concept of the intelligent product. These pioneering developments were the precursors to the notion of ICPS, which is based in part on the intelligent product paradigm. Currently, and as introduced at the beginning of this chapter, the development of ICPS requires the design of autonomous and decision-capable industrial entities, which can be achieved by building on and complementing the work presented in this chapter.

4.5. References

Auzelle, J.-P. (2009). Proposition d'un cadre de modélisation multi-échelles d'un Système d'Information en entreprise centré produit. PhD Thesis, Université Henri Poincaré Nancy I.

Baïna, S. (2006). Interopérabilité dirigée par les modèles : une approche orientée produit pour l'intéropérabilité des systèmes d'entreprise. PhD Thesis, Université Henri Poincaré Nancy I.

Basselot, V., Berger, T., Sallez, Y. (2019). Information chain modeling from product to stakeholder in the use phase – Application to diagnoses in railway transportation. *Manufacturing Letters*, 20, 22–26.

Cardin, O. and Castagna, P. (2012). Myopia of service oriented manufacturing systems: Benefits of data centralization with a discrete-event observer. In *Service Orientation in Holonic and Multi-Agent Manufacturing Control*, Borangiu,T., Thomas, A., Trentesaux, D. (eds). Springer, Cham.

Derigent, W., McFarlane, D., Bril El-Haouzi, H. (2020). Intelligent products through a SOHOMA prism. In *SOHOMA 2020: Service Oriented, Holonic and Multi-Agent Manufacturing Systems for Industry of the Future*, Derigent, W., McFarlane, D., Bril El-Haouzi, H. (eds). Springer, Cham. [Online]. Available at: https://hal.archives-ouvertes.fr/hal-03018048.

Dubromelle, Y., Ounnar, F., Pujo, P. (2012). Service oriented architecture for holonic isoarchic and multicriteria control. In *Service Orientation in Holonic and Multi-Agent Manufacturing Control*, Borangiu,T., Thomas, A., Trentesaux, D. (eds). Springer, Cham.

Fortineau, V., Paviot, T., Lamouri, S. (2013). Improving the interoperability of industrial information systems with description logic-based models – The state of the art. *Computers in Industry*, 64(4), 363–375.

Herrera, C., Berraf, S.B., Thomas, A. (2012). Viable system model approach for holonic product driven manufacturing systems. In *Service Orientation in Holonic and Multi-Agent Manufacturing Control*, Borangiu,T., Thomas, A., Trentesaux, D. (eds). Springer, Cham.

Kärkkäinen, M., Ala-Risku, T., Främling, K. (2003). The product centric approach: A solution to supply network information management problems? *Computers in Industry*, 52(2), 147–159.

Kiritsis, D. (2011). Closed-loop PLM for smart products in the era of the Internet of things. *Computer-Aided Design*, 43(5), 479–501 [Online]. Available at: http://www.sciencedirect.com/science/article/pii/S0010448510000485.

Kubler, S., Derigent, W., Främling, K., Thomas, A., Rondeau, É. (2015). Enhanced product lifecycle information management using communicating materials. *Computer-Aided Design*, 59(0), 192–200.

Le Mortellec, A., Clarhaut, J., Sallez, Y., Berger, T., Trentesaux, D. (2013). Embedded holonic fault diagnosis of complex transportation systems. *Engineering Applications of Artificial Intelligence*, 26(1), 227–240.

McFarlane, D. and Sheffi, Y. (2003). The impact of automatic identification on supply chain operations. *International Journal of Logistics Management*, 14(1), 1–17.

Mekki, K. (2016). Gestion de l'information embarquée dans des matériaux communicants à l'aide de protocoles de réseaux de capteurs sans fil. PhD Thesis, Université de Lorraine.

Meyer, G.G., Främling, K., Holmström, J. (2009). Smart products: A survey. *Computers in Industry*, 60(3), 137–148.

Mezgebe, T.T. (2020). Algorithme inspiré humain pour la conception d'un nouveau système de contrôle dans le contexte de l'usine du futur. PhD Thesis, Université de Lorraine.

Morel, G., Panetto, H., Zaremba, M., Mayer, F. (2003). Manufacturing enterprise control and management system engineering: Paradigms and open issues. *Annual Reviews in Control*, 27(2), 199–209.

Pach, C., Bekrar, A., Zbib, N., Sallez, Y., Trentesaux, D. (2012). An effective potential field approach to FMS holonic heterarchical control. *Control Engineering Practice*, 20(12), 1293–1309.

Pannequin, R. (2007). Proposition d'un environnement de modélisation et de test d'architectures de pilotage par le produit de systèmes de production. PhD Thesis, Université Henri Poincaré Nancy I.

Pujo, P. and Ounnar, F. (2018). Cyber-physical logistics system for physical internet. In *Service Orientation in Holonic and Multi-Agent Manufacturing*, Borangiu, T., Trentesaux, D., Thomas, A., Cardin, O. (eds). Springer, Cham.

Pujo, P., Broissin, N., Ounnar, F. (2009). PROSIS: An isoarchic structure for HMS control. *Engineering Applications of Artificial Intelligence*, 22(7), 1034–1045.

Quintanilla, F.G., Cardin, O., Castagna, P. (2013). Evolution of a flexible manufacturing system: From communicating to autonomous product. In *Service Orientation in Holonic and Multi Agent Manufacturing and Robotics*, Borangiu, T., Thomas, A., Trentesaux, D. (eds). Springer, Cham.

Ranasinghe, D.C., Harrison, M., Främling, K., McFarlane, D. (2011). Enabling through life product-instance management: Solutions and challenges. *Journal of Network and Computer Applications*, 34(3), 1015–1031.

Sallez, Y. (2012). Produit actif tout au long de son cycle de vie. HDR, Université de Valenciennes et du Hainaut Cambrésis.

Tursi, A., Panetto, H., Morel, G., Dassisti, M. (2009). Ontological approach for products-centric information system interoperability in networked manufacturing enterprises. *Annual Reviews in Control*, 33(2), 238–245 [Online]. Available at: http://www.sciencedirect.com/science/article/pii/S1367578809000522.

Valckenaers, P. and Van Brussel, H. (2005). Holonic manufacturing execution systems. *CIRP Annals – Manufacturing Technology*, 54(1), 427–432.

Ventä, O. (2007). Smart products and systems. Technology theme: Final report. Report, VTT Technical Research Centre of Finland, Espoo.

Wan, H., David, M., Derigent, W. (2020). Energy-efficient chain-based data gathering applied to communicating concrete. *International Journal of Distributed Sensor Networks*, 16(8), 1550147720939028.

Wong, C.Y., McFarlane, D., Zaharudin, A.A., Agarwal, V. (2002). The intelligent product driven supply chain. *Proceedings of the IEEE Intetnational Conference on Systems, Man and Cybernetics*, 4.

PART 3

Digitalizing at the Service of Industrial Cyber-Physical Systems

5

Virtualizing Resources, Products and the Information System

Theodor BORANGIU[1], Silviu RĂILEANU[1] and Octavian MORARIU[2]
[1] University Politehnica of Bucharest, Romania
[2] Centre of Research in Robotics and CIM, Bucharest, Romania

5.1. Virtualization – the technology for industrial cyber-physical systems

Virtualization, the technology that allows the creation of virtual counterparts of physical (hardware, process) and non-physical (software, control) elements, is essential for the implementation of cyber-physical systems – systems of autonomous and cooperative informational entities that are strongly coupled between them and with the physical world that is of interest in situation-dependent ways. These informational entities of a CPS provide and simultaneously use Web-based data access and processing services, which, in industrial CPS (ICPS), are related to the various forms of coordinated actions exerted upon the clusters of physical elements: health monitoring, cost-effective assignment and reconfiguring at the failure of *resources and their controllers*, optimal planning and reality-aware rescheduling of activities for *product* making, traceability, supervision and coordination of *processes* at local and global levels.

The physical elements with local automation are virtualized and integrated with higher-level ICPS information systems, with centralized or distributed intelligence,

---

For a color version of all figures in this book, see www.iste.co.uk/cardin/digitalization.zip.

Digitalization and Control of Industrial Cyber-Physical Systems,
coordinated by Olivier CARDIN, William DERIGENT and Damien TRENTESAUX.
© ISTE Ltd 2022.

that perform the coordinated actions. Hence, two types of workloads are virtualized: *individual workloads* – specific for a single physical entity: resource, product, process that is monitored, tracked, parameterized or predicted; and *collective workloads* – specific for global non-physical entities: scheduling, negotiation, optimization, etc. Depending on the workload's nature, the virtualization process may cross one or more of the ICPS information layers: IoT-Node – the distributed, agent-based layer (e.g. the basic holon sets for heterarchical job allocation on resources); IoT-Node, Fog, Middleware, Cloud – the centralized, cloud-based ICPS layer (e.g. high-performance computing tasks for intelligent decision-making).

In the context of ICPS, virtualization is the process of running a virtual instance of a control or computer system in a layer abstracted from the actual hardware support. To the applications running on top of the virtualized machine, it appears as if they are on their own dedicated hardware support, where the operating system, utility programs, task sharing protocol and software tools are unique to the guest virtualized system and unconnected from the host operating system that is seated below it. Virtualization allows: a) segmenting a large supervisor system into many smaller parts, allowing the server to be used more efficiently by a number of different users (resource observers, product orders) or applications with various needs (optimization, high availability, prediction); b) isolation, keeping programs running inside a virtual machine safe from processes taking place in another virtual machine on the same host; and c) decoupling supervision (global, coordinated) from control (local, individual).

Virtualization of the ICPS information systems also involves software workloads that are executed in parallel at different speeds: the supervisory control workload that is directly connected to the reality (the physical plant) is alerted by the sensory devices about the necessity to reschedule activity plans, re-assign activities to valid resources; then a reality-modeling workload is initiated at computing speed (much faster than real-time simulation) based on virtual twins of resources and product orders, which provides predictive situation awareness and facilitates intelligent decision-making.

5.2. Virtualization in the industrial environment

Virtualization in industrial control with computing and information-based system support indicates the creation of virtual versions of computer hardware platforms, computer network resources, industrial equipment or software control systems. There are two virtualization technologies currently available that allow virtual instances of various physical devices to be created on different layers of digital environments including CPUs and process controllers, sensors, storage, networking, communication protocols and interfaces: 1) *digital twins* and 2) *agentification* of reality-reflecting class entities such as activities/processes, outcomes/products, facilities/resources and procedures/orders. The latter is either directly associated with the distribution of intelligence in heterarchical control systems or used as implementation of the framework of the holonic control paradigm.

The **digital twin** (DT) concept has three components (Caputo *et al.* 2019): 1) a physical object in real world, 2) a virtual object in the informational space and 3) a set of connections between the real world and the informational system. At present, the DT concept has evolved to a highly advanced modeling and simulation used in various fields (design, simulation, control, maintenance) and industry domains (Kritzinger *et al.* 2018) such as manufacturing, integrating additional features like process optimization, ability to run test scenarios without needing the physical object to perform them and use of AI to perform preventive maintenance. From the point of view of modeling reality, there are two types of DT: i) with a physical counterpart or *data-driven* DT, which relies on the IoT to collect data; this model is used to synchronize the virtual twin with the physical counterpart; and ii) without a physical counterpart or *model-driven* DT – a digital simulation used for modeling, design, analysis and forecasting (Graessler and Poehler 2018).

Embedded digital twins (EDT) are involved in all activities that imply their physical twins; for example, EDT are part of a resource control or a production management system. The connection between the physical model and its virtual model is established in dual mode by generating real-time data from sensors, and real-time controls from decision-making entities. Thus, the holistic view of status and performances of resources and activity instances (performed processes, used resources, products) including their operating models, execution context and usage cost can be captured in digital twins that provide reality awareness to the control software, and are therefore classified as *intelligent beings* in industrial holonic control architectures (Valckenaers 2020).

The distribution of intelligence within the industrial control system and the need for collaborative decisions of strongly coupled plant entities, such as plant devices in cyber-physical systems, led to the adoption of a new modeling approach for robust and optimized process control with **agent-based** implementing framework: the **holonic control** paradigm. This approach is based on the virtualization of a set of abstract entities: *products* (reflecting the client's needs and value propositions), *resources* (technology, humans – reflecting the producer's profile, capabilities and skills) and *orders* (reflecting business solutions) that are modeled by autonomous holons collaborating in holarchies by means of their information counterparts – *intelligent agents* that are organized in dynamic clusters to reach a common, production-related goal.

A cross-section through the IT landscape of an industrial enterprise would typically show a three-layered architecture, as illustrated in Figure 5.1. The lower layer consists of the plant (shop floor) or physical layer and contains the material flow conditioning, transport and processing **resources** and **products** worked out. The physical software workloads of a plant are proprietary (custom hardware and software) or semi-proprietary (standard hardware and operating system and custom software) and are responsible for the direct control of the physical resources and the material flow routing. Tightly coupled with the physical layer is the computer system used to track, document and optimize the transformation of raw materials in products, for example, the manufacturing execution system (MES) in production enterprises (Valckenaers 2020). The MES is an **information system** that consists of a set of workloads that can be virtualized as:

1) The set of workloads directly connected to the *physical entities* that are seen as agents representing a resource or product (shown in Figure 5.1 as Resource Agent i – RAi and Product Agent i – PAi); these are local workloads of the physical layer, for example, resource monitoring, product routing, dispatching and tracking production order and assigning jobs to resources for products in execution (distributed MES – dMES).

2) The set of workloads connected to *MES computing entities* that are seen as expert or advisor agents acting as optimization engine, machine learning predictor and outlier detector (shown in Figure 5.1 as Scheduler and Predictor); these are global workloads of the production lifecycle coordinated by the MES information system.

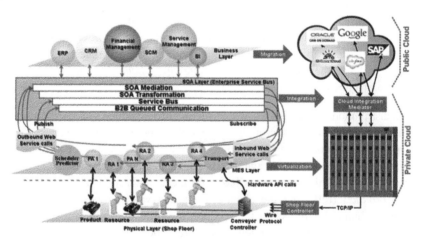

Figure 5.1. *Three-layer service oriented enterprise architecture virtualized in the cloud*

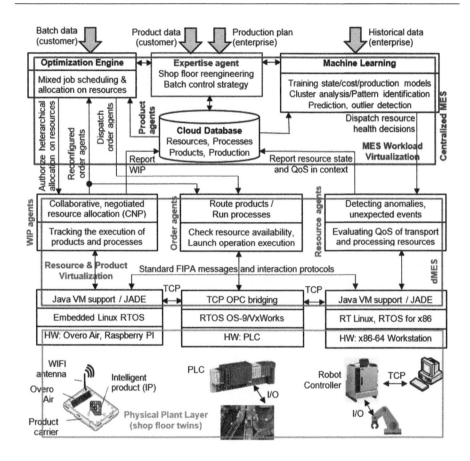

Figure 5.2. *Virtualization of plant and MES workloads in ISA-95 enterprise layers*

Virtualization also represents the main enabling technology for *cloud computing applied to the industrial domain*, regardless of the delivery method considered. Cloud adoption and virtualization for industrial enterprises organized according to the ISA-95 models focuses on level 3, where private clouds can offer support for the virtualized MES (Lydon 2020). The IT model of Cloud Computing (CC) is extended to services that orchestrate operational technology hardware and software elements that monitor and control factory resources, processes, events and products. This dual Cloud Control and Computing model (CCoC) is the real-time partition of the enterprise Cloud Manufacturing (CMfg) model mapped on its technical layer, and which:

– transposes pools of factory resources (robots, machines, transport belts, PLCs, controllers) into on-demand making services;

– enables pervasive, on-demand network access to a shared pool of configurable high-performance computing (HPC) resources – servers, storage and applications that can be rapidly provisioned and released as services to global MES workloads with minimal management.

The CCoC extended cloud model takes over and adapts some cloud computing features: a) product-making services are offered offline by factory re-engineering mechanisms based on agentifying shop floor devices, and rescheduled dynamically in real time by an optimized activity allocator workload of the MES; b) the CC part offers network access to HPC services through a distributed message platform – the enterprise service bus (ESB); c) the shop floor resources of the Cloud Control (CCo) part are grouped in clusters of known location relative to the material flow and dynamically assigned at runtime; d) the CC services can scale rapidly in order to sustain the variable real-time computing demand in activity rescheduling or anomaly detection, respectively, for resources being assigned/released elastically; e) the assigned resources are monitored and controlled and both the MES (service consumer) and the Cloud (service provider) are notified about the usage in the smart control application. The "pay as you go" cost model is used both to establish the cost offers for client orders in the service level agreements, and to weight the resources' offers while negotiating the heterarchical allocation of product operations. Figure 5.2 shows the two virtualization layers: 1) factory entities (*resources, products*) and 2) MES (*information system*).

5.3. Shop floor virtualization of resource and product workloads

The virtualization of physical factory entities – resources and products – represents the key factor for: (1) transversal (big) data transfer from the shop floor to the cloud for global MES workloads: process optimization while keeping resource health; (2) agile local coordination of shop floor resources for the products in current execution by distributing intelligence among agent sets. Virtualization operates in (1) on the full manufacturing cloud computing (CC) stack, while in (2), it addresses the horizontally distributed layer of resource pool at work under cloud operational control (CCo).

5.3.1. *Resource and product virtualization through shop floor profiles*

Global MES workloads virtualized in the cloud call for real-time shop floor (big) data streaming. Data streams are flowing from the plant (shop floor) into the enterprise service bus – a robust queuing system, capable of handling data bursts in a consistent manner; from there, a series of map-reduce aggregations are performed in the cloud, followed by global MES workloads (prediction, optimization) on aggregated streams: (1) *resource streaming*: factory resources send data that is encapsulated in periodic events that monitor operational parameters (e.g. temperature, power consumption, vibration levels) or as a response to unexpected situations (e.g. resource failure). Each of these events has a timestamp in order to assure valid time series streaming; (2) *intelligent product (IP) streaming*: IP data streams contain location and status information. The place where the product is located in the shop floor is relevant information for scheduling and path optimization. Virtualization of shop floor resources and products is necessary when there is a large amount of real-time data processing: i) aggregating at the right logical levels in topics (parameter sets) when data originates from multiple sources; ii) aligning the data streams in normalized time intervals; iii) applying map-reduce operations on these topics data streams to obtain consolidated data stream from which insights are extracted and further used for decision-making in the cloud.

The architecture of industrial resource (e.g. robot, CNC machine) controllers varies depending on the manufacturer, the technology used and the fabrication period, which means that they are not always based on high-level communication protocol standards such as SOAP/REST/JSON that qualify them as "SOA-enabled devices". The resources are integrated in the ISA-95 layer 3 information system by PC-type workstations; the communication between the workstation and the resource can be either standard TCP/IP-based or a proprietary wire protocol. Consequently, there are two alternatives to workload virtualization: a) when the resource can be accessed by TCP/IP directly, the workload is directly virtualized and a virtual network interface is mapped to it, which will be used to control the resource; b) if a proprietary wire protocol is used, the virtualization process becomes more complex as it would involve a local controller on the shop floor to provide the physical interface for the wire protocol (Figure 5.3, left).

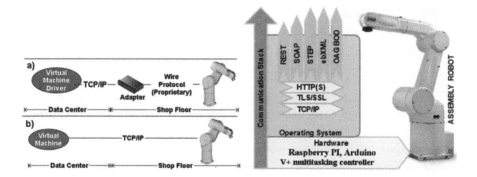

Figure 5.3. *Left: resource access – a) through a specific driver, b) by TCP/IP directly. Right: SOA-enabled shop floor resource – RT controller and external sensors*

This physical interface is virtualized and mapped through a specific driver to the virtualized workload over the network. When standard communication protocols are used by the shop floor resources, the virtualization process is straightforward and does not require additional development. Yet, if proprietary protocols are used, the virtual workloads require custom drivers to communicate with the shop floor controllers mapped over the network. Shop floor data from a resource may originate from its RT controller (e.g. robot controller) and a set of external sensors (e.g. power meters) as in Figure 5.3, right; in this case, the PC workstation acts as a data *aggregation node*.

To be virtualized, resources with a wire protocol need a new type of device on the shop floor, which acts as an extension of the private cloud system. This device hosts the physical communication interface for the shop resources and provides virtualized mapping for the workloads in the cloud (Figure 5.4).

The virtualization process of shop floor entities starts with workload discovery and publication in the service catalog, and is performed in a sequence of steps as follows:

Step 1: Identification of the physical controller's main characteristics for each shop floor resource – hardware requirements, operating system, software stack, certification.

Step 2: Creation of the resource virtual machine templates as per the specifications determined in Step 1. These virtual machines (VM) will contain the complete software stack required to control the physical resources, including the device mapping drivers.

Step 3: Creation of VM templates for each MES component like System Scheduler (SS), staff advisor, ESB, Machine Learning (ML) predictor and classifier.

Step 4: Creation of shared or dedicated VM template for the intelligent products depending on the technology used and the level of distributed intelligence present.

Step 5: Publication of all these virtual machine templates in the service catalog so that they can be deployed in the private cloud infrastructure as actual workloads.

Step 6: Populating the resource catalog with the resource definitions. There are two types of resources in the catalog: cloud resources (like CPU, memory installed on the virtualization blades, installed storage, network devices, etc.) and shop floor resources (like virtual protocol adapters for scenarios where a proprietary wire protocol is used). This step can be done manually by a human production system configurator.

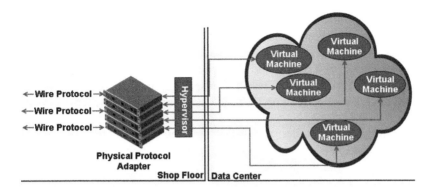

Figure 5.4. *Physical protocol adapter architecture*

At this stage, all the building blocks for a virtualized shop floor and MES are present in the service catalog of the private cloud. This six-step process is shown in Figure 5.5.

The binding between workload templates and virtualized resources is done using *shop floor profiles*. Shop floor profiles are XML files and contain a complete or partial definition of the manufacturing system virtual layout and mappings. The shop floor profile is workload-centric and basically contains a list of workload definitions. The workload refers to a specific revision of a VM published in the service catalog, a number of mapped virtual CPU cores, the amount of RAM memory allocated to the VM and the amount of disk space. The workload also contains references to a list of mapped resources, together with parameters passed.

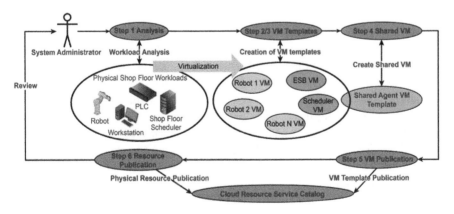

Figure 5.5. *Shop floor workload management process*

Shop floor profiles can also be nested by XML inclusion. This is useful when two or more workloads are defined as a pair. A practical example is when two robots are placed together in the same workspace on the shop floor and can perform collaborative tasks and operations. In this scenario, it is easier to manage the two corresponding workloads and resource mappings in a sub-profile that can be included in various shop floor profiles and thus reused whenever needed.

The shop floor profiles are loaded by the Provisioning Manager (PM) component. The PM is responsible for parsing the shop floor profiles and creates the workload instances in the private cloud platform based on their definition. The PM also maps and binds virtualized resources to the VMs deployed in the cloud, running on the virtualization blades by using either standard network drivers, for TCP/IP accessible resources, or by using custom drivers for proprietary communication protocols. To do so, the PM calls the *hypervisor* APIs. This concept is illustrated in Figure 5.6.

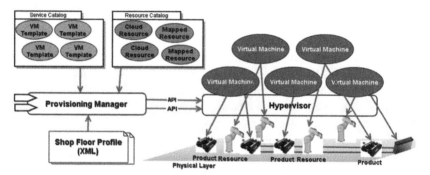

Figure 5.6. *Provisioning manager and provisioning profiles*

The PM loads all the provisioning profiles available but only one main shop floor profile is active at a time, together with all the nested sub-profiles. Switching between shop floor profiles requires: 1) saving the state of all workloads running in the current shop floor profile; 2) de-allocating the virtual resources from the workloads and returning them to the resource pool; 3) de-provisioning workloads from the virtualization blades and storing them in suspended mode; 4) loading the workloads defined in the new profile, either from the VM catalog if the profile is executed for the first time, or from their suspended state if the profile was executed before; 5) allocating the virtual resources to each workload; and 6) starting the VMs or restoring their state on the virtualization blades. The feature of the PM that allows quick switching between shop floor profiles provides an industrial system with a high level of flexibility, especially during the initial configuration phases, when many tests are required, and during the configuration change (resource added/failed). The PM also provides monitoring of VM statuses and fail-over assurance. A workload crash can be detected and the related VM can be restarted or re-provisioned, reducing the system downtime to a minimum.

5.3.2. *Virtualization of collaborative product and resource workloads*

On the distributed MES layer, the local workloads are directly connected to the plant's physical entities: resources and products in current execution. This means that the virtualization of these entities allows the management of hardware and software control resources at runtime in a pool model, allowing multiple beneficiaries – the product orders – to use these resources as needed. This approach leads directly to higher resource utilization, which represents the primary goal and benefit for cloud operational control (CCo) of any model in large-scale production systems.

The agents that are virtualizing the generic classes of factory entities: resources, products and orders, instantiate them at the production run for two types of local workload – (a) *individual* resource state, behavior and performance monitoring, respectively tracking product execution; (b) *collaborative* activity, scheduling and allocating resources for products that add up to the factory's capacity of simultaneous execution. This local collaborative workload is typical for heterarchical production scheduling, which can be chosen either as a scheduling mode for the entire batch or in the short term at resource breakdown until shop floor reconfiguring and the global plan are updated. The workload concerns the dynamic scheduling of operations for N products on resources virtualized by m Resource Agents RA_j, $1 \leq j \leq m$; the products are virtualized from the type perspective by Product Agents PA_k, $1 \leq k \leq t$, $t \leq N$, that have N *instances* virtualized by Order Agents OA_i, $1 \leq i \leq N$. The *real-time representation* of OA_i is expressed by $p \leq N$ Work-in-Process Agents WIP_i, $1 \leq i \leq p$ that virtualize *packets of p products in simultaneous execution* in the shop floor.

PA are passive agents that act as information servers for OA and WIP agents, for whom they provide data about the execution mode of product types; they reside in the MES database. RAs offer information about the operations that can be performed by resources: types, parameters, constraints, performances and usage cost (duration, energy consumption), thus allowing the instantiation of PAs in the set of OAs. RAs configure and command the physical resources, and execute these tasks on IBM PC-type industrial resource terminals; RAs and resource controllers communicate through the Ethernet with a TCP/IP protocol. OAs include data about the execution of individual products; therefore, they are hosted by the factory device that is most generally used to route products between resources – the factory PLC (programmable logic controller). For the heterarchical product scheduling workload, a limited number of p OAs are successively created and maintained for the parallel execution of products at maximum processing capacity in the shop floor by the interaction between the real-time counterparts of the OA_i, $1 \leq i \leq p$ – the WIP_i agents and the RAs of valid resources in the m-dim. shop floor pool. WIP agents mirror the way the p shop floor PA instances are completed in real time by accompanying the products routed by the PLC for execution. WIP agents virtualize products with embedded intelligence (IP) which result from the temporary aggregation (during their production lifecycle) of: 1) the physical product to be progressively made by resources, 2) the decision module, for example, computer-on-module on which the WIP agent executes, and 3) the carrier on which the product on pallet and the processor are placed.

The connection between the sets of RAs (executing on PCs), OAs (running on the PLC) and WIP agents (executing on IPs) that virtualize factory resources and products can be realized by an Ethernet network. The shop floor hardware units: PCs, Resource Controllers, PLC and IEDs (intelligent embedded devices on IPs) are connected to an Ethernet switch that offers support for the wireless communication of the IEDs; IPs can thus connect through an *access point* to this switch. Real-time WIP agents hosted by IEDs on products (IPs) play a central role in the collaborative dMES workload: a) in the *initialization stage*, the active WIP agents ask the PA defining a product type to send the data necessary to manufacture the instance entering the shop floor: the operation list and execution order, set up data and user requirements; b) in the *product scheduling stage*, operations are assigned to resources by the interactions of WIP agents with RAs based on Contract Net Protocol communication (FIPA); and c) in the *product execution stage*, the OAs residing on the PLC (product routing controller) apply the instance execution commands to the selected RAs while the WIP agents track the instances' execution status by collecting operation data from RAs via PLC and context data from sensor agents such as power meters measuring resource energy consumption.

Figure 5.7 shows aggregated components of an intelligent product with mobility capability (IP) and is virtualized by the order agent (OA) storing the product's execution schedule (the associations operation–resource and the routes between work stations) that is managed by the transportation PLC and the WIP agent that updates the product's execution status (McFarlane *et al.* 2020).

When the product carrier enters the shop floor, a unique ID is assigned to its RFID tag that will be used in Stage 2 for pallet identification and locating in the workstations. Intelligent products communicate on the dMES layer with the PCs hosting resource agents and with the PLC hosting order agents for product routing, as shown in Figure 5.8.

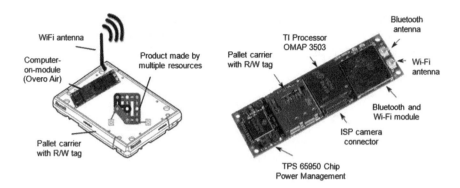

Figure 5.7. *Product with local embedded intelligence (left); virtualization with IED (right)*

The lifecycle of an intelligent product comprises three stages:

1) *Aggregation of components*: pallet carrier, IED processor and product assignment.

2) *Collaborative product execution*: three phases with the earlier defined actions:

– *Knowledge update*: the WIP agent initialization phase, in which the PAs in the MES database are interrogated about the product execution data and the RAs are queried about the status and occupancy of resources.

– *Decision*: the IP assigns product operations to resources by CNP negotiation with RAs and agreement with the OAs already routing their products. A new OA is created and transferred to the PLC while its WIP agent runs in the IED.

– *Execution*: the WIP agent tracks the execution of the new OA in the context of parallel execution with the other existing OAs in the shop floor.

3) *Product removal*: when the physical product is completed and exits the factory, its IP is recycled by assigning it to the next product to be executed.

The communication between the set of IPs and the PLC can be realized by a TCP-OPC bridge protocol which is a C# software application containing: i) a TCP/IP server communicating through a socket with the TCP/IP client developed in the WIP multi-agent application, ii) an OPC client that communicates with the OPC server installed on the PLC and performs related data read/write tasks. The TCP/IP server opens a socket for each WIP agent created in the "Decision" phase of Stage 2. Object linking and embedding for Process Control (OPC) is a real-time communication standard that allows heterogeneous industrial hardware devices to interact (Lange *et al.* 2016).

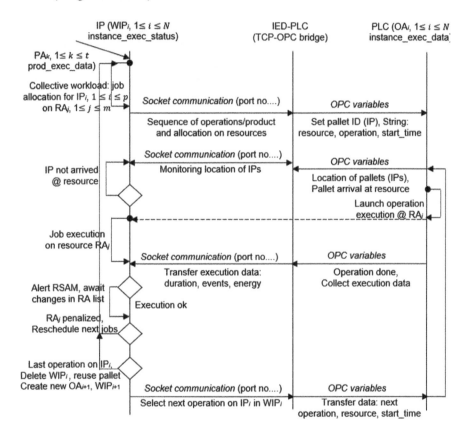

Figure 5.8. *IP – PC, PLC protocols for creating and real-time managing product orders*

The local dMES collaborative workload for scheduling products on resources with route selection may be performed in the "Decision" phase in one of the following two strategies (Răileanu *et al.* 2017) defined in Table 5.1.

Strategy	Description	Expected results
Heterarchical negotiated (HN)	Schedules of *all operations* for each active OA are computed through communication with all simultaneously executing OAs.	Minimize the execution time of all products that are simultaneously processed.
Heterarchical non-negotiated (HNN)	There is no global scheduling and only the *next operation* is successively selected on the first resource found free.	Minimize the impact of Perturbations.

Table 5.1. *Strategies for virtualized dMES product scheduling*

An extended version of Contract Net Protocol is used in the interaction of the real-time OA(s) with the set of valid RAs in order to overcome some limits of the standard CNP protocol: extending the CNP design beyond the virtual environment (i.e. actions may not start immediately after confirmation); relaxing the necessity of interrogating all participants even if they are of no interest; providing direct synchronization between multiple initiators; allowing an initiator to manage more than one single job which is awarded to a single participant; and dealing with fault tolerance aspects, such as when a participant disappears (e.g. resource failure) during the time interval from job award to service receipt (Borangiu *et al.* 2014). The sequence of actions for the collaborative product execution of an OA (Stage 2 of IP) in HN mode includes the steps (Figure 5.9):

1) Update the RSAM (resource performance and cost model) in the MES database with data about the most recent services performed by resources.

2) Search necessary operations for the associated product entering the shop floor.

3) Send Call for Proposals (cfp) to m-specific RAs (virtualizing useable resources).

4) If current product cannot be executed, then exit (and load new product data).

5) Iterative operation allocation on the available RAs (n – number of RAs that have responded to the cfp; i – number of negative responses (reject) to the cfp sent ($i < \psi n$); j – number of positive responses (accept) to the cfp sent ($j < \psi n - \leftarrow i$).

6) Inform all RAs ←one offer accepted< k $\Im \leftarrow j - \leftarrow 1$ offers refused).

7) Start execution {transport, processing, quality control}.

8) For each operation:

a) Check whether it can be realized:

i) no – go to step 5;

ii) yes – start operation.

b) Operation execution.

c) Reception of the message describing how the operation was executed:

i) if the operation was successfully executed go to next operation, step 7;

ii) if operation execution doesn't succeed mark OA as failed and go to step 9.

9) Delete the OA and its WIP agent, exit the finished product, aggregate a new IP.

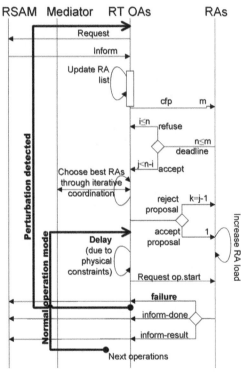

WIP agents: real-time (*rt*) OAs that are affected by resource breakdown and those of new introduced products initiate rescheduling and, respectively, new schedules. They inform the other OAs that are not affected that they must send their schedules to a *mediator*.

The WIP agent selected as mediator solves possible conflicts generated by OA schedules that use the same resources in overlapping time intervals. The usual election rule is "the oldest OH in production is elected mediator".

The mediator forms a Gantt chart describing the utilization of resources in time by proposed/existing schedules. The conflicting allocations are cancelled and postponed in an iterative process.

Figure 5.9. *CNP-based interaction of real-time OAs with RAs for product scheduling*

5.4. MES virtualization in the cloud (vMES)

MES virtualization involves the migration of MES workloads that were traditionally executed on physical machines to the private cloud platform as *virtual workloads*. The idea is to run the global MES software controlling the plant infrastructure for full batch production in a virtualized environment and keep only the physical resources with their dedicated RT controllers on the shop floor. This separation between hardware resources and global control software provides a new level of flexibility and agility to the production control problem. ISA-95 level 3 functions are mapped in separate workloads at the MES layer; from the virtualization perspective, the profile and scalability requirements of these workloads relative to the system load are (Morariu *et al.* 2015):

– *Global production scheduling*: the process that determines operation sequencing and resource allocation for the entire production order. The scheduling problem is often an NP-complete problem and finding a near-optimal solution is computing-intensive. The workload is active before the actual production begins and may be updated after an operation completes, whenever changes in the same direction are detected in the resources' usage cost. After the schedule is computed, the workload becomes idle; its workload profile tends to be CPU-intensive. The scalability of this workload depends highly on the algorithm used for schedule computation. An algorithm that can be executed in parallel allows for horizontal workload scaling (i.e. provisioning of multiple virtual machines for parallel computation depending on the batch size). On the other hand, a monolithic algorithm would require scaling by resource allocation to a single virtual machine (i.e. by allocating more CPU cores or physical memory to a given virtual machine executing the algorithm).

– *Production dispatching*: this workload has a similar temporal pattern as the global production scheduling, being active for a short time after the schedule is computed and before execution starts. For this reason, this workload is collocated with the scheduler workload; it is not resource-intensive, especially in an MSB-integrated environment, as it is just responsible for sending a set of messages across the MSB.

– *Production execution*: this workload deals with the hierarchical execution of the schedule by generating RT commands to the lower levels of the stack, specifically to the resource controllers. It becomes active after dispatching the global schedule and remains active throughout the entire batch process. This workload interacts in RT with other workloads and shop floor components in event-driven architecture; it has a high I/O profile, as data flows from various directions via events from many MES/shop floor devices; it can be scaled horizontally using a *load balancer*.

– *Automated control*: handles unexpected scenarios (e.g. resource breakdown) that affect the initially computed schedule. It is implemented as automatically switching control to the agents running on dMES with distributed intelligence. The workload is resource-intensive, being provisioned at disturbances or unexpected events.

– *Resource instrumenting and health management*: involves (big) data streaming from shop floor entities. This information flow is used for both RT resource health monitoring and predictive system scheduling. Dividing the messaging platform into separate topics (parameter domains – resource data and intelligent product data) with established producer–consumer relations helps in logically dividing the load (Morariu *et al.* 2020). This workload is I/O-intensive and has a real-time profile.

– *Historical data management*: consists of a relational database management system that stores manufacturing data (e.g. energy consumption/operation/resource) in a structured and accessible format. Depending on the granularity and size of stored data, this workload needs to access a large disc space and has an I/O-intensive profile.

– *Machine learning (ML)*: extracts real-time insights from aggregated data streams originating from the shop floor resources and products. The computation is parallel for all resource channels and product orders. This workload is CPU-intensive for three functions: *prediction*: deep learning of patterns and measurement variations (e.g. energy data), forecasting the evolution of values; *classification*, i.e. finding classes for feature vectors received; *clustering*, i.e. searching and identifying similarities in non-tagged, multi-dimension data and tagging each feature vector suitably. Recording and storing historical data are needed to train multiple resource behavior patterns (resource topic) and product execution models (IP topic).

The MES workloads above are interconnected using a real-time version of the enterprise service bus integration model – an adaptation to production enterprises of the ESB software architecture. In addition to the key characteristics inherited from the ESB: a) message routing across enterprise layers; b) decoupling of modules by asynchronous messaging; c) reusability of utility services; d) message transformation and translation, allowing easy integration of legacy applications, this real-time version acts as a service bus for MES virtualized in the cloud, offering new features of robust queuing, capable of handling shop floor data bursts in a consistent manner (Figure 5.10):

1) *Event-driven communication*: the main role of the implementation is to perform the event dispatch operation, allowing shop floor resources and intelligent products to exchange information in an event-driven fashion.

2) *Workflows*: along with event dispatching, the real-time ESB (RT-ESB) is able to launch and execute predefined workflows (successive operations) associated with specific events requiring complex logic to handle them, like resource breakdowns.

3) *Synchronous and asynchronous communication*: the implementation offers both synchronous and asynchronous communication modes.

4) *Message persistence*: in asynchronous mode, the messages reside in logical queues from where they are consumed. The RT-ESB implementation stores the queues in a persistent highly available storage (a network file system or a distributed database) that allows production state recovery in case of a system crash.

5) *Message transformation*: the shop floor level integrates a wide range of software modules (e.g. computing energy consumption per operation) and hardware devices (e.g. power meter, IED). The communication protocols and the message formats used can be a simple +5 V DC signal, proprietary line protocols or even high-level TCP-based protocols. MSB transforms these messages to and from the proprietary protocols in a common standardized format, by allowing the development of message converters at any entry point and exit point of the bus.

6) *Message validation*: the RT-ESB performs message validation according to pre-defined rules and logic before dispatching; this approach prevents errors down stream in map-reduce procedures like those used in Big Data transfer from shop floor resources and IPs to the cloud for global MES workloads (see Figure 5.10).

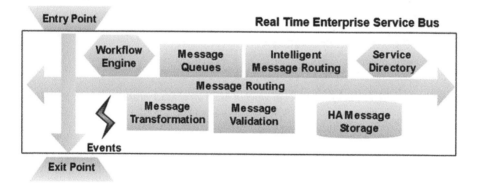

Figure 5.10. *Logical view of RT-ESB for vMES workload transfer in the cloud*

Along with the classic *hypervisor virtual machine* approach (VM) to virtualize MES workloads, some more advanced techniques can be used to further optimize resource usage and improve performance. Container-based architectures have increasingly been adopted over the last years, especially due to better standardization in the containerization technologies, the transition to micro-service-based architectures and the employment of agile methodologies. A *container* is a virtualization environment that emulates the operating system, in contrast with hypervisors that emulate the hardware layer. A container lifecycle is managed by a container engine that runs on top of the OS kernel.

The main difference between containers and virtual machines is that a virtual machine requires a hypervisor running on the operating system of the hardware server. The virtual machine has its own operating system on which the applications offering the services run. The container is much lighter and requires only an operating system on which the container is running; the container is composed only by a runtime which offers the support files for the application to run, and the application itself which offers the service (Mavridis and Karatza 2019).

Combining hypervisor and container virtualization can yield benefits in cloud vMES scenarios. Figure 5.11 offers a comparison of three approaches to virtualization.

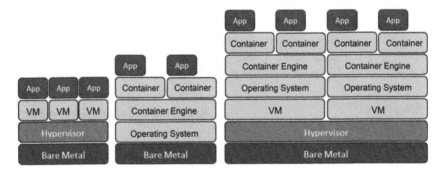

Figure 5.11. *High-level view of MES workload virtualization approaches: left – VM; middle – container; right – hybrid*

Depending on the requirements of the workload, there are some considerations on which approach is appropriate to virtualize resource, product and MES workloads:

– *Compute intensive workloads*: workloads that deal with data processing and are intensive in terms of resource consumption are generally executed in a cloud-based environment, either private or hybrid. In a private cloud environment, a *hybrid virtualization* approach would give the best results. The hypervisor layer assures isolation between workloads because of hardware emulation; at the same time, containers provide consolidation options, so applications can be grouped together on virtual machines, thus improving hardware utilization. The hybrid virtualization approach gives architects the tools to balance between isolation requirements of workloads and flexibility of containers. When porting legacy applications to a virtualized environment, this hybrid architecture proves to be the most flexible, as it provides transparent virtualization of the operating system layer.

– *Real-time workloads*: these workloads operate in real time and in close relation with intelligent products and shop floor resources. From the virtualization perspective, the main requirements for these types of workflows are low latency and reliability. It is also important to keep these workloads as lightweight as possible, as some of them are executed on embedded devices. Using container-based virtualization is a good approach because container technology does not virtualize hardware, so code execution can be guaranteed almost the same as with non-virtualized applications. Containers are lightweight in comparison to VMs from a storage perspective, containing only the binaries and libraries required for the application to run. This is a relevant aspect, especially where workloads are provisioned dynamically during the manufacturing process, as the overhead is significantly reduced.

In the industrial domain, using cloud services offered in IaaS infrastructure must take into account the dynamic nature of the workloads to be virtualized in the cloud and hence the timing for deploying MES-related services. The basic approaches are:

1) deploying services inside the cloud system *before production starts*;

2) deploying the services *on-demand*, whenever they are needed.

In the first case, the services are offered just before the production starts and the industrial control system (the MES) can start production without any delay (a typical situation is the offline optimization of mixed operation scheduling and allocation on resources – a computing-intensive workload). The problem is that the resources must be pre-provisioned and the load of services must be predicted. Online reconfiguration or deployment of the services (like in the semi-heterarchical MES control mode) adds downtime to the services caused by restarting the virtual machines implied in the process. This approach will use more resources than needed and is less flexible; hence, it can be adopted if the processes and their control are not changing dynamically from the point of view of the cloud services needed, and the number of services can be predetermined before the production starts. If at production runtime a service needs to be deployed in the cloud, then a delay will occur. This approach can be used if the delay is acceptable or if the MES can predict the need of the service and generate the service request before this service is needed (Anton *et al.* 2019).

In the second approach, the resources are consumed in an efficient way; however, being an IaaS system, service provisioning will require time which is translated in production execution delays. The solution to use containers is flexible because it offers elastic services and scales faster than virtual machines. The size of a container is also much smaller than a VM and the provisioning process is much faster. This solution can be used in highly dynamic industrial control environments due to the speed of service provisioning, but with the cost of a set of resources which are allocated by default by the VM which offers the containers.

The best solution is to use a combination of virtual machines deployed in the cloud before the start of the production, while the services will run in containers executed on the virtual machines. In this case, the VMs accessed as services in the IaaS cloud will be the base for offering the static part of the services, and the containers which are deployed much faster than virtual machines will cover the dynamic services. The solution of using containers inside virtual machines is also adequate from the security perspective, even if running the container in a VM causes a slight drop of performance compared with running it on the operating system directly installed on the server. VMs will be combined with containers in complex environments where two types of cloud services are needed: *heavy load services* (offered using VMs) and *dynamic light services* (offered using containers).

5.5. Perspectives offered by virtualization to industry of the future

Future industrial systems will be conceived as cyber-physical systems (CPS) that use strongly coupled virtual entities (software agents, holons or virtual twins) which represent (or are embedded in) physical components that sense, actuate, process, control, compute and communicate through several networks, including the Internet, in order to reach global goals – making products, delivering services efficiently and safely. The drivers of industrial CPS are resource, product and system virtualization (Cardin 2019), and distribution of intelligence in IT systems that virtualize workloads through cloud services. MES virtualization reduces operational costs and improves flexibility, agility, reconfigurability and maintainability of the production system. The factory data streams and global MES functions are mapped to specific workloads in the cloud, defined in terms of activity scheduling, resource assignment and behavior forecast.

Virtualization also brings many advantages on the industrial system reliability by allowing full system snapshots and backups and quick recovery in case of failures, as well as providing built-in redundancy. Most private cloud implementations offer these features by default and can be directly adopted. MES workload virtualization allows decoupling between the physical resources and the controlling information system. The most important advantage introduced by this decoupling is the possibility of having multiple versions of the MES workload with different configurations and switch between them as required. This reconfiguring capability is very useful when initial configuration or changes need to be tested and implemented in the production line. With virtualized MES workloads, a redundancy mechanism with active/active or active/passive workloads can be implemented.

Adoption of virtualization and cloud-related functionality, like automatic provision and de-provision of workloads and predictive resource allocation, represent the first steps for implementing highly flexible industrial systems designed on SOA concepts and patterns. In recent years, a great deal of effort has been invested in these cloud platforms by both academia and cloud vendors. Production enterprises have a new opportunity to take advantage of this and move from legacy systems to highly scalable and flexible solutions based on cloud platforms (Trentesaux *et al.* 2016). Future work is directed towards developing an integrated framework for resource, product and information systems virtualization, such as vMES, based on the concepts presented.

5.6. References

Anton, F.D., Borangiu, T., Anton, S., Răileanu, S. (2019). Deploying on demand cloud services to support processes in robotic applications and manufacturing control systems. *Proceedings of the 23rd International Conference on System Theory, Control and Computing*, 9–11 October, Sinaia, Romania [Online]. Available at: https://ieeexplore.ieee.org/document/8885712.

Borangiu, T., Răileanu, S., Trentesaux, D., Berger, T., Iacob. I. (2014). Distributed manufacturing control with extended CNP interaction of intelligent products. *Journal of Intelligent Manufacturing*, 25, 1065–1075.

Caputo, F., Greco, A., Fera, M., Macchiaroli, R. (2019). Digital twins to enhance the integration of ergonomics in the workplace design. *International Journal of Industrial Ergonomics*, 71, 20–31 [Online]. Available at: https://doi.org/10.1016/j.ergon.2019.02.001.

Cardin, O. (2019). Classification of cyber-physical production systems applications: Proposition of an analysis framework. *Journal Computers in Industry*, 104, 11–21.

Graessler, I. and Poehler, A. (2018). Intelligent control of an assembly station by integration of a digital twin for employees into the decentralized control system. *Procedia Manufacturing*, 24, 185–189.

Kritzinger, W., Karner, M., Traar, G., Henjes, J., Sihn, W. (2018). Digital twin in manufacturing: A categorical literature review and classification. *IFAC-PapersOnLine*, 51(11), 1016–1022.

Lange, J., Iwanitz, F., Burke, T. (2016). *OPC from Data Access to Unified Architecture*, 4th edition. VDE Verlag, Frankfurt.

Lydon, B. (2020). ISA95 in the IoT & digitalization era. Technical report, International Society of Automation [Online]. Available at: https://www.automation.com/en-us/articles/2020/isa95-in-the-iot-digitalization-era.

Mavridis, I. and Karatza, H. (2019). Combining containers and virtual machines to enhance isolation and extend functionality on cloud computing. *Future Generation Computer Systems*, 94, 674–696.

McFarlane, D., Ratchev, S., Thorne, A., Parlikad, A.K., de Silva, L., Schönfuß, B., Hawkridge, G., Terrazas, G., Tlegenov, Y. (2020). Digital manufacturing on a shoestring: Low cost digital solutions for SMEs. In *Service Oriented, Holonic and Multi-Agent Manufacturing Systems for Industry of the Future*, Borangiu, T., Trentesaux, D., Leitão, P., Giret Boggino, A., Botti, V. (eds). Springer, Cham.

Morariu, O., Morariu, C., Borangiu, T. (2015). vMES: Virtualization aware manufacturing execution system. *Journal of Computers in Industry*, 67, 27–37.

Morariu, C., Morariu, O., Răileanu, S., Borangiu, T. (2020). Machine learning for predictive scheduling and resource allocation in large scale manufacturing systems. *Journal Computers in Industry*, 120, 103244.

Răileanu, S., Anton, F., Iatan, A., Borangiu, T., Anton, S., Morariu, O. (2017). Resource scheduling based on energy consumption for sustainable manufacturing. *Journal of Intelligent Manufacturing*, 28(7), 1519–1530.

Trentesaux, D., Borangiu, T., Thomas, A. (2016). Emerging ICT concepts for smart, safe and sustainable industrial systems. *Journal Computers in Industry*, 81, 1–10.

Valckenaers, P. (2020). Perspective on holonic manufacturing systems: PROSA becomes ARTI. *Journal Computers in Industry*, 120, 103226.

6

Cybersecurity of Industrial Cyber-Physical Systems

Antoine GALLAIS and Youcef IMINE

LAMIH UMR CNRS 8201, Université Polytechnique Hauts-de-France, Valenciennes, France

The digital transition in the industry is resulting in new services based on data from various objects (sensors, actuators, robots). More specifically, industrial cyber-physical systems (ICPS) now enable sophisticated interactions between connected devices and humans to make informed decisions. These objects range from sensors and actuators to vehicles and production machines. They are used in the fields of industry, energy, mobility, the smart home and the smart city. The rapid evolution of the number of objects and the tasks performed on them has increased the attack surface of ICPS, significantly increasing the risk of cyber incidents at the same time. Recent sophisticated attacks, exploits and flaws in software and hardware designs (e.g. Stuxnet, WannaCry, Mirai, Meltdown) thus testify to the importance of cybersecurity for industrial cyber-physical systems. Indeed, digital control systems make decisions that are reflected towards the physical elements of ICPS, thus posing security and safety risks incurred in the infrastructures relying on these ICPS (e.g. road safety, nuclear safety). In order to determine the decisions to be taken, these systems use data exchanged within or between several ICPS. Numerous solutions used today in the Internet make it possible to secure data

For a color version of all figures in this book, see www.iste.co.uk/cardin/digitalization.zip.

Digitalization and Control of Industrial Cyber-Physical Systems,
coordinated by Olivier CARDIN, William DERIGENT and Damien TRENTESAUX.
© ISTE Ltd 2022.

exchanges, guaranteeing in particular the confidentiality of contents, their integrity and the authentication of sources and destinations.

However, after the emergence of the Internet of Things, where data is stored and processed within remote infrastructures (e.g. cloud), there are now many reasons for carrying out these operations as close as possible to the source objects (e.g. reactivity of real-time applications, optimization of bandwidth, limitation of the risk of data leakage). The security solutions deployed in the context of the Internet must therefore be adapted, or even rethought, in order to take into account the specific characteristics of ICPS.

6.1. What are the risks involved?

Within the ICPS, the data and decision-making mechanisms are vulnerable to attacks from the outside or inside. The motivation and skill levels of attackers vary depending on the products handled by the targeted ICPS and the security systems in place to protect them. The significant growth in the number of connected devices in these environments has only amplified this phenomenon. Among other things, security issues inherent to communications are becoming predominant, with potential attacks at all levels of the communication stack (e.g. jamming, sleep denial, frame relay and injection, identity theft). Existing and deployed solutions for the Internet, however, are inadequate, mainly due to the limited resources available to objects and the complex environments in which they operate (Kouicem *et al.* 2018).

However, the applications envisaged in the field of transport or health present important safety or public health issues (e.g. road safety, remote assistance; Panchal *et al.* 2018). Assisted or autonomous decision-making must therefore rely on available services and potentially confidential data. In order to control access to these data and services, it is necessary to first authenticate the actors who interact with these resources. It is then possible to grant authorizations corresponding to the role of each entity in the ICPS. Depending on the nature of the data generated and exchanged during these processes, it is crucial to define a level of privacy protection.

6.1.1. *Unavailability of systems*

The devices deployed in these scenarios are doubly exposed, due to their geographical position (uncontrolled environment) and connectivity (more and more communication standards, for example IEEE 802.11p, NFC, IEEE 802.15.4). Some of the attacks aim to make these systems unavailable, by preventing them from performing their usual tasks. The blocking of physical devices transmitting data can thus lead to the denial of service for the systems using them. The latter can also be the target of attacks that cause them to stop functioning. As a result, without data to process or without a system to do so, the ICPS are deprived of the control functions essential to their operation. These attacks are all the more dangerous as their detection requires being able to distinguish them from usual disturbances such as instabilities (i.e. intermittent connectivity) or drops in performance (e.g. delivery rates, delays).

Therefore, protecting these systems while keeping their indispensable properties (e.g. energy saving) represents a major challenge (Merlo *et al*. 2015), *a fortiori* in a context where new attacks are emerging.

– **Jamming**: jamming attacks are designed to disable some or all communications. These attacks can target a variety of wireless technologies, including GPS, mobile communications and Wi-Fi. The mere emission of an interference signal in the frequency bands used can be enough to block communication on a wireless channel. While simple to execute, they can be very dangerous and difficult to detect. For example, in the field of smart meters, the regularly transmitted readings make it possible for attackers to predict the most damaging periods during which to disrupt the signals. They can then settle for short jamming times, which ensure low detection probabilities (Algin *et al*. 2017).

The objective of an active jammer is to keep the channel busy, even when it is not in use. A reactive jammer, on the other hand, observes channel activity and only begins jamming when the channel is in use. Jamming attacks can also be aimed at draining the resources of battery-operated devices, thus putting the entire system at risk. Nevertheless, the design and implementation of such effective security mechanisms remains challenging, due to the limited computational and memory resources available on the targeted devices (Tiloca *et al*. 2015, 2019).

– **Denial-of-Service** (DoS): a DoS attack is when a system is unable to provide the service(s) it normally provides. These attacks disrupt access to resources and can delay the execution of urgent operations. As a result, the system is unable to respond to legitimate requests. Attackers can also coordinate multiple compromised devices (or accomplices) to launch a denial-of-service attack on a target. In this case, we refer to it as a distributed denial-of-service (DDoS) attack, such as in the attacks that led to a power outage for several hundred thousand Ukrainians in 2015 (Lee *et al*. 2016).

Figures 6.1–6.3 illustrate such an attack carried out by hijacking TCP connection establishment. Figure 6.1 shows a typical connection initiation. It begins with the transmission of a SYN packet from the legitimate user. If the server responds favorably (with a SYN/ACK packet), then the sender of the request can confirm its request (with an ACK packet) and thus finalize the establishment of a TCP flow.

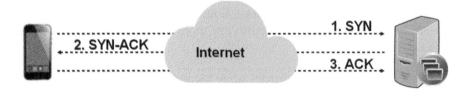

Figure 6.1. *Establishing a TCP connection between a legitimate client and a server that now has three established connections*

In this example, we assume that the server already had two TCP clients connected and thus ends up with three established connections. Subsequently, an attacker can initiate a TCP connection with a server by sending it a SYN packet, without following up on the SYN–ACK packet it receives in return. The server, for its part, keeps a so-called semi-open connection (in addition to the three already established), for which context information is stored in memory (see Figure 6.2).

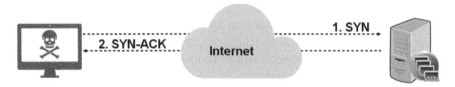

Figure 6.2. *SYN/ACK attack where the malicious client requests synchronization with the server, without ever finalizing the TCP connection establishment*

This means that multiple synchronized attackers can target a server by sending SYN packets simultaneously, without being followed by ACK packets. Since the targeted server must handle a large number of semi-open connections, it will become unable to process SYN packets from legitimate clients that have been subjected to a DDoS attack, as shown in Figure 6.3.

Here are the attack vectors that allow us to realize a denial of service:

– Botnets: botnets are networks of objects infected with malware that become controllable in a centralized manner by attackers. These infected objects will thus participate in increasing the scale of a DDOS attack and cause more damage in the target system. This is how the Mirai botnet, consisting of several tens of millions of IP addresses, was able to disable the Dyn provider, then preventing any address resolution from an entire part of the Internet (Antonakakis *et al.* 2017).

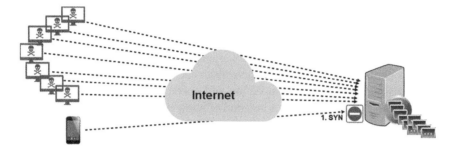

Figure 6.3. *Example of the distributed denial of service using SYN/ACK attacks*

– Reflection-based attacks: a reflection attack consists of sending packets to machines accessible via the network (reflectors) using the victim's IP address as the source IP address. As a result, the reflectors generate unsolicited responses to the victim.

– Amplification attacks: this type of attack is often carried out by exploiting the properties of certain protocols (DNS, for example) in order to maximize the volume of traffic generated. The protocols exploited during an amplification attack are generally protocols whose response size is much larger than the request size. As a result, when the cost disparity is amplified by numerous requests, the resulting volume of traffic can disrupt the network infrastructure due to the large sizes of the responses sent back.

6.1.2. *Loss of confidentiality or integrity*

Emerging systems such as ICPS are based on a collaborative model between several objects. In most cases, these objects use remote services (storage or computing power) offered by other entities in the network (i.e. gateways or data sinks). However, the use of these services requires the confidentiality of data for sensitive applications to be guaranteed, for example, military, health, safety. Many attacks on ICPS can cause data leaks, such as those observed in 2020 from Visser Precision. The publication of data relating to products supplied by this American company affected several of its customers (e.g. Boeing, Lockheed Martin, SpaceX, Tesla).

Eavesdropping

This so-called passive attack consists simply of observing the operation of the system, without altering its functioning. The adversary can thus intercept any information communicated by the system. ICPS are particularly sensitive to eavesdropping, which makes it possible for an attacker to analyze the traffic. For example, if the appropriate security mechanisms are not in place, an attacker could collect the control data sent back by the various sensors making up an ICPS. These attacks jeopardize confidentiality at several levels. They could enable attackers to collect sensitive data on the organization and operation of the ICPS. They would also give access to the personal information of users interacting with these ICPS.

Key compromise attack

The compromise of a key means that an attacker now has the ability to access data encrypted with that key. Such a key should only be known by trusted third parties who are authorized to manipulate the data. In general, the security of a key is based on three criteria: (1) the size of the key used, (2) the security of the process of transmitting the key to its bearer object in the cyber-physical system and finally (3) the secure storage of the key in the various components of the ICPS.

An attacker may obtain the key via a brute force attack (i.e. reverse engineering, testing all possible keys until the correct one is found; Garfinkel 2015), or as a result of a security flaw in the transmission process. The success of such an attack makes it possible for the attacker to access the secured data, without the knowledge of the legitimate entities (e.g. correspondents on a radio channel). The attacker can also use the compromised key to analyze the key generation algorithms used in the cyber-physical system. This enables the attacker to compute additional keys in case the ICPS implements weak cryptographic mechanisms (e.g. vulnerabilities discovered in Haier SmartCare home automation system (Arias *et al.* 2017)). The attacker can then access other secure communications or resources.

Advanced persistent threats (APT)

According to the NIST definition (Dempsey *et al.* 2011), APTs are attacks with (1) specific targets and clear objectives and (2) highly organized and well-resourced attackers. The approach followed in these attacks is a repetitive process that extends over time and uses stealthy and evasive techniques (e.g. use of zero-day exploits) to hijack the security mechanisms implemented in the ICPS. APTs follow an attack approach known by the name *cyber kill chain* (Yadav and Rao 2015), comprising the following phases:

1) Reconnaissance: this preliminary phase of the attack aims to gather as much information as possible that will be useful for breaking into the target system and executing the attack. Here, the adversary seeks to answer the following questions:

– What methods of attack will offer the highest degree of success?

– Which are the easiest to execute in terms of investment?

2) Weaponization: in this phase, the attacker becomes active and begins to prepare their infiltration into the target system. The attacker creates malware (e.g. virus, worm) to exploit the vulnerabilities identified during the reconnaissance phase.

3) Delivery: in this phase, the attacker begins their intrusion and transmits the malicious payload prepared during the arming phase. There are two types of delivery mechanisms: (1) direct delivery, where the attacker manages to introduce the malicious payload through an identified entry point into the system (e.g. a vulnerable sensor, an open port in the ICPS administrator's machine). (2) Stealthy indirect delivery, where the attacker transmits the malicious payload using a third party approved by the target but compromised (e.g. via a phishing attack that targets an ICPS administrator).

4) Exploitation and installation: in this phase, the attackers have initial unauthorized access to the target system and will begin by installing the necessary tools to carry out the attack. Once the anchor point is established inside the system, the attackers attempt a privilege escalation, in order to gain more access rights in the target system.

5) Command and control: during this phase, adversaries control the assets of the target system, enabling further exploitation of the system. To evade detection, attackers typically use legitimate services and publicly available tools (e.g. DNS, ICMP, HTTP(S)) and also make lateral moves into the target system to identify other points of vulnerability and locations of sensitive data.

6) Data exfiltration: the theft of sensitive data is among the main objectives of an APT attack. Data exfiltration consists of transmitting the stolen data to an internal (previously installed) transfer point, where it will be processed (e.g. compression, encryption) before being transmitted to external locations controlled by the attackers. In order to mask the transmission process, APT actors often use secure protocols (e.g. TLS).

In the context of ICPS, APTs typically target Supervisory Control and Data Acquisition (SCADA) systems in order to gain strategic advantage, not only through data theft, but also through compromising the operation of the control system itself. Among the most well-known attacks on SCADA systems, the Stuxnet computer worm was able to spy on and reprogram industrial systems at Iran's Natanz nuclear facility (Kushner 2013).

6.1.3. *Bypassing access and authentication controls*

ICPS have been developed in many industrial fields (e.g. water industry, chemical engineering, healthcare, power transmission, manufacturing, transportation). Directly linked to people's daily lives, the various ICPS applications are thus confronted with identity theft and access rights violations caused mainly by the following threats.

Man in the middle

This type of attack is based on eavesdropping. The attacker manages to insert themselves in the middle of a legitimate communication. This makes it possible for the attacker to intercept information and data from either party, or even modify them. When the data is related to authentication (e.g. key exchange), this attack can make it possible to spy on a victim.

Replay attack

A replay attack consists of intercepting a transmission and repeating it later. This replay of traffic aims to deceive legitimate recipients and alter the operation of the system. An attacker can thus intercept data messages and resend them (modified or not) at the moment they consider appropriate. The consequences of such an action are erroneous decisions or an overconsumption of energy by the relay and recipient objects. The attacker can also replay control messages in order to modify the operation of the targeted ICPS (e.g. change the configuration of the control system).

Internal threats

These threats are usually caused by people with certain appropriate access rights to an information system. They then abuse these privileges by carrying out attacks in order to circumvent the security mechanisms in place (Bishop and Gates 2008). For example, a malicious employee could take advantage of the trust placed in them and the internal knowledge acquired on an ICPS to cause the propagation of a worm (e.g. introduction of the Stuxnet worm via a USB key). The measures deployed to defend against external malicious actions are then useless against the threat from entities within the system. The internal threat affects every infrastructure and can cause far more damage to the organization than any external threat.

6.2. What means of protection?

In the face of the attacks detailed so far, the design and implementation of effective security mechanisms remains challenging, due to the limited computational and memory resources available on the targeted objects. Yet, responsiveness in case of attacks is essential, both for detection and protection of targeted services (Granjal *et al.* 2015). Attacks affect each level of the protocol stack, whether it is the physical and MAC layers (e.g. denial of service), routing (e.g. replay of alert packets to prevent responses to legitimate requests, injection of fake signaling packets to generate or stop congestion, hijacking of sensitive data) or application (e.g. corruption of the geolocation system or injection of viruses in connected vehicles (Hasrouny *et al.* 2017)).

6.2.1. *Ensuring availability*

To ensure the availability of an ICPS, its administrators must be able to detect any anomalies that occur in the system as soon as possible. Among the denial-of-service attacks targeting ICPS, jamming attacks can be countered using radio channel observations and learning methods (Karagiannis and Argyriou 2018). Other threats require solutions such as filtering communications using firewalls or intrusion detection as a last resort. It should be noted that when such protections are put in place, it is essential to conduct regular audits to test the relevance and effectiveness of the rules defined in these tools.

Communication filtering

The protection of an ICPS requires filtering of communications and data entering and leaving the system. Such filtering mechanisms are used in firewalls, which observe network traffic and apply static or dynamic rules. The former is used when firewalls filter according to the raw data contained in packets (e.g. source and destination addresses, protocol used, packet size). The latter analyzes the role of each packet in relation to the more global context in which it occurs. For example, it is thus possible to detect and block a DDoS attack based on a flood of SYN packets, as discussed previously in Figures 6.1–6.3. In such a case, a firewall could incorporate a rule to only accept new connection requests within a suitable time interval.

In the context of ICPS, communication filtering operations are carried out by an industrial firewall. This device aims to secure the connections between two connected networks in an industrial environment. It recognizes industrial protocols (e.g. PROFINET, ETHERCAT) and can be configured to block all incoming network traffic, except those explicitly required to maintain proper system operations (Huang *et al.* 2015).

Intrusion detection

Intrusion detection systems (IDS) are distinguished first and foremost by the location in which they are installed. Host-based IDS (HIDS) are installed on all or part of the machines that make up the system. They analyze events triggered at the operating system level. Network-based IDS (NIDS) are deployed near network equipment (e.g. switches, routers) in order to observe the traffic passing through.

Whether HIDS or NIDS, these systems differ in how they characterize intrusions. Static IDSs rely on sets of known attack rules and signatures, while dynamic IDSs attempt to characterize the usual behavior of the system in order to alert administrators when actions deviate from it. Each of these approaches has its advantages and disadvantages. A rule-based IDS is immediately effective against known attacks. However, it will not be able to detect new threats, unlike a dynamic IDS that can automatically evolve its attack signature base. This type of evolving IDS requires learning based on observations made on the system to be protected (Flaus and Georgakis 2018; Yao *et al.* 2019). Intrusions are then detected when the observed behavior differs from the one usually characterized (Hussain *et al.* 2021). IDSs also differ in the way they analyze traffic, in real time or *a posteriori*. The former allows increased responsiveness but requires significant resources, while the latter allows easier discovery of new intrusion patterns (Abdel-Basset *et al.* 2020).

The tools described here can be used to ensure the availability of services provided and used within an ICPS. It should also be noted that there are vulnerability assessment tools. These are designed to proactively protect cyber assets by identifying and then mitigating or removing vulnerabilities before they are exploited. Tools such as Nessus and OpenVas can contribute to this proactive protection (McMahon *et al.* 2018; Chhetri and Motti 2020) to verify these systems with numerous constraints (e.g. scaling). Other work has also focused on automating penetration testing so that analysts can cope with the increasing number of new cyber threats (Vezzani *et al.* 2019; Pozdniakov *et al.* 2020). This work consists of implementing intelligent agents that execute different attack sequences aimed at finding vulnerabilities in a target system. This execution phase is accompanied by a learning phase that aims to improve the logic of penetration testing by learning and exploring new attack sequences.

While these safeguards enable data exchanges to continue, they are not sufficient to protect the data in the event of interception.

6.2.2. *Ensuring confidentiality*

Before discovering the methods and tools used to guarantee confidentiality, it is imperative to understand some basic notions of cryptography. Indeed, data encryption guarantees confidentiality by making the encrypted information incomprehensible to any third party not involved in the communication.

Many encryption algorithms are distinguished according to whether they use symmetric or asymmetric keys. In the first case, the two communicating entities share an identical key that allows them to encrypt and decrypt the data they exchange (e.g. AES). In the second case, each entity has a pair of keys, one of which is public and can be distributed, while the other is private and must be kept safe.

Solutions based on symmetric encryption guarantee the confidentiality of data, as long as the key remains unknown to unauthorized actors. The simplicity of symmetric encryption mechanisms (e.g. basic logic operations, shift registers) makes them easy to implement on constrained objects. Moreover, the encryption/ decryption of a data item is not very resource-intensive for any entity that has the key. On the other hand, it must be possible to exchange this key between legitimate entities, without a malicious actor being able to copy it. Existing solutions for this purpose are based on the principles of the Diffie–Hellman key exchange (Diffie and Hellman 1976). Two entities exchange data necessary to generate a symmetric (i.e. identical) key for each. However, this data is not sufficient for any third party to use it to generate the same key. This method relies on the use of cyclic finite groups (e.g. the multiplicative group of integers modulo p, where p is a prime number) or elliptic curves. In the case of finite groups, the data that a third party could intercept are only the remainders of Euclidean divisions by a prime number. The problem that the third party then faces is that of the discrete logarithm, which is impossible to solve from certain data sizes (e.g. prime numbers p of size 2048 bits, i.e. about 600 digits in decimal writing).

Asymmetric encryption methods rely on a public/private key pair and thus avoid the complexity of sharing a symmetric key. Their security lies in the complexity of decomposing large integers into products of prime factors. The most widely used algorithm, RSA (Rivest *et al.* 1978), uses a public key consisting of an exponent and a divisor, and a private key that is another exponent. The encryption of a datum is the remainder of the Euclidean division of that datum raised to the power of the public exponent by the public divisor. Only the entity with the private exponent associated with these two numbers can then retrieve the original data. Asymmetric cryptography avoids the need to share an identical key kept secret, as in symmetric cryptography. However, it requires heavier operations (e.g. exponentiation).

This is why the two approaches are most often used together. Asymmetric encryption is then used only to encrypt the only critical information in symmetric cryptography: the shared secret key. In this way, both parties have this secret key and can use simple symmetric encryption algorithms. The cost of asymmetric encryption (e.g. RSA) will only have been paid for the transmission of the symmetric key (e.g. AES).

Asymmetric cryptography also allows us to ensure the integrity of data using electronic signatures. The principle is simple: encrypt a fingerprint of the data using the private key. The fingerprint is calculated using one-way hash functions[1] (e.g. SHA-512). Any entity will then be able to decrypt this signature using the public key in order to compare the resulting fingerprint with the one calculated on the received data. If the two match, it means that the data is indeed the one that was signed.

However, the advantages of using asymmetric cryptography are accompanied by several costs that may prove prohibitive for some ICPS equipment. For example, on some embedded architectures, the hundreds of milliseconds required for a signature with a 2048-bit RSA (private) key[2] could affect the responsiveness of the steering or decision-making system (Malina *et al.* 2016). Trust in the data feeding these systems could then rely on the authentication of their sources.

6.2.3. *Implementing authentication mechanisms*

The authentication service is the entry point to any security system. It consists of verifying the identity of entities in a system. Authentication protocols can be classified into three main families (Brainard *et al.* 2006):

– "Something you know" protocols: in this family of protocols, an entity in the system will be authenticated based on its knowledge of secret information that is also known by the authenticating entity (e.g. password).

---

1. It must be very difficult to retrieve the data from the fingerprint alone, and even minor changes to the data must lead to a very distant fingerprint.

2. Minimum size recommended by the French National Agency for Information Systems Security (*Agence, Nationale de la Sécurité des Systèmes d'Information*, ANSSI).

– "Something you have" protocols: in this family of protocols, an entity in the system will be authenticated if it proves that it has something specific in its possession (e.g. certificate, security token, SIM card). In practice, the something you know and something you have approaches are combined to achieve a so-called multi-factor authentication (e.g. online payment requiring the possession of a credit card and the knowledge of a secret code in order to authenticate the bearer and validate the transactions).

– "Something you are" protocols: in this family of protocols, an entity in the system will be authenticated based on biometric information. Many types of biometric systems are in use or under development today. These include authentication systems based on voice, fingerprint, retina, signature or keystroke pattern recognition. Biometric systems are extremely robust in terms of security, as they circumvent the problems associated with the use of objects that can be stolen or revealed. However, they can only be applied in cases where we have direct interaction with humans.

These different protocol families can be implemented at different levels of ICPS. For example, the something you have solutions are the only ones able to ensure authentication between physical components of the system (e.g. actuators, sensors). The something you know and something you are solutions are more suitable when human intervention is required, usually in the context of ICPS control and command operations (e.g. password or fingerprint authentication in a smart industry monitoring system).

6.2.4. Controlling access, permissions and logging

The aim here is to study authentication and authorization mechanisms between services processing common data. In an ICPS, the physical sensors will provide data to the control and decision-making systems. In the case of the connected vehicle, for example, a control system could use data from the numerous communicating objects onboard (e.g. signs, speed limit) and from equipment not integrated in the vehicle (e.g. driver's pedometer), in order to assist the decision-making of human or software actors (e.g. detection of driver's pause time). Therefore, two services (i.e. health and road safety applications) have to share the same data, without having the same access rights on it (e.g. data anonymized in the road safety context and not in the health application, which is more personalized). The security protocols defined by the IEEE 1609.2 standard (IEEE 2016) guarantee confidentiality, authentication and integrity, but anonymity is limited (Ucar et al. 2018). Also, the transit and processing of data across separate systems raises the question of their protection.

For these reasons, the objective here is to secure the data and implement access control policies governing the rights of each service mobilized during the processing flow.

An access control system must rely on an authentication system to verify the identity of a service wishing to perform an operation on a resource. An authorization system must then validate (or not) the request of a given service. Authorization can be seen as both the definition and application of rules controlling access to resources. The management of authorizations (issuance, verification) is even more complex when considering a diverse set of services, provided by entities with different properties and exploiting several types of resources (Mehta and Sandall 2017).

There are two types of access control: physical and logical. Physical access control systems regulate physical access to resources, such as access to a factory, campus, buildings, etc. On the other hand, logical access control regulates logical access to a digital resource (e.g. access to the network, access to data in a system). These two access control systems share the following concepts:

– object: an entity that contains or receives information;

– subject: an active entity that performs tasks in the system;

– operation: an active process invoked by a subject;

– permission (privilege): an authorization to perform an action on the system.

In order to protect the components of an industrial cyber-physical system and manage access rights and permissions to different resources, it is essential to deploy logical access control mechanisms. These mechanisms can be defined as logical modules that serve to receive an access request from the subject and then decide and enforce the access decision according to a previously defined policy (Hu *et al.* 2013). These mechanisms are usually based on access control models defined as follows:

1) Discretionary access control (DAC): in this access control model, access rights can be defined at the discretion of the owner or any other entity that controls access to a resource in the system.

2) Mandatory access control (MAC): access rights in this model are regulated by a central authority that defines the security policies of the system on several levels. The term mandatory implies that access control is based on clearly defined rules that must be followed throughout the system.

3) Identity-based access control (IBAC): this model relies on mechanisms such as access control lists (ACLs) to identify which components are allowed to access a resource.

4) Role-based access control (RBAC): the system assigns a predefined role to each component. Each role has a specific set of privileges that allow the role holder to access the different resources of the system.

5) Attribute-based access control (ABAC): each component in this model is identified by a set of attributes. Attributes are characteristics (or values) of a component involved in an access event. This access control analyzes the attributes of a component and evaluates its access right through a set of rules, policies and relationships built on the basis of the different attributes of the system.

Cryptographic access control is a paradigm designed for a global federation of information systems. This paradigm represents an access control mechanism that relies exclusively on cryptography to ensure the confidentiality and integrity of data managed in the system. In addition, it provides effective access control in untrusted (in terms of security) environments, such as ICPS. In the following, we present the most widely used cryptographic access control methods in the literature that can be implemented in the data management layer of ICPS.

1) **Identity-based encryption (IBE)** is an advanced method of public key encryption (Boneh and Franklin 2001). A user's public key is generated using identity information (e.g. an administrator's email address in an ICPS). In the IBE scheme, a central trusted authority generates system parameters (a public/master key pair) and publishes a part of these generated system parameters (public parameters). A sender who has access to the public parameters can encrypt a message using unique information identifying the recipient as an encryption key. On the other hand, the receiver must obtain its decryption key from the central authority, which established the public parameters, in order to successfully decrypt the encrypted data.

2) **Attribute-based encryption (ABE)** is an approach that goes even further than IBE, by defining the identity of users as a set of attributes that form a private key (e.g. the characteristics of a component in an ICPS such as its type and role in the system). The main idea of ABE is to encrypt data according to an access policy that specifies the attributes that other components must have in order to access the encrypted data. The access policy (also known as the access tree) is a logical expression combining several attributes via logical operators. The leaf nodes

of the access tree represent the attributes used in encryption, while the non-leaf nodes represent threshold gates used to bind the leaf nodes (attributes) together. A component verifies its authorization to access encrypted data if the attributes stored in its private key satisfy the access policy defined during encryption.

In attribute-based encryption, we distinguish two main approaches:

– key-policy attribute-based encryption (KP-ABE; Goyal *et al.* 2006);

– cipher-text policy attribute-based encryption (CP-ABE; Bethencourt *et al.* 2007).

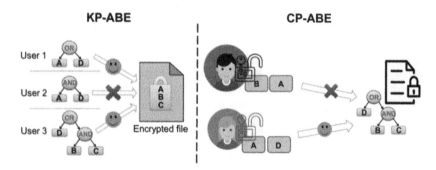

Figure 6.4. *Comparison between the KP-ABE and CP-ABE approaches*

KP-ABE associates encrypted data with a set of descriptive attributes, while access policies are applied on user keys. Therefore, a data owner has no control over who has access to its encrypted data. This is because the data owner does not set the access policy and their control is limited to the choice of descriptive attributes associated with the encrypted data.

On the contrary, CP-ABE makes it possible to define access policies for data encryption. Thus, this approach offers more flexibility and gives more control to the data owner. Figure 6.4 illustrates how the KP-ABE and CP-ABE approaches work.

6.3. Conclusion

ICPS are made up of communicating physical objects capable of feeding their control and decision-making systems. Data exchange and processing within an ICPS must be done in complete security, in order to protect the equipment, the information and ultimately the users. This protection consists of ensuring data confidentiality, integrity and authentication of their sources and destinations.

In the same way as the interconnection of autonomous systems that led to the current Internet, there is already an interest in exchanging data and information between ICPS, for example, for collaborative purposes. This is why it seems critical to protect these exchanges, by defining and applying access control, filtering and intrusion detection methods.

Securing an ICPS thus requires an in-depth study of the machines, users and services that make it up, as well as the protocols that govern communications. Beyond the notions presented in this chapter, it is crucial that ICPS security be described through policies. These policies enable the entities that consult them to determine the level of trust that they can have in the ICPS. These entities may be external ICPS with which data should be exchanged, or simply the actors of the ICPS in question, who seek to ensure the robustness of their system. The security procedures are in fact intended to be audited.

The security assessment of ICPS depends on several factors related to the system usage patterns, the topology of the network interconnecting its different components, as well as the attack patterns identified in the system in question. Among the approaches used in the literature to address this issue, we find model-based approaches (Nguyen et al. 2017). These approaches assess the security of the ICPS based on its workflow. The security of the ICPS then develops throughout its lifecycle. This also provides a (semi-)automated (formal) verification and validation of the security of each process provided in the ICPS.

Finally, we have not dealt with data protection aspects. The deployment of ICPS for sensitive applications (e.g. smart mobility, remote assistance) could lead to rethinking the data security and guaranteeing its protection, at scales not encountered so far (Lopez et al. 2017). To address this issue, the evolution of storage and processing approaches (e.g. from Cloud to Edge computing) may have been accompanied by increased availability and varying degrees of data anonymization (Lu et al. 2017). At the European level, these personal data protection requirements are contained in the General Data Protection Regulation (GDPR). This EU text and other international data protection texts (e.g. Australia, Brazil, California, Canada) have resulted in the international standard ISO 27701 that identifies privacy-enabling security techniques (ISO/IEC 2019).

6.4. References

Abdel-Basset, M., Chang, V., Hawash, H., Chakrabortty, R.K., Ryan, M. (2020). Deep-IFS: Intrusion detection approach for IIoT traffic in fog environment. *IEEE Transactions on Industrial Informatics*, 1–1.

Algin, R., Tan, H.O., Akkaya, K. (2017). Mitigating selective jamming attacks in smart meter data collection using moving target defense. *Proceedings of the 13th ACM Symposium on QoS and Security for Wireless and Mobile Networks*, Q2SWinet '17, Association for Computing Machinery, New York, 1–8 [Online]. Available at: https://doi.org/10.1145/3132114.3132127.

Antonakakis, M., April, T., Bailey, M., Bernhard, M., Bursztein, E., Cochran, J., Durumeric, Z., Halderman, J.A., Invernizzi, L., Kallitsis, M., Kumar, D., Lever, C., Ma, Z., Mason, J., Menscher, D., Seaman, C., Sullivan, N., Thomas, K., Zhou, Y. (2017). Understanding the Mirai botnet. In *26th USENIX Security Symposium (USENIX Security 17), USENIX Association*, Vancouver, B.C., 1093–1110 [Online]. Available at: https://www.usenix.org/conference/usenixsecurity17/technicalsessions/presentation/antonakakis.

Arias, O., Ly, K., Jin, Y. (2017). Security and privacy in IoT era. *Smart Sensors at the IoT Frontier*. Springer, Cham.

Bethencourt, J., Sahai, A., Waters, B. (2007). Ciphertext-policy attribute-based encryption. *IEEE Symposium on Security and Privacy (SP '07)*, 321–334.

Bishop, M. and Gates, C. (2008), Defining the insider threat. *Proceedings of the 4th Annual Workshop on Cyber Security and Information Intelligence Research: Developing Strategies to Meet the Cyber Security and Information Intelligence Challenges Ahead*, 15, 1–3.

Boneh, D. and Franklin, M. (2001). Identity-based encryption from the weil pairing. *Annual International Cryptology Conference*. Springer, Cham.

Brainard, J., Juels, A., Rivest, R.L., Szydlo, M., Yung, M. (2006). Fourth-factor authentication: Somebody you know. *Proceedings of the 13th ACM Conference on Computer and Communications Security*, 168–178.

Chhetri, C. and Motti, V. (2020). Identifying vulnerabilities in security and privacy of smart home devices. *National Cyber Summit*. Springer, Cham.

Dempsey, K., Johnson, L., Scholl, M., Stine, K., Clay, A., Orebaugh, A., Chawla, N., Johnston, R. (2011). Information Security Continuous Monitoring (ISCM) for Federal Information Systems and Organizations. Special Publication (NIST SP), National Institute of Standards and Technology, Gaithersburg, MD [Online]. Available at: https://doi.org/10.6028/NIST.SP.800-137 [Accessed 10 January 2022].

Diffie, W. and Hellman, M. (1976). New directions in cryptography. *IEEE Transactions on Information Theory*, 22(6), 644–654.

Flaus, J.-M. and Georgakis, J. (2018). Review of machine learning based intrusion detection approaches for industrial control systems. *Computer & Electronics Security Applications Rendez-vous (C&ESAR) Conference*, Rennes.

Garfinkel, S.L. (2015). De-identification of personal information. *National Institute of Standards and Technology*. October.

Goyal, V., Pandey, O., Sahai, A., Waters, B. (2006). Attribute-based encryption for fine-grained access control of encrypted data. *Proceedings of the 13th ACM Conference on Computer and Communications Security*, 89–98.

Granjal, J., Monteiro, E., Silva, J.S. (2015). Security for the Internet of Things: A survey of existing protocols and open research issues. *IEEE Communications Surveys & Tutorials*, 17(3), 1294–1312.

Hasrouny, H., Samhat, A.E., Bassil, C., Laouiti, A. (2017). VANET security challenges and solutions: A survey. *Vehicular Communications*, 7, 7–20.

Hu, V.C., Ferraiolo, D., Kuhn, R., Friedman, A.R., Lang, A.J., Cogdell, M.M, Schnitzer, A., Sandlin, K., Miller, R., Scarfone, K (2013). Guide to attribute based access control (ABAC) definition and considerations (draft). *NIST Special Publication*, 800(162), 1–54.

Huang, S., Zhou, C.-J., Yang, S.-H., Qin, Y.-Q. (2015). Cyber-physical system security for networked industrial processes. *International Journal of Automation and Computing*, 12(6), 567–578.

Hussain, B., Du, Q., Sun, B., Han, Z. (2021). Deep learning-based DDoS-attack detection for cyber–physical system over 5G network. *IEEE Transactions on Industrial Informatics*, 17(2), 860–870.

IEEE (2016). IEEE standard for wireless access in vehicular environments – Security services for applications and management messages. IEEE Std 1609.2-2016 (Revision of IEEE Std 1609.2-2013), 1–240.

ISO/IEC (2019). Security techniques – Extension to ISO/IEC 27001 and ISO/IEC 27002 for privacy information management – Requirements and guidelines. ISO/IEC 27701:2019.

Karagiannis, D. and Argyriou, A. (2018). Jamming attack detection in a pair of RF communicating vehicles using unsupervised machine learning. *Vehicular Communications*, 13, 56–63.

Kouicem, D.E., Bouabdallah, A., Lakhlef, H. (2018). Internet of Things security: A top-down survey. *Computer Networks*, 141, 199–221.

Kushner, D. (2013). The real story of stuxnet. *IEEE Spectrum*, 50(3), 48–53.

Lee, R., Assante, M., Conway, T. (2016). Analysis of the cyber attack on the Ukrainian power grid. *Defense Use Case*, SANS ICS.

Lopez, J., Rios, R., Bao, F., Wang, G. (2017). Evolving privacy: From sensors to the Internet of Things. *Future Generation Computer Systems*, 75, 46–57.

Lu, R., Heung, K., Lashkari, A.H., Ghorbani, A.A. (2017). A lightweight privacy-preserving data aggregation scheme for fog computing-enhanced IoT. *IEEE Access*, 5, 3302–3312.

Malina, L., Hajny, J., Fujdiak, R., Hosek, J. (2016). On perspective of security and privacy-preserving solutions in the Internet of Things. *Computer Networks*, 102, 83–95.

McMahon, E., Patton, M., Samtani, S., Chen, H. (2018). Benchmarking vulnerability assessment tools for enhanced Cyber-Physical System (CPS) resiliency. *IEEE International Conference on Intelligence and Security Informatics (ISI)*, 100–105.

Mehta, M. and Sandall, T. (2017). How Netflix is solving authorization across their cloud [Online]. Available at: https://www.youtube.com/watch?v=R6tUNpRpdnY.

Merlo, A., Migliardi, M., Caviglione, L. (2015). A survey on energy-aware security mechanisms. *Pervasive and Mobile Computing*. Special Issue on Secure Ubiquitous Computing, 24, 77–90.

Nguyen, P.H., Ali, S., Yue, T. (2017). Model-based security engineering for cyber-physical systems: A systematic mapping study. *Information and Software Technology*, 83, 116–135.

Panchal, A.C., Khadse, V.M., Mahalle, P.N. (2018). Security issues in IIoT: A comprehensive survey of attacks on IIoT and its countermeasures. *IEEE Global Conference on Wireless Computing and Networking (GCWCN)*, 124–130.

Pozdniakov, K., Alonso, E., Stankovic, V., Tam, K., Jones, K. (2020). Smart security audit: Reinforcement learning with a deep neural network approximator. *International Conference on Cyber Situational Awareness, Data Analytics and Assessment (CyberSA)*, IEEE, 1–8.

Rivest, R.L., Shamir, A., Adleman, L. (1978). A method for obtaining digital signatures and public-key cryptosystems. *Commun. ACM*, 21(2), 120–126 [Online]. Available at: https://doi.org/10.1145/359340.359342.

Tiloca, M., Guglielmo, D.D., Dini, G., Anastasi, G., Das, S.K. (2015). Defeating jamming with the power of silence: A game-theoretic analysis. *IEEE Transactions on Wireless Communications*, 15(5).

Tiloca, M., Guglielmo, D.D., Dini, G., Anastasi, G., Das, S.K. (2019). DISH: Distributed shuffling against selective jamming attack in IEEE 802.15.4e TSCH networks. *ACM Transactions on Sensor Networks*, 15(1), 1–28.

Ucar, S., Ergen, S.C., Ozkasap, O. (2018). IEEE 802.11p and visible light hybrid communication based secure autonomous platoon. *IEEE Transactions on Vehicular Technology*, 67(9), 8667–8681.

Vezzani, G., Gupta, A., Natale, L., Abbeel, P. (2019), Learning latent state representation for speeding up exploration. arXiv preprint. arXiv:1905.12621.

Yadav, T. and Rao, A.M. (2015). Technical aspects of cyber kill chain. *International Symposium on Security in Computing and Communication*. Springer, Cham.

Yao, H., Gao, P., Zhang, P., Wang, J., Jiang, C., Lu, L. (2019). Hybrid intrusion detection system for edge-based IIoT relying on machine-learning-aided detection. *IEEE Network*, 33(5), 75–81.

PART 4

Controlling Industrial Cyber-Physical Systems

7

Industrial Agents: From the Holonic Paradigm to Industrial Cyber-Physical Systems

Paulo Leitão[1], Stamatis Karnouskos[2], and Armando Walter Colombo[3]

[1] *Research Centre in Digitalization and Intelligent Robotics (CeDRI), Instituto Politécnico de Bragança, Portugal*
[2] *SAP, Walldorf, Germany*
[3] *Institute for Industrial Informatics, Automation and Robotics (I2AR), University of Applied Sciences Emden/Leer, Emden, Germany*

Traditional control approaches are based on centralized and hierarchical structures, following the well-known (ANSI/ISA-95 2010) standard, also known as the automation pyramid, which presents good production optimization, but a weak response to condition change and reconfigurability due to the rigidity, monolithic structure and centralization of their control structures (Colombo *et al.* 2021). These control approaches are not designed or prepared to respond to the current demanding requirements of responsiveness, scalability, reconfigurability and robustness (Leitão 2009a).

The advent of Industry 4.0 (Kagermann *et al.* 2013; Leitão *et al.* 2020) led to the use of distributed control structures, the use of the decentralization of control nodes and the introduction of intelligence to transform the existing assets into smart

---

Digitalization and Control of Industrial Cyber-Physical Systems,
coordinated by Olivier Cardin, William Derigent and Damien Trentesaux.
© ISTE Ltd 2022.

processes and machines, and also considering smart products (Barbosa *et al.* 2016) as important players in this ecosystem. Multi-agent systems (MAS) and holonic systems are suitable for facing these demanding requirements since they offer an alternative way to design and implement such innovative systems, taking advantage of their capability to decentralize the management over distributed structures towards modularity, scalability, robustness, fault-tolerance, reconfigurability and reusability (Leitão *et al.* 2016b; Karnouskos and Leitão 2017). The development of Industry 4.0-compliant solutions will constitute a new opportunity to use MAS and holonics to realize these innovative and emergent industrial cyber-physical systems (ICPS) that foster the backbone of Industry 4.0 (Colombo *et al.* 2015, 2017; Leitão and Karnouskos 2015; Leitão *et al.* 2016b; Karnouskos *et al.* 2020). This is evident in the efforts within the industrial cyber-physical systems (ICPS) that have emerged over the last few years (Colombo *et al.* 2017), where the MAS have the potential to significantly enhance different aspects of ICPS, such as decision-making, and enable them to address a wide variety of industrial challenges (Leitão *et al.* 2016a).

This chapter introduces the main conceptual foundations of MAS and holonic systems and presents the framing of industrial agents as an instantiation of such technological paradigms to face industrial requirements such as, for example, those posed by ICPS. The alignment of industrial agents with RAMI 4.0 (Deutsches Institut fuer Normung 2016) is also addressed, and, in particular, the use of industrial agents to realize ICPS, to concretely enhance the functionalities provided by the asset administration shells (AAS), which play an important role in developing and implementing Industry 4.0 components (Boss *et al.* 2020). Finally, this chapter discusses some research challenges and directions that currently arise from the deployment of industrial agents.

7.1. Overview of multi-agent systems and holonics

7.1.1. *Multi-agent systems*

MAS is a technological paradigm derived from the distributed artificial intelligence field that is suitable for implementing flexible, adaptive and responsive ICPS (Leitão *et al.* 2016a), based on a set of intelligent autonomous entities called agents that cooperate to achieve the system goals.

There is not a unique or universal definition for agents, for example there are those given in Russel and Norvig (1995) and Wooldridge (2002), but a suitable definition is that an agent is an "autonomous component that represents physical or logical objects in the system, capable to act in order to achieve its goals, and being able to interact with other agents, when it does not possess knowledge and skills to reach alone its objectives" (Leitão 2009a). From such a definition, it is clear that autonomy (i.e. the capability of performing their own decisions without the direct intervention of external entities) and cooperation (i.e. the capability of interacting with other agents to achieve their objectives) are important characteristics of agents. However, according to Wooldridge and Jennings (1995), an agent may also exhibit other characteristics, such as intelligence (i.e. the capability of reasoning and performing cognitive procedures), reactivity (i.e. the capability of sensing the environment and quick response to changes), proactivity (i.e. the capability of taking the initiative) and social capabilities (i.e. the capability of interacting with other agents, and possibly humans, via a communication language).

Rare applications consider agents in an isolated manner, but, instead, they generally consider a set of agents to solve complex problems, constituting a MAS, that can be defined as a society of agents that may represent physical or logical objects of a system, capable of interacting in order to achieve their individual goals when they do not have enough knowledge and/or skills to achieve their objectives individually (Leitão 2009a).

As illustrated in Figure 7.1, a MAS system comprises a society of agents, each one representing one object, with a set of goals and possessing a set of skills and local knowledge. Each agent is regulated by internal behaviors that are responsible for performing the required actions towards the execution of its goals, which are its functionalities encapsulated as services.

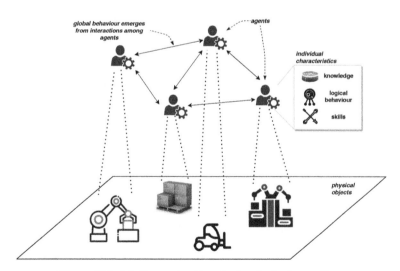

Figure 7.1. *Multi-agent system technological paradigm*

In such systems, since each agent has a partial view of the system, as well as partial knowledge and skills to execute its goals, agents need to interact with each other, performing different forms of cooperation, for example, collaboration and negotiation, to achieve its goals. The global system function emerges from the interaction among the distributed agents, each one contributing with its knowledge and skills. For this purpose, agents follow a heterarchical structure organization characterized by the high level of autonomy and cooperation, which ensure modularity, plugability, robustness, scalability and reconfigurability on-the-fly.

Compared to traditional centralized control strategies, MAS offers an alternative way to design large-scale and complex systems by decentralizing the control of the system, and distributing the control between autonomous and cooperative agents, ensuring the capabilities to adapt to emergence without external intervention (Wooldridge 2002). In fact, MAS replaces the centralized control with a distributed functioning where the interactions among individual agents lead to the emergence of "intelligent" global behavior. This ensures a high degree of autonomy without a fixed client–server structure.

Agents are computational pieces of code that exhibit the described characteristics, namely intelligence, autonomy and cooperation, based on a distributed system infrastructure. An agent-based system can be developed using a programming language, but the development of agent-based applications requires the implementation of features that are not supported by usual programming languages, such as message transport, encoding and parsing, yellow and white page services, and agent lifecycle management services, which increases the programming effort and complexity. In order to simplify their development, debugging and maintenance, they are usually developed using agent development frameworks that provide these features. As an example, the Java Agent DEvelopment (JADE) framework (Bellifemine et al. 2007) is a well-known agent development platform that provides a set of services, namely a naming service and yellow page services, message transport and parsing services, a library of the Foundation for Intelligent Physical Agents (FIPA 2002) interaction protocols, agent lifecycle management services and debug tools, in order to develop agent-based (FIPA 2002) compliant systems.

7.1.2. Holonic paradigm

Holonic paradigm translates the Köstler's observations and Herbert Simon's theories into a set of appropriate concepts for distributed control systems.

In the mid-1960s, Köstler (1967) introduced the word holon to describe the basic unit of organization in living organisms and social organizations. Based on Simon's theories that complex systems are hierarchical systems formed by intermediate stable forms, which do not exist as auto-sufficient and non-interactive elements but, on the contrary, they are simultaneously a part, and a whole, Köstler concluded that, although it is easy to identify sub-wholes or parts, wholes and parts in an absolute sense do not exist anywhere (Leitão 2009b).

Having this in mind, Köstler proposed the word *holon* to represent this hybrid nature, which is a combination of the Greek word *holos*, meaning whole, and the suffix *on*, meaning particle. Similar to agents, autonomy and cooperation are the major characteristics of holons, which are autonomous and cooperative entities that can represent physical or logical objects, for example, a robot, a machine, an order or a product. As illustrated in Figure 7.2, it can comprise a communication part, an information processing part and a physical processing part, where the physical part of the holon represents a physical device, such as a product, a transport module, a machine or an industrial robot (Colombo *et al.* 2001; Leitão 2009b). This feature can be considered as the inspiration for the CPS concept in the sense of combining cyber and physical counterparts.

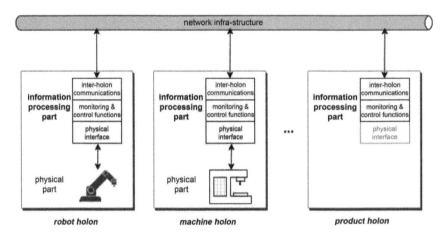

Figure 7.2. *Highlights of the constitution of holons*

A holarchy is a society of holons, organized in a hierarchical structure, operating as autonomous wholes in supra-ordination to their parts and as dependent parts in sub-ordination to controls on higher levels. Holons cooperate with each other to achieve system goals by combining their individual skills and knowledge. In a holarchy, the holon behaviors and activities are determined through the cooperation with other holons, following appropriate interaction patterns, as opposed to being determined by a centralized mechanism.

Each holarchy has fixed rules and directives, and a holon can dynamically belong to multiple holarchies at the same time, which is an important difference from the traditional concept of hierarchies. In fact, each holon can integrate a holarchy and simultaneously preserve their autonomy and individuality. This allows the best of two worlds to be obtained: preserving the stability of hierarchy while providing the dynamic flexibility of heterarchy structures.

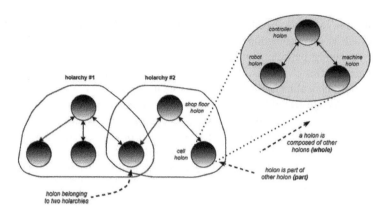

Figure 7.3. *Main features of holonics paradigm*

In holonics, the design of complex problems can be simplified by dividing the initial problem into several small problems. This is possible through the inherent recursivity capability associated with the holon, and particularly with the Janus effect, i.e. a holon is simultaneously a self-contained whole to its subordinated parts and a dependent part when seen from the higher levels. As illustrated in Figure 7.3, a holon representing a cell can be simultaneously the whole, encapsulating holons representing the cell resources and the part when considering the shop floor system. In other words, a holon can be part of another holon or a holon can be broken into several other holons, which in turn can be broken into further holons.

These characteristics provide many advantages that are well adapted for the semi-structured environment of ICPS. The next section of this chapter introduces the technical aspects of implementation in the context of ICPS. The next chapter is intended to provide some insights about the most successful holonic architectures in the literature for architecturing the implementation.

7.2. Industrial agents

7.2.1. *Definition and characteristics*

In the context of MAS, a software agent can be defined as "an encapsulated computer system that is situated in some environment and that is capable of flexible, autonomous action in that environment in order to meet its design objectives" (Jennings and Wooldridge 1998). As previously referred to, these agent-based systems provide several benefits, namely flexibility, robustness, reconfigurability and scalability, to developing large and complex systems (Leitão and Karnouskos 2015).

Industrial agents inherit the software agent principles, such as intelligence, autonomy and cooperation, but their application domains are related to industrial environments and then face industrial requirements, for example, specific hardware integration, reliability, fault-tolerance, scalability, industrial standard compliance, quality assurance, resilience, manageability and maintainability (Leitão et al. 2016b). The degree of importance of each requirement is different and depends on the operational and business contexts. Additionally, Karnouskos and Leitão (2017) elaborate on the key factors, which include design, technology, intelligence/algorithms, standardization, hardware, challenges, application and cost, that play important roles in the acceptance of agent-based solutions in the industry.

In this sense, according to Unland (2015), an industrial agent is an

> agile and robust software entity that intelligently represents and manages the functionalities and capabilities of an industrial unit. While it reveals the common features of an advanced agent, it also has some specifics. It understands and efficiently handles the interface and functionality of (low-level) industrial devices. Usually, it belongs to an agent-based industrial application system within which it acts and communicates in an efficient, intelligent, collaborative, and goal-oriented way. In principle, it is an autonomous and self-sustained unit. Nevertheless, it accepts and follows company guidelines, codes of conduct, general laws, and relevant directives from higher levels. Moreover, especially in emergency and real-time scenarios, its autonomy may be compromised in order to permit fast and efficient reactions.

Apart from inheriting the software agent principles, industrial agents also inherit several insights from the holonics principles, mainly in terms of the integration of physical assets, through the interaction of the computational intelligent part (the information processing part in holonics) and the physical asset. The design principles provided by holonics can also be used by monitoring and control applications that are based on industrial agents.

The industrial agent context imposes strong requirements that may affect the adequacy of the existing agent development frameworks and consequently compromise the industrial adoption of the agent technology. In this context, the development of new, light and industrial-oriented agent development frameworks is fundamental to attending the industrial requirements, considering the communication between industrial agents, the structure to interconnect the physical assets and the legacy systems and the compliance with industrial standards (Colombo et al. 2006).

Another important issue to be addressed is the target applications that can better benefit from the use of industrial agents. Due to the intrinsic characteristics of industrial agents, and particularly the need for interaction among agents to achieve the global behavior, they are particularly suited for soft real-time operations, for example, monitoring, simulation, planning, scheduling and system self-organization under condition changes. The implementation of hard real-time control strategies usually requires us to combine industrial agents with traditional industrial controllers, for example, programmable logic controllers (PLCs) and computer numerical control (CNC), that maintain the nominal system operation and ensure the system responsiveness (Colombo *et al.* 2001; Leitão *et al.* 2021).

7.2.2. *Interfacing with physical assets*

Along with the holonics principles, an industrial agent usually has an associated physical hardware counterpart, which increases the deployment complexity. For example, consider one software agent associated with a punching machine to monitor and optimize its health condition or a software agent associated with a smart metering device to gather the current consumption data. In this context, the interface between the software agent and the low-level automation control devices, illustrated in Figure 7.4, assumes a crucial role. Due to the heterogeneity of the counterparts, this interface can be implemented in different ways, following proprietary or more standard technologies, without having a universal standard that allows the easy, fast and transparent integration (Schoop *et al.* 2002).

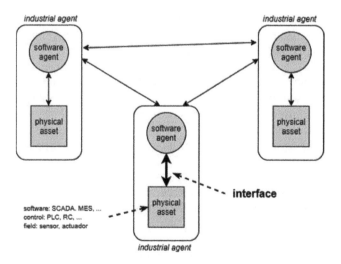

Figure 7.4. *Interface between the software agent and the physical asset*

The recently established IEEE 2660.1-2020 standard on Recommended Practice on Industrial Agents (IEEE 2021) addresses this problem by defining a method to recommend the best interfacing practice for a particular application scenario, taking into account the feedback from experts in implementing and using different interfacing practices (Leitão *et al.* 2021). For this purpose, this method scores and compares the existing interface practices according to specific criteria, and also indicates their strong and weak points.

7.3. Industrial agents for realizing industrial cyber-physical systems

In the CPS and their evolution towards in ICPS, as analyzed by Colombo *et al.* (2017), several challenges arose, many of which have been researched via the utilization of MAS in different application domains (Leitão *et al.* 2016b). MAS and holonics have been applied in industrial environments, namely, in smart production, smart grids and smart logistics, for more than 20 years (Lastra and Colombo 2006; Leitão and Karnouskos 2015; Leitão *et al.* 2016b). Nowadays, industrial agents can play an important role in the ICPS context since, in these emergent solutions, they can naturally provide autonomy, proactivity and cooperation. In fact, industrial agents are potentially suited to realize ICPS by adding a brain set of capabilities that include knowledge, decision-making algorithms and negotiation algorithms to the AAS, and thus contributing to the realization of more autonomous and intelligent I4.0 components.

7.3.1. *Supporting the development of intelligent products, machines and systems within cyber-physical systems*

Adopting Industry 4.0-compliant digitalization and networking technologies for the migration of the traditional hierarchical industrial architectures and associated technologies (Colombo *et al.* 2010, 2014b) which are implemented on the basis of IEC 62264/IEC 61512, the transformation leads to a distributed, asynchronously networked and functionally flat infrastructure, driven by the interaction among the different services (Colombo *et al.* 2005). This infrastructure is composed of a set of cyber-physical nodes, also identified as I4.0 components and systems. Each node is a fusion of mechatronics, communication, information and service-based business technologies (Colombo *et al.* 2014a).

According to DIN SPEC 91345, which describes the reference architecture model for Industry 4.0 (Deutsches Institut fuer Normung 2016), an initial physical object, positioned within the ISA'95/ISA'88 standard enterprise architecture, is called an "asset". Each of these assets can be digitalized and networked following the six-layer specifications addressed by the vertical dimension of the 3D-RAMI 4.0 model. Such a digitalized and networked asset becomes a cyber-physical component/system, recognized as an I4.0 component/system.

The concrete specification and implementation of a cyber-physical component or an I4.0 component are performed by means of the asset administration shell (AAS), as illustrated in Figure 7.5 (Boss *et al.* 2020). The AAS is a uniquely addressable digital/cyber representation of functionality and data/information for each type and instance of an asset. In this sense, it supports the Internet-based communication and the networking of a digitalized asset with other assets in the Industry 4.0-compliant system.

NOTE.– The relationship between this specification of ICPS and the definition introduced in Chapter 1 of this book can be better understood following the schema shown in Figure 17.1 of Chapter 17.

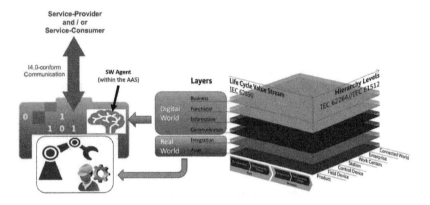

Figure 7.5. *Positioning of industrial physical agents within RAMI 4.0*

Following the latest reported results about the specification and implementation of the AAS, it is possible to summarize a set of characteristics such as:

1) the AAS creates cross-vendor interoperability because it contains data and information associated with different phases of the lifecycle of the digitalized and networked asset;

2) the AAS specifies the entire lifecycle of products, equipment, machinery and production systems, following the standard specification IEC 62890;

3) the AAS enables "digital" consistent value chains being considered as the implementation of different "digital twins" of the asset(s).

The AAS is composed of submodels which are the data and information containers associated with different lifecycle phases of the digitalized asset.

Any asset located within the IEC 62264 standard architecture can become a CPS or I4.0 component, i.e. products, sensors and actuators, controllers, stations, lines, IT-/Management systems such as manufacturing execution systems (MES), enterprise resource planning (ERP), customer relationship management (CRM), etc. These I4.0 components and systems cyber-physical components and systems, are able to perform business in a service-oriented fashion, and for each business to be developed and implemented, I4.0 components have to fulfill a dedicated set of service-level agreements (SLAs).

An innovative concrete step for integrating agent- and holonic-technology with I4.0-compliant solutions is to include essential capabilities of agents/holons, such as decision-making functions as well as negotiation services, as a set of new submodels, as schematically depicted in Figure 7.6.

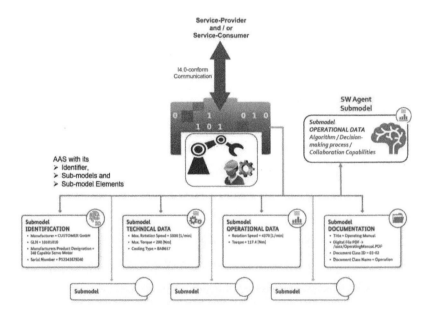

Figure 7.6. *Industrial agent as a submodel within the AAS*

7.3.2. *Implementing an industrial multi-agent system as ICPS*

The proposal to enhance the AAS structure by, for example, a submodel with agent capabilities, has major consequences. On the one side, the AAS is designed to be available for both non-intelligent and intelligent digitalized assets, which is also a digital basis for autonomous components and systems. On the other side, the set of I4.0 components with intelligent decision-making and negotiation capabilities, that is, the set of networked AAS with intelligence, constitutes the basis of an I4.0-compliant "industrial multi-agent system". It is here where MAS and holonics technologies find their way into the Industry 4.0 and CPS contexts. The AAS are in charge of managing their own physical agents, and the SLA-based business interaction protocol manages the whole I4.0 ecosystem-based MAS/holonic systems.

7.4. Discussion and future directions

Concepts and technologies pertinent to industrial agents and holonic systems have been researched and prototyped over the last few decades (Colombo *et al.* 2001, 2006; Leitão and Karnouskos 2015; Leitão *et al.* 2016b). However, the influences of each era of computing and communication paradigms and associated technologies are evident (Ribeiro *et al.* 2017), and have heavily influenced how this research and these prototypes have evolved, and recently this is due to the emergence of Industry 4.0 (Leitão *et al.* 2020), and, specifically, the ICPS (Karnouskos *et al.* 2020). The promising directions are towards the power relation that rely on the combination of CPS and agents that can lead to enhanced capabilities, management, engineering, infrastructures, ecosystems and information systems (Colombo *et al.* 2021).

From a technology viewpoint, there are several horizontal challenges that pertain to industrial agents and CPS that are identified and, to a degree, also prioritized (Leitão *et al.* 2016a, 2016b; Colombo *et al.* 2017; Karnouskos *et al.* 2020). Ever-relevant directions that agents can address include integration, modularity, servification and collaboration in order to realize the autonomous and intelligent infrastructures envisioned. In addition, the direction of combining the intelligent aspects of agents with the modern machine learning capabilities can further lead to approaches that deal with better planning, learning, knowledge representation and control, all of which are at the heart of modern CPS systems and services (Ribeiro *et al.* 2008; Nagorny *et al.* 2012; Karnouskos *et al.* 2020).

Beyond the core technology aspects for the powerful combination of agents and CPS, the operationalization of these in concrete scenarios is also of research interest. This is especially promising in the direction of human–machine interaction where agents can mediate and bring together both humans and machines. Today these areas are under active development via the utilization of modern technologies with successful realization such as sophisticated chatbots, augmented/virtual reality, personal assistants, etc.

Agent-based modeling and simulation have been an active area of agents, and approaches can be extended to the new CPS-based infrastructures. Simulation of complex CPS infrastructures, as well as large ecosystems with their own goals and capabilities, is of interest. In addition, providing monitoring, management and control solutions for such complex systems while hiding complexity and, in parallel, offering self-management is also another promising direction.

Finally, because most of the discussed solutions go beyond the traditionally highly controlled industrial environments, key issues relevant to security, trust, privacy, resiliency, safety and ethics are also promising directions to investigate, as future agent-based systems are expected to be designed, developed and operated in real-world constellations with high uncertainties.

While, for engineers, priorities are initially on the technology and product/solution development, it is necessary to consider that other non-technical aspects may be the determining factors for success. As analyzed by Karnouskos and Leitão (2017), the key factors for the acceptance of agents in industrial environments include design, technology, intelligence/algorithms, standardization, hardware, challenges, application and cost. The case of the agent-based system Production 2000+ at the Mercedes-Benz (now Daimler) factory plant in Stuttgart, Germany (Colombo *et al.* 2006) exemplifies why agents should not be looked at solely as a technology, but in their entirety, including the business aspects (Karnouskos *et al.* 2020). The introduction of agent-based solutions enhanced reconfiguration and adaptation in the assembly line, and was in operation for five years before being decommissioned, despite the evidenced robustness and higher productivity increase of 20%, because its technical advantage did not imply an immediate and measurable economic advantage (Schild and Bussmann 2007).

In conclusion, it can be pointed out that several promising directions exist (Karnouskos *et al.* 2020) for agents and their associated concepts, which, however, need to carefully balance technological as well as operational and business factors (Karnouskos and Leitão 2017). The current combination of agent concepts, modern technologies and the emergence of cyber-physical infrastructures today provides the most fruitful ground where agent-based approaches can be designed, realized, operated and assessed. As can be seen, industrial agents and their associated concepts may yet have another chance to enter the mainstream and achieve the long-promised impact (Karnouskos and Leitão 2017).

7.5. References

ANSI/ISA-95 (2010). ANSI/ISA-95.00.01-2010 (IEC 62264-1 mod). Enterprise-control system integration – Part 1: Models and terminology. Standard, International Society of Automation.

Barbosa, J., Leitão, P., Trentesaux, D., Colombo, A.W., Karnouskos, S. (2016). Cross benefits from cyber-physical systems and intelligent products for future smart industries. *14th IEEE International Conference on Industrial Informatics (INDIN'16)*.

Bellifemine, F., Caire, G., Greenwood, D. (2007). *Developing Multi-Agent Systems with JADE*. John Wiley & Sons, Ltd., Chichester.

Boss, G.B., Malakuti, S., Lin, S.-W., Usländer, T., Clauer, E., Hoffmeister, M., Stojanovic, L. (2020). Digital twin and asset administration shell concepts and application in the industrial internet and industrie 4.0. Technical report, Industrial Internet Consortium and Plattform Industrie 4.0 [Online]. Available at: https://www.plattform-i40.de/PI40/Redaktion/DE/Downloads/Publikation/Digital-Twin-and-Asset-Administration-Shell-Concepts.html.

Colombo, A.W., Neubert, R., Schoop, R. (2001). A solution to holonic control systems. *8th International Conference on Emerging Technologies and Factory Automation (ETFA)*. IEEE.

Colombo, A.W., Jammes, F., Smit, H., Harrison, R., Lastra, J., Delamer, I. (2005). Service-oriented architectures for collaborative automation. *31st Annual Conference of IEEE Industrial Electronics Society, 2005. IECON 2005*. IEEE.

Colombo, A.W., Schoop, R., Neubert, R. (2006). An agent-based intelligent control platform for industrial holonic manufacturing systems. *IEEE Transactions on Industrial Electronics*, 53(1), 322–337.

Colombo, A.W., Karnouskos, S., Mendes, J.-M. (2010). Factory of the future: A service-oriented system of modular, dynamic reconfigurable and collaborative systems. In *Artificial Intelligence Techniques for Networked Manufacturing Enterprises Management*, Benyoucef, L. and Grabot, B. (eds). Springer, London.

Colombo, A.W., Bangemann, T., Karnouskos, S. (2014a). IMC-AESOP outcomes: Paving the way to collaborative manufacturing systems. *2014 12th IEEE International Conference on Industrial Informatics (INDIN)*. IEEE.

Colombo, A.W., Bangemann, T., Karnouskos, S., Delsing, J., Stluka, P., Harrison, R., Jammes, F., Lastra, J.L. (eds). (2014b). *Industrial Cloud-Based Cyber-Physical Systems*. Springer, Cham.

Colombo, A.W., Karnouskos, S., Mendes, J.M., Leitão, P. (2015). Industrial agents in the era of service-oriented architectures and cloud-based industrial infrastructures. In *Industrial Agents: Emerging Applications of Software Agents in Industry*, Leitão, P. and Karnouskos, S. (eds). Elsevier, Amsterdam.

Colombo, A.W., Karnouskos, S., Kaynak, O., Shi, Y., Yin, S. (2017). Industrial cyberphysical systems: A backbone of the fourth industrial revolution. *IEEE Industrial Electronics Magazine*, 11(1), 6–16.

Colombo, A.W., Karnouskos, S., Yu, X., Kaynak, O., Luo, R.C., Shi, Y., Leitão, P., Ribeiro, L., Haase, J. (2021). The IES 70 year evolution journey through industrial revolutions – ICT perspective. *IEEE Industrial Electronics Magazine*, 15(1), 115–126.

Deutsches Institut fuer Normung (2016). Reference architecture model industrie 4.0 (rami4.0). DIN SPEC 91345.

FIPA (2002). Foundation for Intelligent Physical Agents (FIPA) [Online]. Available at: http://www.fipa.org.

IEEE (2021). IEEE recommended practice for industrial agents: Integration of software agents and low-level automation functions. IEEE Standard.

Jennings, N.R. and Wooldridge, M. (1998). Applications of intelligent agents. In *Agent Technology: Foundations, Applications and Markets*, Jennings, N.R. and Wooldridge, M. (eds). Springer, Berlin Heidelberg.

Kagermann, H., Wahlster, W., Helbig, J. (2013). Securing the future of German manufacturing industry: Recommendations for implementing the strategic initiative industrie 4.0. Technical report, ACATECH.

Karnouskos, S. and Leitão, P. (2017). Key contributing factors to the acceptance of agents in industrial environments. *IEEE Transactions on Industrial Informatics*, 13(2), 696–703.

Karnouskos, S., Leitão, P., Ribeiro, L., Colombo, A.W. (2020). Industrial agents as a key enabler for realizing industrial cyber-physical systems: Multiagent systems entering industry 4.0. *IEEE Industrial Electronics Magazine*, 14(3), 18–32.

Köstler, A. (1967). *The Ghost in the Machine*. Hutchinson, London.

Lastra, J.L.M. and Colombo, A.W. (2006). Engineering framework for agent-based manufacturing control. *Engineering Applications of Artificial Intelligence*, 19(6), 625–640.

Leitão, P. (2009a). Agent-based distributed manufacturing control: A state-of-the-art survey. *Engineering Applications of Artificial Intelligence*, 22(7), 979–991.

Leitão, P. (2009b). Holonic rationale and self-organization on design of complex evolvable systems. *HoloMAS '09: Proceedings of the 4th International Conference on Industrial Applications of Holonic and Multi-Agent Systems: Holonic and Multi-Agent Systems for Manufacturing*, Mařík, V., Strasser, T., Zoitl, A. (eds). Springer, Berlin Heidelberg.

Leitão, P. and Karnouskos, S. (eds) (2015). *Industrial Agents: Emerging Applications of Software Agents in Industry*. Elsevier, Amsterdam.

Leitão, P., Colombo, A.W., Karnouskos, S. (2016a). Industrial automation based on cyber-physical systems technologies: Prototype implementations and challenges. *Computers in Industry*, 81, 11–25.

Leitão, P., Karnouskos, S., Ribeiro, L., Lee, J., Strasser, T., Colombo, A.W. (2016b). Smart agents in industrial cyber-physical systems. *Proceedings of the IEEE*, 104(5), 1086–1101.

Leitão, P., Pires, F., Karnouskos, S., Colombo, A.W. (2020). Quo vadis industry 4.0? Position, trends, and challenges. *IEEE Open Journal of the Industrial Electronics Society*, 1, 298–310.

Leitão, P., Strasser, T., Karnouskos, S., Ribeiro, L., Barbosa, J., Huang, V. (2021). Recommendation of best practices for industrial agent systems based on the IEEE 2660.1 standard. *IEEE 22nd International Conference on Industrial Technology (ICIT'21)*.

Nagorny, K., Colombo, A.W., Schmidtmann, U. (2012). A service- and multi-agent-oriented manufacturing automation architecture: An IEC 62264 level 2 compliant implementation. *Computers in Industry*, 63(8), 813–823.

Ribeiro, L., Barata, J., Colombo, A.W. (2008). MAS and SOA: A case study exploring principles and technologies to support self-properties in assembly systems. *2008 Second IEEE International Conference on Self-Adaptive and Self-Organizing Systems Workshops*. IEEE.

Ribeiro, L., Karnouskos, S., Leitão, P., Strasser, T.I. (2017). A community analysis of the IEEE IES Industrial Agents Technical Committee. *IECON 2017 – 43rd Annual Conference of the IEEE Industrial Electronics Society*. IEEE.

Russel, S. and Norvig, P. (1995). *Artificial Intelligence, A Modern Approach*. Prentice-Hall, Englewood Cliffs.

Schild, K. and Bussmann, S. (2007). Self-organization in manufacturing operations. *Communications of the ACM*, 50(12), 74–79.

Schoop, R., Colombo, A.W., Suessmann, B., Neubert, R. (2002). Industrial experiences, trends and future requirements on agent-based intelligent automation. *IEEE 2002 28th Annual Conference of the Industrial Electronics Society. IECON 02*. IEEE.

Unland, R. (2015). Industrial agents. In *Industrial Agents: Emerging Applications of Software Agents in Industry*, Leitão, P. and Karnouskos, S. (eds). Elsevier, Amsterdam.

Wooldridge, M. (2002). *Introduction to Multiagent Systems, Volume 30*. John Wiley and Sons, Ltd., Chichester.

Wooldridge, M. and Jennings, N.R. (1995). Intelligent agents: Theory and practice. *The Knowledge Engineering Review*, 10(2), 115–152.

8

Holonic Control Architectures

Olivier CARDIN[1], William DERIGENT[2] and Damien TRENTESAUX[3]

[1] *LS2N UMR CNRS 6004, Nantes University, IUT de Nantes, France*
[2] *CRAN CNRS UMR 7039, University of Lorraine, Nancy, France*
[3] *LAMIH UMR CNRS 8201, Université Polytechnique Hauts-de-France, Valenciennes, France*

8.1. Introduction

Over the last 20 years, holonic control architectures (HCAs) have been widely studied and developed in the field of manufacturing production (Morel *et al.* 2019) as a relevant solution for system control. Several scientific state of the arts (Shen and Norrie 1999; Monostori *et al.* 2006; Shen *et al.* 2006; Leitão 2009; Trentesaux 2009) have presented HCAs and highlighted their advantages and disadvantages. These have been particularly highlighted by the various industrial applications of the paradigm that are described in the literature, from early applications in the automotive industry (Bussmann and Sieverding 2001) to railway systems (Le Mortellec *et al.* 2013), and more recently to pharmaceuticals (Borangiu *et al.* 2019).

The objective of this chapter is to present a study of existing holonic architectures in order to identify the contributions of this type of control architecture to industrial cyber-physical systems. First, their historical characteristics are presented, and demonstrate an interesting performance in the physical part of ICPS. This chapter then presents the evolutions of this concept that have led to a relevant integration in the cyber part of ICPS.

Digitalization and Control of Industrial Cyber-Physical Systems,
coordinated by Olivier CARDIN, William DERIGENT and Damien TRENTESAUX.
© ISTE Ltd 2022.

It is structured as follows: section 8.2 presents a brief definition of the fundamental principles of HCAs, complementing the fundamental principles of the holonic paradigm expressed in the previous chapter. The integration of different architectures in the physical part of ICPS is then detailed in section 8.3, before section 8.4 shows their relevance in the cyber part. Sections 8.5 and 8.6 focus respectively on the possibility of integrating artificial intelligence tools into HCAs and on their contribution to the digitization of control architectures.

8.2. HCA fundamentals

Decision-making is a fundamental property of HCAs. Research on the topic of decision-making by artificial entities has been conducted for several decades (Pomerol 2012). In the world of industrial engineering, deciding is the activity of narrowing down a set of possibilities. A related notion is the concept of "degree of freedom". From this point of view, classical decision-making activities can be derived: choice (set reduced to one), ranking (order of integration in the set), etc. both in discrete (set of resources) and continuous (speed of rotation, energy consumption) domains. Within HCAs, given the importance of the physical aspects, deciding is an activity merged into a larger process that can be called a decision process. Extending the basic ideas of Simon (1996), a decision process is composed of several activities: monitoring, initiation, design of possible decisions, *a priori* evaluation of decisions, decision, implementation and *a posteriori* evaluation of decisions.

The decision process (holon behavior) can be reactive (reflex as an automated response to a stimulus) or proactive (goal-directed response). A holon that implements reactive behavior perceives stimuli in its environment and responds to them using pre-programmed behaviors. A proactive holon is not only an entity that reacts to a stimulus, but can also act to further its own goals. In any case, holons are rational in the sense that they always try to choose an optimal decision (local and/or global). To make a good decision, the holon can use simulation or optimization models. Given the recursive aspect of a holarchy, this decision process is also recursive and can be implemented in layers of holons. For example, the triggering activity of a quality control holon can be decomposed into a decision process managed by lower-level holons to decide, through a learning strategy, the best triggering level to avoid overreaction if it is too low, or to avoid customer loss if it is too high.

A holon operates in a constantly changing environment that is difficult to predict. The predefined goals of a holon may not remain valid (or optimal) if a change occurs in the holon's environment. Adaptability is then required so that the holon can modify its goals according to its knowledge of the environment. This also means that a holon must learn from its experience and environment in order to be able to adapt its behavior correctly. Here, learning means generating new knowledge from the data acquired about the production system.

Autonomy is another fundamental property. It is defined as the degree of freedom of each holon with respect to its decision capacity, whatever the holon level (Giret and Botti 2004). It can also be associated with a set of constraints on a search space when using optimization tools. The autonomy level can be set during the design phase by the designer themselves, but it can also be adjusted by a higher-level holon with application to a lower level during the operation phase. For example, a supervisor holon decides to restrict the set of possible resource holons to be chosen by the lower-level product holons due to an upcoming maintenance operation on one of these resource holons. This decision-making autonomy must be accompanied by operational autonomy, allowing the holon to implement its decisions and monitor the execution of its plans, with the possibility of taking corrective actions in case of disruptions.

Cooperation between holons allows for the restriction or expansion of holon autonomy. For example, a direct peer-to-peer negotiation protocol (Smith 1980) or an indirect use of pheromone-based communication by the environment (Valckenaers and Van Brussel 2005; Pannequin 2007) can lead holons to improve the quality of their decisions by prohibiting search spaces to avoid local optima during a dynamic task allocation process. This property also includes the possibility of cooperating with a human operator. Another important aspect is the flexibility of the architecture, namely the ability to integrate or delete holons with minimal external intervention (plug and play concept), as well as the ability to change dependencies or hierarchical relationships between holons with minimal external intervention (McFarlane and Bussmann 2003).

Due to these characteristics for a holon and an HCA, it is expected that emergent behaviors will appear (Mataric 1993; Pach *et al.* 2012). From our perspective, an emergent behavior is the observation of a property at a higher level of an HCA that has not been explicitly embedded (programmed) in the holons composing that HCA. Emergent behaviors are sometimes positive with respect to the performance of the whole system, but can also lead to blockages or inefficient situations.

8.3. HCAs in the physical part of ICPS

Historical architectures are a category that include all of the "pioneer" reference architectures proposed in the early stages of HCAs. These early architectures implement some properties of the holonic paradigm such as cooperation, autonomy and decision-making (reactive and proactive). They focused first on a change of the control paradigm within the physical part of the ICPS (Derigent *et al.* 2021).

Van Brussel *et al.* (1998) described the first reference architecture resulting from an IMS project called holonic manufacturing systems (HMS) in 1996. Its acronym is PROSA, which stands for "Product–Resource–Order–Staff Architecture" (see Figure 8.1), referring to the four holons that make up the architecture: Product Holons (PH), in charge of knowledge of production process data; Resource Holons (RH), in charge of asset management; Order Holons (OH), in charge of process execution; and Staff Holons (SH), not shown in the figure, acting as global advisors for the entire architecture.

This architecture is the most referenced in the literature. It is often the basis for later architectures as it is the most generic. This architecture was the first of a series, developed for different domains (i.e. production, logistics, maintenance, etc.). For example, PROSIS (Product, Resource, Order, Simulation for Isoarchy Structure) was designed to provide a different organization paradigm using the concept of isoarchy (Pujo *et al.* 2009). In an isoarchy, there are no hierarchical links of subordination between holons. At the same decision level, the different decision entities are equal in the decision-making mechanism. In the PROSIS architecture, the Holon Staff, which is useless in such an isoarchy context, has been replaced by the Holon Simulation, which is able to simulate the evolution of the production system from its current state, computed through active listening and analysis of the interactions between all other holons.

The implementation of architectures from a control system perspective is an issue that needs to be studied, and several architectures have been derived from PROSA in order to benefit from the theories and tools developed in the multi-agent field. Among them, HCBA (holonic component-based architecture, Chirn and McFarlane (2000)) is the first architecture based on a fusion of different concepts from component-based development, multi-agent systems (MAS) and HMS. The objective of this fusion is to develop a highly decentralized architecture, built from autonomous and modular, cooperative and intelligent components, able to manage the different changes quickly, focusing on the reconfigurability of the system.

HCBA consists of two types of components in the production system: the resource component and the product component. The resource component consists of a physical part and a virtual control part. The resources manage the scheduling of operations, while seeking to optimize their use. The product component is composed of a physical part and an informational part. Its physical part can represent materials, parts, pallets, etc. In addition, the informational part manages the production program, including routing control, process control, decision-making and production information. The informational part is composed of virtual agents with specific roles. Each product component refers to a product coordinator that creates WIP (Work in Process) agents. Both monitor the execution of orders, but at different levels. The product coordinator monitors the production of a batch, while the WIP agents are responsible for monitoring the production of an individual part. As a result, the WIP agents negotiate with the resource community to define the processing of parts on the shop floor. These negotiations are done within the framework of a goal set by the product coordinator (see Figure 8.2).

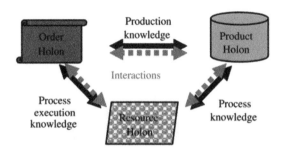

Figure 8.1. *Simplified architecture of PROSA*

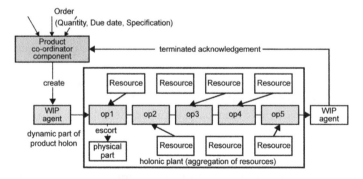

Figure 8.2. *Structure of the HCBA architecture*

ADACOR (ADAptive holonic COntrol aRchitecture) is an HCA proposed by Leitão and Restivo (2006). This architecture has a decentralized control structure but also considers centralization in order to move towards a global optimization of the system. The holons belong to the following classes: Product Holons (ProdH),

Task Holons (TH), Operation Holons (OpH) and Supervisor Holons (SupH), interconnected through the schema represented in Figure 8.3.

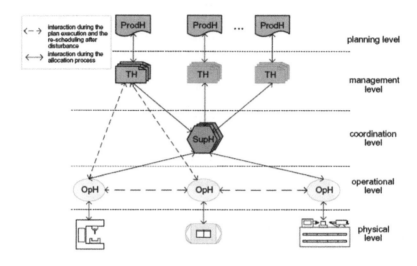

Figure 8.3. *Holon repartition of ADACOR (Leitão and Restivo 2006)*

SupH are based on biological systems and are different from PROSA's SH. In normal execution, the ADACOR architecture maintains the production system in a steady state, where holons are organized in a hierarchical structure, with OH following the optimized schedules proposed by SupH, for TH. However, when a production problem occurs (delay, machine failure, etc.), the global system enters a transient state, characterized by the reorganization of the holons needed to react to the disturbance. To do this, ADACOR uses a pheromone-like diffusion mechanism to distribute the global information. Thanks to this mechanism, ADACOR introduces the possibility of dynamically changing the holarchy between the steady state and the transient state.

8.4. Dynamic architectures, towards a reconfiguration of the physical part from the cyber part of ICPS

HCAs naturally seek responsiveness since they were designed with this in mind, to overcome the main drawback of centralized architectures. Thus, all previous historical architectures can react quickly to disturbances. However, the global behavior of the system is constant and does not change. Therefore, the design of dynamic control architectures is probably one of the most promising current trends in the HCA literature (Cardin *et al.* 2017). This is based on the assumption that the system behavior can be dynamically modified to adapt to changes in the environment, and thus reduce transient states and the associated performance loss. Several dynamic architectures have been proposed in the literature, all of which are characterized by a "switching mechanism" to switch from one holonic architecture to another. Jimenez *et al.* (2017) conducted a literature review of the different types of switching mechanisms and their use in dynamic holonic architectures. Here, we will mainly present four of them.

ORCA (Pach *et al.* 2014) was one of the first dynamic architectures formalized in the literature (see Figure 8.4). In ORCA, a global optimizing holon controls the local optimizing holon at a lower level. A switch mechanism, allowing the local holon to decide, occurs if a disturbance arrives and prohibits the application of a predefined schedule. This switch allows the holonic architecture to adapt to disturbances, but there is no rollback mechanism. In Borangiu *et al.* (2015), a mechanism was proposed to switch from a centralized to a decentralized holonic architecture in the presence of disruptions, in order to ensure both global optimization and agility to batch order changes as long as possible during production. This switchover is bidirectional (see Figure 8.5).

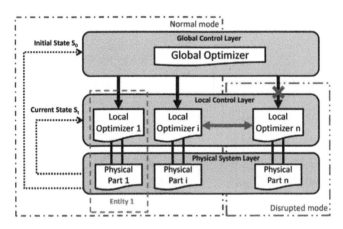

Figure 8.4. *Overall organization of ORCA (Pach et al. 2014)*

An evolution of the ADACOR mechanism was also presented in Barbosa *et al.* (2015) and called ADACOR². The aim is to make the system evolve dynamically through online discovered configurations, not only between a stationary and a transient state. The rest of the architecture is nevertheless quite similar to ADACOR.

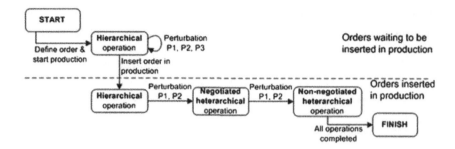

Figure 8.5. *Bidirectional HCA switching (Borangiu et al. 2015)*

A more recent dynamic HCA is named POLLUX (Jimenez *et al.* 2017). The main novelty is focused on the architecture adaptation mechanism, using governance parameters that expand or limit the behavior of low-level holons with respect to the perturbations observed by the higher level. The simulation of the performance consequences of several switching options ("what-if" scenarios) is proposed since in POLLUX, the number of possible switches at a given time is high compared to ORCA, for instance. Each switching decision is therefore justified by an increase in performance compared to the other switching options (see Figure 8.6).

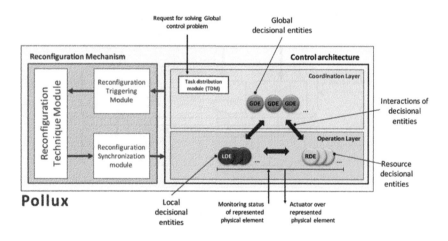

Figure 8.6. *Mechanism from POLLUX (Jimenez et al. 2017)*

The advantages of this type of architecture come from their ability to better cope with real-time uncertainties: the architecture is adjusted according to events as they occur. Nevertheless, these architectures suffer from two main disadvantages related to their possible nervousness (too frequent, too fast configuration change) and their possible time myopia (configuration change that is not actually necessary). The cost of switching is therefore not yet mastered.

8.5. HCAs and Big Data

In recent years, due to the advent of Big Data-oriented methods, the need to control the data flows carried by the architecture has emerged. The interest in using HCAs is to be able to take advantage of the recursiveness of the architecture to succeed in rationalizing the flow of data, information and knowledge, and thus limit the explosion of the volume of data to be processed in the cyber part as much as possible.

The SURFER architecture (Le Mortellec *et al.* 2013) illustrates this objective well, through the example of maintenance and monitoring of very complex systems (in this case trains). The proposed generic holonic architecture model for diagnosis is presented in Figure 8.7. This model is composed of recursive diagnostic structures, including subsystems and associated diagnostic methods. Each diagnosed system is composed of a control part and a controlled part, associated with a context. The control part executes an algorithm to control the controlled part and, in return, the controlled part adopts an expected behavior. At the lowest level of the holonic structure, the controlled part is usually composed of physical elements (e.g. sensors, switches, actuators) that are bound by mechanical and electrical constraints.

This architecture is designed to handle a huge amount of data, as its direct application envisions monitoring complex systems with hundreds of sensors. In a traditional approach, the Big Data streams would have been aggregated in one place to characterize and understand the data and the relationship between them. In the SURFER architecture, the aggregation of holons creates an architecture where data is processed locally and propagated to the rest of the architecture at a higher semantic level. To do this, each holon can gather and understand data from the lower level. This data is already processed and is only transmitted globally. Through this mechanism, each layer of the architecture adds value to the semantics of the data in order to minimize the explosion of data to be processed by a single level (Trentesaux and Branger 2018). Data is then only sent when it is relevant. This example is further developed in Chapter 13, including the use made of this data in the cyber section.

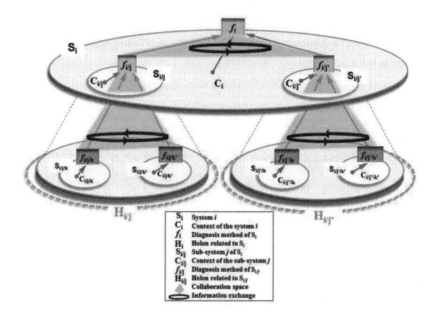

S_i	System i
C_i	Context of the system i
f_i	Diagnosis method of S_i
H_i	Holon related to S_i
S_{ij}	Sub-system j of S_i
C_{ij}	Context of the sub-system j
f_{ij}	Diagnosis method of S_{ij}
H_{ij}	Holon related to S_{ij}
	Collaboration space
	Information exchange

Figure 8.7. *Basics of the SURFER architecture*

8.6. HCAs and digital twin: towards the digitization of architectures

The concept of the digital twin in the industrial sector has become increasingly important in recent years. Its use is often seen as a standard interface between heterogeneous devices and the IT infrastructure in large and small production systems. Indeed, the possibilities it offers to induce an omniscient view of the real state and behavior of the system are key to many applications, from control to predictive maintenance, through virtual reality or online simulation. Therefore, this twin concept is positioned as a credible possibility to establish the link between the physical and cyber part of an ICPS.

This deeper interoperability has been integrated into a new reference architecture, aiming both to clearly demonstrate the existence of the digital twin and provide a new terminology, disconnected from that of production, which might be misunderstood and underestimated in other contexts. This architecture is referred to as ARTI (Activity Resource Type Instance) (Valckenaers 2020) and is represented as a cube (see Figure 8.8).

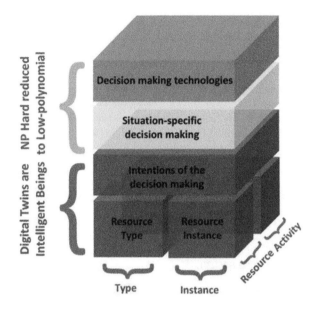

Figure 8.8. *ARTI reference architecture (Valckenaers 2020)*

The digital twin is present in the blue cubes, where each element of the physical twin can find its virtual equivalent. The yellow and green cubes are represented in this figure as control cubes, but any other software can conveniently connect to the blue cubes to collect the image of the current state of the physical twin. Note that the blue cubes are not necessarily represented as holons, so the classic HCAs can be fully integrated into the green and yellow cubes. This HCA is the first to clearly show a digital twin layer and the various elements integrating both the cyber and physical layers of the ICPS.

8.7. References

Barbosa, J., Leitão, P., Adam, E., Trentesaux, D. (2015). Dynamic self-organization in holonic multi-agent manufacturing systems: The ADACOR evolution. *Computers in Industry*, 66, 99–111.

Borangiu, T., Răileanu, S., Berger, T., Trentesaux, D. (2015). Switching mode control strategy in manufacturing execution systems. *International Journal of Production Research*, 53(7), 1950–1963.

Borangiu, T., Răileanu, S., Oltean, E.V., Silicsteanu, A. (2019). Holonic hybrid supervised control of semi-continuous radiopharmaceutical production processes. *Advanced Control Techniques in Complex Engineering Systems: Theory and Applications*. Springer, Cham.

Bussmann, S. and Sieverding, J. (2001). Holonic control of an engine assembly plant: An industrial evaluation. *IEEE International Conference on Systems, Man and Cybernetics. e-Systems and e-Man for Cybernetics in Cyberspace (Cat.No.01CH37236)*, 7–10 October, Tucson, AZ, 1, 169–174. DOI: 10.1109/ICSMC.2001.969807.

Cardin, O., Trentesaux, D., Thomas, A., Castagna, P., Berger, T., El-Haouzi, H.B. (2017). Coupling predictive scheduling and reactive control in manufacturing hybrid control architectures: State of the art and future challenges. *Journal of Intelligent Manufacturing*, 28(7), 1503–1517.

Chirn, J.L. and McFarlane, D.C. (2000). A holonic component-based approach to reconfigurable manufacturing control architecture. *Proceedings of the 11th International Workshop on Database and Expert Systems Applications*, 4–8 September, London. DOI: 10.1109/DEXA.2000.875030.

Derigent, W., Cardin, O., Trentesaux, D. (2021). Industry 4.0: Contributions of holonic manufacturing control architectures and future challenges. *Journal of Intelligent Manufacturing*, 32(7), 1797–1818.

Giret, A. and Botti, V. (2004). Holons and agents. *Journal of Intelligent Manufacturing*, 15(5), 645–659.

Jimenez, J.F., Bekrar, A., Zambrano-Rey, G., Trentesaux, D., Leitão, P. (2017). Pollux: A dynamic hybrid control architecture for flexible job shop systems. *International Journal of Production Research*, 55(15), 4229–4247.

Leitão, P. (2009). Agent-based distributed manufacturing control: A state-of-the-art survey. *Engineering Applications of Artificial Intelligence*, 22(7), 979–991.

Leitão, P. and Restivo, F. (2006). ADACOR: A holonic architecture for agile and adaptive manufacturing control. *Computers in Industry*, 57(2), 121–130.

Le Mortellec, A., Clarhaut, J., Sallez, Y., Berger, T., Trentesaux, D. (2013). Embedded holonic fault diagnosis of complex transportation systems. *Engineering Applications of Artificial Intelligence*, 26(1), 227–240.

Mataric, M.J. (1993). Designing emergent behaviors: From local interactions to collective intelligence. *Animals to Animats 2. Proceedings of the Second International Conference on Simulation of Adaptive Behavior*, August, Honolulu, Hawaii.

McFarlane, D.C. and Bussmann, S. (2013). Holonic manufacturing control: Rationales, developments and open issues. *Agent-based Manufacturing*, Deen, S.M. (ed.). Springer, Berlin, Heidelberg.

Monostori, L., Váncza, J., Kumara, S.R.T. (2006). Agent-based systems for manufacturing. *CIRP Annals-Manufacturing Technology*, 55(2), 697–720.

Morel, G., Pereira, C.E., Nof, S.Y. (2019). Historical survey and emerging challenges of manufacturing automation modeling and control: A systems architecting perspective. *Annual Reviews in Control*, 47, 21–34.

Pach, C., Bekrar, A., Zbib, N., Sallez, Y., Trentesaux, D. (2012). An effective potential field approach to FMS holonic heterarchical control. *Control Engineering Practice*, 20(12), 1293–1309.

Pach, C., Berger, T., Bonte, T., Trentesaux, D. (2014). ORCA-FMS: A dynamic architecture for the optimized and reactive control of flexible manufacturing scheduling. *Computers in Industry*, 65(4), 706–720.

Pannequin, R. (2007). Proposition d'un environnement de modélisation et de test d'architectures de pilotage par le produit de systèmes de production. PhD Thesis, Université Henri Poincaré Nancy I.

Pomerol, J.-C. (2012). *Decision-Making and Action*. ISTE Ltd, London, and John Wiley & Sons, New York.

Pujo, P., Broissin, N., Ounnar, F. (2009). PROSIS: An isoarchic structure for HMS control. *Engineering Applications of Artificial Intelligence*, 22(7), 1034–1045.

Shen, W. and Norrie, D.H. (1999). Agent-based systems for intelligent manufacturing: A state-of-the-art survey. *Knowledge and Information Systems, An International Journal*, 1, 129–156.

Shen, W., Hao, Q., Yoon, H.J., Norrie, D.H. (2006). Applications of agent-based systems in intelligent manufacturing: An updated review. *Advanced Engineering Informatics*, 20(4), 415–431.

Simon, H.A. (1996). *The Sciences of the Artificial*, 3rd edition. MIT Press, Cambridge.

Smith, R.G. (1980). The contract net protocol: High-level communication and control in a distributed problem solver. *IEEE Transactions on Computers*, 29(12), 1104–1113.

Trentesaux, D. (2009). Distributed control of production systems. *Engineering Applications of Artificial Intelligence*, 22(7), 971–978.

Trentesaux, D. and Branger, G. (2018). Foundation of the surfer data management architecture and its application to train transportation. *International Workshop on Service Orientation in Holonic and Multi-Agent Manufacturing, Studies in Computational Intelligence*. Springer, 111–125.

Valckenaers, P. (2020). Perspective on holonic manufacturing systems: PROSA becomes ARTI. *Computers in Industry*, 120, 103226.

Valckenaers, P. and Van Brussel, H. (2005). Holonic manufacturing execution systems. *CIRP Annals – Manufacturing Technology*, 54(1), 427–432.

Van Brussel, H., Wyns, J., Valckenaers, P., Bongaerts, L., Peeters, P. (1998). Reference architecture for holonic manufacturing systems: PROSA. *Computers in Industry*, 37(3), 255–274.

PART 5

Learning and Interacting with Industrial Cyber-Physical Systems

9

Big Data Analytics and Machine Learning for Industrial Cyber-Physical Systems

Yasamin Eslami[1], Mario Lezoche[2] and Philippe Thomas[2]
[1] LS2N UMR CNRS 6004, Ecole Centrale de Nantes, France
[2] CRAN CNRS UMR 7039, University of Lorraine, Nancy, France

9.1. Introduction

The objective of this chapter is to illustrate, through the concepts of Big Data and machine learning, how it is possible to exploit the immense mass of data that can be capitalized at the level of the cyber layer of industrial cyber-physical systems (ICPS).

Indeed, an ICPS is more than the networking and exploitation of information technology. Information and knowledge are embedded in objects within their physical part and are connected to their cyber part. By integrating perception, communication, learning, behavior generation and reasoning into these systems, a new generation of intelligent and autonomous systems can be developed. Industry 4.0 technologies used in production are an example of this. Linked to cyber-physical systems, the Internet of Things (IoT) and cloud computing, they can generate benefits from a circular economy perspective, as they make it possible for circularity to be designed from information gathered from customers as well as across the entire production process (de Sousa Jabbour *et al.* 2018).

For a color version of all figures in this book, see www.iste.co.uk/cardin/digitalization.zip.

Digitalization and Control of Industrial Cyber-Physical Systems,
coordinated by Olivier Cardin, William Derigent and Damien Trentesaux.
© ISTE Ltd 2022.

Regardless of the application context of ICPS, the component concept is central. It serves as a model for representing the properties of an ICPS, for example, real objects in a production environment connected to virtual objects and processes. A component of an ICPS can be a production system, a transportation system, a piece of equipment, an individual machine or an assembly within a machine. Some of the fundamental concepts of ICPS can be traced back to research and technologies related to sensor nodes and sensor networks. A sensor node integrates sensors, actuators, computing elements (a processor, memory, etc.), communication modules and a battery. The sensor network interconnects many small sensor nodes via a wireless or wired connection (Golatowski *et al.* 2003) (Figure 9.1). Referred to as wireless sensor networks (WSNs), a large number of sensor nodes equipped with a wireless network connection can be deployed in the physical phenomenon environment. These sensor nodes can provide raw data to the nodes responsible for data fusion or they can process the raw data using their computational capabilities and relay the required part to other sensor nodes (see Chapter 3).

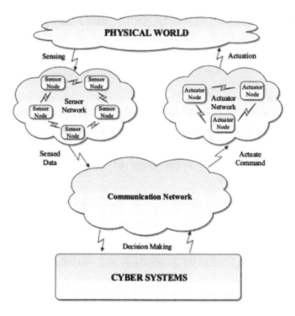

Figure 9.1. *Holistic view of CPS (Gunes* et al. *2014)*

The main objective of the implementation of new technologies is related to the effective and efficient customer-oriented adaptation of products (and thus production) and services in order to increase the added value for industrialists, raising their competitive position, while improving customer satisfaction and loyalty

(Roblek *et al*. 2016). To achieve this goal, companies producing goods and services need to develop and manage new knowledge that is crucial for the organization's decision-making process and the achievement of related business objectives (Abubakar *et al*. 2019). Therefore, the data generated by ICPS needs to be analyzed and contextualized, to make it a relevant source of information. In the context of the factory of the future, this makes ICPS, and, in particular, their cyber part, in charge of capitalizing these masses of data, a source of information integrating, often implicitly, relationships on the environment and the business domain. This information and these relationships constitute a potential source of knowledge that must be extracted, formalized and reused.

9.2. Data massification in industrial cyber-physical systems

ICPS are based on technological advances that affect the production process of goods (advanced manufacturing systems, autonomous robots, additive manufacturing) and services (healthcare system, transportation), the use of smart systems and products and/or data and analytics tools (Porter and Heppelmann 2014).

Typically, in the context of manufacturing production, within the manufacturing process, the adoption of autonomous and/or collaborative robotics (Adamson *et al*. 2017) or 3D printing opens up new opportunities to create new knowledge about products and processes (Anderson 2012). At the same time, smart products and "data-driven technologies" successfully acquire useful data from multiple sources within organizational boundaries, as well as from customers and suppliers (Klingenberg *et al*. 2019). Thus, ICPS are huge data potentials that can be used in real time, enriching contextual knowledge or generating new approaches in the way products can be manufactured and used, as well as in practices regarding value generation (from product to service), which can enable companies to take actions and make decisions based on these insights (Tao *et al*. 2018).

These technological advances have improved data collection to an unprecedented degree within the ICPS. It is estimated that the amount of data acquired worldwide doubles every 11 hours. However, if collecting, archiving and structuring data is a necessary condition to understand, control and monitor an industrial system, it is not sufficient. It is also necessary to use the databases thus constituted. However, the processing time required to transform this data into knowledge is extremely time-consuming in terms of human time. This means that very often the only use of the collected data is to perform some simple calculations (comparison to a threshold, calculation of averages and standard deviations, etc.) or even simply to be stored waiting for a possible use. Can't we do better and more with these data, which are expensive to collect and store? Answering this question means equipping ICPS with automatic or semi-automatic data analysis capabilities. ICPS then "learns" from the data it collects, as shown in Figure 1.5 in Chapter 1.

Analyzing data is often linked to "knowledge discovery in databases" and "data mining" methods. It is common to confuse "data mining" with "knowledge discovery in databases". Knowledge discovery in databases (KDD) is a complex process that takes place in a succession of operations, of which data mining is one and corresponds to the art of extracting knowledge from data. Data mining is a process to identify and validate new behaviors by using previously collected data (Patel and Panchal 2012), which can be performed using different approaches such as artificial intelligence, machine learning and statistics.

Many data mining techniques are available for the analysis of these large masses of data. In the context of ICPS, two of them are developed in this chapter: multi-relational data mining and machine learning.

9.3. Big Data and multi-relational data mining (MRDM)

A permanent and important limitation in the field of data mining is the fact that the majority of data mining and machine learning algorithms work with a single table, whereas potential knowledge is stored in data spread across many tables, databases and even in raw formats such as tweets, blogs and online comments. There may be relationships between the dimensions represented by the data that come from the same or different sources. Each dimension may have a relationship with one or more other dimensions, in which case the dimensions are interrelated. These data are then qualified as "multi-relational data" and can be represented in databases. For their use, it is possible to use MRDM approaches that will search for patterns involving several tables (relationships) of a relational database. Below, we present a method of this family of approaches, in particular, the method of formal concept analysis (FCA), which has aroused much interest.

9.3.1. *Formal concept analysis (FCA)*

Formal concept analysis, introduced in Wille (1982), analyzes unary datasets. They are composed of objects and attributes that characterize them. It is an algebraic method that aims to discover the abstractions, called formal concepts, of such datasets.

9.3.1.1. *Formal context*

A formal context is a triplet **K** = (**O**, **A**, **I**), where **O** is called the set of objects, **A** is called the set of attributes and **I** ⊆ **O** x **A** is a binary relation called an incidence relation. A formal context is a representation of a unary dataset. It can be represented by a unary array. Let us present an example that will illustrate all the definitions and its representations. Consider four cats: Demetra (de), Lea (le), Pepita (pe) and Talpi (tp). Among the different characteristics of these cats, we highlight the following properties:

– always being hungry (sa);

– always wanting cuddles (co);

– having a single colored coat (mc);

– always protecting their territory (te).

K	sa	co	mc	te
de	x			x
le	x		x	
pe			x	x
tp		x		x

Table 9.1. *Example of a formal context*

From this information, we can define a formal context **K** = (**O**, **A**, **I**), where **O** = { **de, le, pe, tp** } is the set of objects, and **A** = { **sa, co, mc, te** } is the set of attributes. Such a context can be represented as a unary array, where the elements of **O** correspond to the rows, the elements of **A** to the columns and the incidence relation **I** is identified by the crosses. A representation is given in Table 9.1. A cross in the box **K** [o_i, a_j] indicates that the object **oi** has the attribute a_j.

9.3.1.2. *Derivation operators*

The FCA method aims to extract sets of objects with common attributes. Before defining the notion of a formal concept, it is necessary to introduce the basic operation of the FCA method, called derivation, which is crucial for the understanding of a formal concept. The derivation operation on objects is an application from **P(O)** to **P(A)**. For a set of objects **X P(O)**, its derivative, denoted **X'**, is given by:

$$X' = \{a \in A \mid \forall o \in X, (o,a) \in I\} = \bigcap_{o \in X} \{a \in A \mid (o,a) \in I\} \qquad [9.1]$$

Symmetrically, the attribute derivation operation is an application from **P(A)** to **P(O)**. For a set **Y** P(A), its derivation, denoted **Y'**, is given by:

$$Y' = \{o \in O \mid \forall a \in Y, (o,a) \in I\} = \bigcap_{a \in Y} \{o \in O \mid (o,a) \in I\} \qquad [9.2]$$

Thus, the derivation of a set of objects **X** is the set of attributes of **A** jointly carried by all objects **X**. In a dual way, the derivation of a set of attributes **Y** is the set of objects of **O** jointly carrying all the attributes of **Y**. The following example shows these definitions on the formal concept defined in Table 9.1:

– {'le, de}' = {'sa'.};

– {pe, de}' = {te};

– {te}' = {tp, pe, de};

– {mc, te}' = {pe}.

9.3.1.3. *Formal concepts*

A pair $C = (X,Y)$ P(O) x P(A) such that $Y = X'$ and $X = Y'$ is called a formal concept. **X** is called the scope, and **Y** is called the intent, of the concept **C**. Concepts are the fundamental abstractions that the FCA method aims to extract from a formal context. A formal context can be represented in different ways:

– with a two-part graph;

– as a maximum rectangle of crosses after ordering the rows and columns of the table.

However, regardless of the preferred graphical representation, the rationale behind the formal concept is always the following – a concept is a pair of sets of objects and attributes, such as:

– the objects carry all the attributes and are the only ones in the context that carry all the designated attributes together;

– each of the objects carries all the attributes, and no other attribute of the context is common to all the objects of the concept.

Formal concepts can be characterized as closures and are intrinsically linked to the notion of equivalence class. The unique maximum of an equivalence class is called a closure (Ganter and Wille 1999). It contains one or more minimal elements. An element $U \in [Y'']$ is said to be minimal if for any $V \subset U$, $V \notin [Y'']$. These minima are called class generators. Finally, since formal concepts are described by the set $\{(Y', Y'') \mid Y \in P(A)\}$, the set of closures of equivalence classes corresponds exactly to the set of intentions of formal concepts.

9.3.1.4. Concept lattice

Let $K = (O, A, I)$ be a formal context. Let us denote:

– C_K as the set of all formal concepts of $P(O) \times P(A)$;

– $\leq_K$ as the inclusion relation on the extensions of concepts.

The partial ordered set (poset) $L_K = (C_K, \leq_K)$ forms a complete finite lattice. It is called a lattice of concepts of context K (Ganter and Wille 1999).

Similarly, selecting the inverse inclusion relation on the intensities of the concepts yields the same lattice of concepts (Ganter and Wille 1999). The representation of the Hasse diagram in Table 9.1 is illustrated comprehensively in Figure 9.2. Each concept is represented by a box with three sections which, from top to bottom, are the concept identification number, its intent and its extension.

Figure 9.2(a) and (b) present the same understanding of the contextual concepts presented in Table 9.1. Figure 9.2(b) is a compressed representation of Figure 9.2(a). Each identically numbered vertex on both grids presents exactly the same concept. The reading of a concept in compressed representation is thus interpreted as follows:

– the intent of a concept is the set of attributes of the represented intents of the concept under consideration and of any super-concept;

– the extension of a concept is the set of objects of the represented extensions of the considered concept and any sub-concept.

The organization of the concepts, in the form of a lattice in the Hasse diagram representation, enables the quick extraction of all the closures and generators existing on a context.

9.3.2. Relational concept analysis (RCA)

Formal concept analysis, as described here, aims to extract knowledge, in the form of association rules, which are distilled on a homogeneous dataset. The extension of this method to the multi-relational paradigm is called relational concept analysis (RCA), and is presented in Rouane-Hacene et al. (2013). The RCA method, introduced in Huchard et al. (2002), aims to extend the FCA method to relational data compatible with the entity-association model (Chen 1976). Such a model considers binary relationships between objects. The RCA method enriches the description of the objects by integrating so-called relational attributes, which reveal the relationships between the objects. RCA is a multi-relational data mining (MRDM) method and therefore exploits different types of objects as well as the links between them.

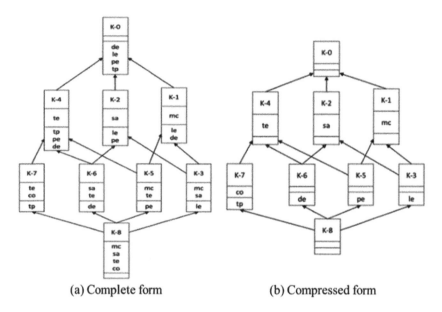

(a) Complete form   (b) Compressed form

Figure 9.2. *Hasse diagram of Table 9.1*

9.3.2.1. *Relational family of contexts*

Consider two formal contexts $\mathbf{K}_i = (\mathbf{O}_i, \mathbf{A}_i, \mathbf{I}_i)$ and $\mathbf{K}_j = (\mathbf{O}_j, \mathbf{A}_j, \mathbf{I}_j)$. A relation with domain $\mathbf{K}_i$ (also called the source) and co-domain $\mathbf{K}_j$ (also called the target) is a binary relation subset of $\mathbf{O}_i \times \mathbf{O}_j$. We denote $\mathbf{R}_{i,j,k}$ the kth relation of domain $\mathbf{K}_i$ and co-domain $\mathbf{K}_j$. The FCA method does not allow for the direct use of the information included in such a relationship. Thanks to the integration of a system of scales, RCA makes it possible to extend FCA to integrate this information and thus characterize the objects of a source context according to the relationships maintained with other objects. A relational context family (RCF) is a pair $(\mathbf{K}, \mathbf{R})$ such that:

– $\mathbf{K}$ is a set of formal contexts $\mathbf{K}_i = (\mathbf{O}_i, \mathbf{A}_i, \mathbf{I}_i)$;

– $\mathbf{R}$ is a set of relationships $_{i,j,k} \subseteq \mathbf{O}_i \times \mathbf{O}_j$ for $\mathbf{i}, \mathbf{j}$ $\{1, ..., |\mathbf{K}|\}$.

9.3.2.2. Propositionalization and gradation operator

Lachiche defined *propositionalization* as a process explicitly transforming a relational dataset into a propositional dataset (Lachiche 2011), i.e. a set of literals of arity 1. The main interests of propositionalization include the construction of features that can be combined into hypotheses (Srinivasan *et al.* 1996) and the reduction of the search space (Lachiche 2011). It should be noted that this linguistic bias (the choice of operators) does not guarantee that it is possible to reconstruct the complete information of the dataset with all propositionalization statements (Krogel 2008). A propositionalization operator makes it possible to transform a class, via a relation, into an attribute.

The *gradation* consists of extending a context $K_i = (O_i, A_i, I_i)$ from a relational family of contexts by integrating relational information, in the form of attributes. The relational attributes translate the links between the objects of the two contexts into a relationship. The resulting RCA lattices are difficult to interpret because of these relational attributes. Resulting extraction methods are based either on fixed-point descriptions that can be recursive and not very easy to interpret, or on inherently circuit-free models that do not cover the general case.

9.3.2.3. Rules of association

The ultimate goal of the lattice construction procedure is the extraction of knowledge in the form of association rules. Furthermore, the concept lattice serves as the basis for extracting a compact representation of the set of association rules. Whether a lattice is produced in an FCA or RCA process, the process of extracting rules is the same: for each concept C, we extract all rules $g \rightarrow Y \setminus g$, where g is a generator of C, and Y is either the intention of C or that of a concept that is the immediate predecessor of C.

However, the RCA method introduces relational attributes, which, like non-relational attributes, are incorporated into the rules. Now, for a rule to be usable, it must be possible to interpret it, in particular by resolving references to the concepts of these attributes. Indeed, a rule of the form $a1, a2 \rightarrow a3, pr : C_{j,k}$ provides no information if we cannot characterize $C_{j,k}$. Thus, there are several options for clarifying these relational attributes:

Extension. Since the extension of the concepts is kept throughout the iterations, we can replace the reference to the concept by it. In this case, a relational attribute characterizes the direct links between objects. However, this type of modeling denotes the very nature of association rules, which is to identify patterns, free from instances, by means of abstractions. It seems unpromising when the list of objects of a relational attribute is large.

Intention. On the other hand, if we decide to replace the reference by the intention of the concept, several ambiguities appear. First of all, a choice must be made about the definition of the concept, since it presents several options. By choosing the option of the evolving concept, several stages of the intention are possible. In purely informational terms, for a concept, the most accurate way to describe its objects is the fixed-point intention. However, in this framework, a problem inherent to RCA emerges: cyclic dependencies. Indeed, the relational paths of the multigraph can form circuits. Interpreting such circuits is a difficult case and requires the use of the smallest fixed point theory, as pointed out by Baader and Sertkaya (2009). Finally, by considering canonical generators to represent a concept in a cycle-free relational attribute, this allows for rule extraction.

9.4. Machine learning

9.4.1. *Basics of machine learning*

Machine learning includes different tools that can be used to perform this step of data mining such as naive Bayes, decision tree, random forest, k nearest neighbors, support vector machine, multilayer perceptron (**MLP**) and deep learning. Although deep learning is currently the most popular tool, it is not necessarily the most suitable tool for industrial data. Indeed, deep learning is well suited to model problems that are stable over time and for which we have very large datasets (object detection, natural language processing, etc.). However, industrial systems are, by nature, evolving (production line reorganization, cutting tool wear, machine change, etc.). It is therefore necessary to build models using reduced datasets, to adapt these models to the evolutions of the modeled system and to handle data that may be heavily polluted by noise and outliers. The rest of this chapter focuses on the use of the MLP, which has the advantages of being simple to implement and being able to handle very diverse problems such as classification or regression while ensuring good performance in terms of accuracy and generalization.

9.4.2. *Multilayer perceptron (MLP)*

9.4.2.1. *Structure of MLP*

The classic MLP is a feedforward neural network with only one hidden layer. The activation function of the hidden neurons is a sigmoidal function such as the hyperbolic tangent. The neurons of the output layer integrate an activation function that will also be sigmoidal to treat a classification problem, or linear to treat a regression problem. Previous works have shown that this type of network is a universal approximator (Cybenko 1989; Funahashi 1989), i.e. a model able to approximate any nonlinear function with the desired accuracy. Its structure is given by (for output k):

$$z_k = g_2\left(\sum_{i=1}^{n_1} w_{ki}^2 \cdot g_1\left(\sum_{h=1}^{n_0} w_{ih}^1 \cdot x_h^0 + b_i^1\right) + b_k\right)$$ [9.3]

where z_k are the n_2 outputs and x_h^0 are the n_0 inputs of the MLP, w_{ih}^1 are the weights connecting the input layer to the hidden layer, b_i^1 are the biases of the hidden neurons, $g1(.)$ is the activation function of the hidden neurons (classically, the hyperbolic tangent), w_{ki}^2 are the weights connecting the hidden neurons to the output k, b_k is the weight of the output neuron k, and $g_2(.)$ is the activation function of the output neurons, which will be chosen to be sigmoidal in the case of a classification problem and linear in the case of a regression problem.

Like any machine learning problem, learning an MLP means finding the parameters (weights and biases connecting the layers) that minimize a global criterion (quadratic criterion) (Figure 9.3). In order to evaluate the generalization capacity of the model thus built, the database is subdivided into three bases:

– a learning base that will be used for the actual learning;

– a validation base that will make it possible to evaluate the risk of overfitting;

– a test base that will allow us to evaluate the generalization capacity of the model.

It is important to ensure that these three databases contain distinct data so that the validation and test databases play their roles correctly. This risk is particularly acute when using data augmentation algorithms. Indeed, it may happen that the database is considered too small to ensure good learning of the model. In this case, we may have to use a data augmentation algorithm, but this must be done on the three databases separately and not on the global database. In order to obtain a good model, several classic problems must be addressed.

The first of these problems is due to the fact that the learning algorithm used is a local minimum search algorithm based on gradient backpropagation. This implies that the performance of the final model depends on the starting point of the training, i.e. the initialization.

The second problem common to any machine learning approach is the problem of rote learning or *overfitting*. This problem is due to the fact that industrial data are polluted by noise and outliers. If we push the learning too much, the model ends up learning the noise on the system more than the behavior of the system itself. Of course, this problem does not arise in the case of a totally deterministic problem, but industrial problems are rarely deterministic problems.

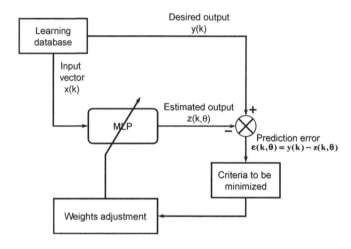

Figure 9.3. *Principle of supervised learning*

The third important problem to be taken into account in the case of an industrial application consists of adapting the model to the evolutions of the system. Indeed, as previously mentioned, industrial systems evolve over time. However, an MLP is only a mathematical equation whose parameters have been determined at a given time. With time, a shift will progressively (wear of a cutting tool, clogging of a filter, etc.) or brutally (replacement of a machine, modification of a range, etc.) occur. It is therefore necessary to detect and correct such a shift. In the following sections, we will deal with each of these problems in a little more detail.

9.4.2.2. *Initialization and local minimum*

As explained earlier, parameter learning corresponds to a local search for the minimum that is performed along the direction indicated by the gradient. Figure 9.4 illustrates this problem in the simple case of a function with a single parameter w. This figure represents the evolution of the cost (criterion to be minimized) as a function of this parameter. It can be seen that, depending on the starting point chosen, the optimum found will be the global minimum or a local minimum that is very far from the local minimum sought, even though the two starting points are very close to each other.

The choice of the initial parameters is therefore crucial. To obtain a good initialization, two characteristics must be sought:

– correctly select the weights to correctly position the starting point in the configuration space;

– be able to start from another point if the learning has not converged to a satisfactory optimum.

The first point requires adjusting the amplitude of the weights according to the amplitude of the inputs. Many initialization algorithms do not take care of this point, which requires a pre-step of normalization. The second point requires a random or pseudo-random initialization of the parameters.

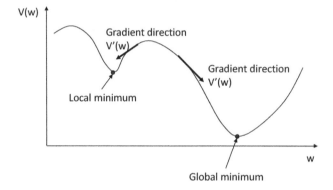

Figure 9.4. *The local minimum problem*

Many initialization algorithms have been proposed in the past (Thomas and Bloch 1997), from purely random initialization (Rumelhart *et al.* 1986) to algorithms integrating orthogonalization (Lehtokangas *et al.* 1995). The best-performing algorithm remains that of Nguyen and Widrow (1990). Whatever the algorithm used, it is necessary to perform several training sessions from different initial parameter sets in order to maximize the chances of finding a good local minimum that is close to the global minimum sought.

9.4.2.3. *Overlearning problem*

The data on which the learning is performed are industrial data. They are therefore noisy and polluted by outliers. Some authors have evaluated the percentage of outliers in industrial data in a range from 1% to 10% (Hampel *et al.* 2011). The objective of the learning is to model the system behavior while discarding the influence of noise and outliers.

Most of the learning algorithms are based on the exploitation of the gradient backpropagation (Rumelhart *et al.* 1986). Two main families have been proposed: the first-order algorithms, also known as gradient descent algorithms (conjugate gradient, stochastic gradient, etc. (Robbins and Monro 1951)), and the second-order algorithms, also known as Hessian algorithms (Levenberg 1944; Marquardt 1963). These algorithms are iterative, with gradient descent algorithms requiring more iterations than Hessian algorithms to converge, but Hessian algorithms possess a higher computational cost at each iteration (Thomas *et al.* 2019). However, regardless of the type of algorithm chosen, its behavior during learning can be represented in Figure 9.5. This figure shows the classic evolution of the criterion to be minimized as a function of the number of iterations performed on the learning and validation sets. We can see that this criterion constantly decreases on the learning set while it first decreases and then increases on the validation set. The first part of the curve corresponds to the learning of the system behavior, while the second part corresponds to the learning of the noise on the system, thus to the overlearning or overfitting.

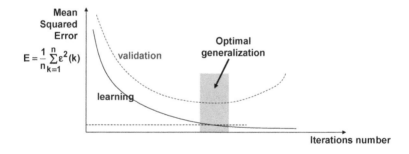

Figure 9.5. *Typical evolution of the E criterion on the learning and validation bases during the learning process*

To prevent this overfitting, several strategies can be used and combined. The first, and most obvious, is to stop learning when the criterion starts to deteriorate on the validation set. This is called early stopping (Drucker 2002). The second approach consists of reducing the number of degrees of freedom of the model to prevent the learning of noise. This can be done by adding a regularization term in the criterion to be minimized in order to constrain the parameters (Williams 1995). Another strategy is to determine the optimal size of the model (choice of useful inputs, number of hidden neurons, number of connections). This determination of the optimal structure of the model can be done in a constructive or destructive way (pruning). The constructive approach consists of adding hidden neurons and/or layers until the optimum is reached (Chentouf and Jutten 1996). Pruning consists of eliminating inputs, hidden neurons and superfluous parameters from a deliberately over-parameterized structure (Thomas and Suhner 2015). This last approach has the advantage of simultaneously performing input selection (feature selection). All the strategies described above can be combined.

9.4.2.4. Adapting the model to change

The last important point to address concerns the adaptation of the model to change. Indeed, the training of the MLP has been done in such a way that the MLP has the same behavior as the modeled system at the time of training. Many systems remain sufficiently constant over time that this is not a problem. For example, when faced with a problem of detecting objects in a scene, time will be of little consequence; a dog will continue to look like a dog for many years to come.

Industrial systems, on the contrary, are in constant evolution, whether it is at the level of the production tool (wear of a tool, replacement of a machine, etc.), at the level of the product (change of range, etc.) or of the control system (moving from a FIFO rule to an Earliest Due Date rule, etc.). It is therefore necessary to adapt the model to this type of evolution. To do this, various approaches can be implemented. The most classic one consists of adapting the model to each arrival of new data. This approach is called stream-based active learning (Dasgupta et al. 2005; Lowrance and Lauf 2019). Another approach is to monitor the accuracy of the model over time. If the behaviors of the system and the model are too divergent, then a relearning is performed to recalibrate the model to the system (Noyel et al. 2016). A control chart is used to determine when the system has drifted too far for the model to remain relevant. A Page–Hinkley test (Basseville 1988) is used to determine on which database the relearning should be performed. This second approach has the advantage of being able to check whether the drift that has occurred between the system and the model is due to normal system behavior, in which case the model must be relearned, or whether, on the other hand, this drift is due to abnormal behavior (failure, breakdown, wear and tear, etc.), in which case it is the system that must be corrected.

9.5. Illustrative example

We illustrate these concepts in the context of an ICPS dedicated to a manufacturing production (see Chapter 11 for more information on the concept of a cyber-physical production system). ACTA Mobilier is a high-end lacquerer that produces panels (in MDF) for kitchen shops, stores, living rooms, etc. At the heart of its industrial tool is a lacquering robot (in series with a drying oven) that constitutes the bottleneck. However, due to the high level of quality required for the products, this robot is subject to a high rate of non-quality. This high rate of non-quality, which is damaging in itself, has the additional consequence of greatly disrupting the production flow. In order to control this non-quality rate, a prediction model of the non-quality risk was built using a machine learning approach with the help of an MLP (Noyel *et al.* 2016) and integrated into the cyber part of the ICPS. The database used combines data from several sources and related to various concepts (product, process, environment) that had to be consolidated. Figure 9.6 shows a possible exploitation of the constructed model. The objective here is to simulate an experimental design in order to determine the limit values of the control parameters according to the measured but not controlled parameters (meteorological condition, product characteristics, etc.).

The training database was collected over a period of the year that was representative of certain weather conditions. During the use of the model throughout the year, new weather conditions were encountered which required re-learning phases. In a second phase, this prediction model was used in a holonic control system in order to optimize the control of flows (see Chapter 8). Each holon, associated with each batch, embeds an instance of the quality prediction model and, in the case of non-quality risk, a local reordering decision is made by consensus between the batches present in the robot's feed queue (Zimmermann *et al.* 2018).

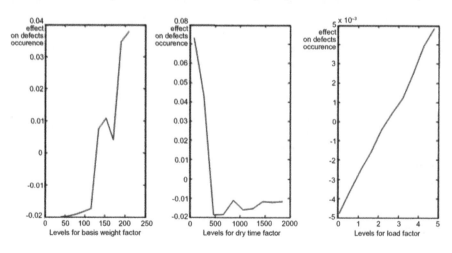

Figure 9.6. *Simulation of an experimental design*

9.6. Conclusion

Today's technology enables the use of information and knowledge embedded in physical objects. ICPS incorporate such components, capable of producing not only goods and services, but also large amounts of data. A large-scale ICPS can therefore be envisioned as millions of networked intelligent devices, sensors, and actuators embedded in the physical world that can sense, process and communicate data over the network. The management of this huge mass of data must be entrusted to algorithms that process them together with the different contexts to structure information and knowledge. Capitalized and managed in the cyber part, the data produced by ICPS often have an internal relational structure that allows the use of MRDM techniques to extract implicit semantics and make them available to artificial agents. The formalization of data and knowledge allows the use of various machine learning techniques. Typically, the MLP presented in this chapter is simple to implement and at the same time capable of handling very different problems.

9.7. References

Abubakar, A.M., Elrehail, H., Alatailat, M.A., Elçi, A. (2019). Knowledge management, decision-making style and organizational performance. *Journal of Innovation & Knowledge*, 4(2), 104–114.

Adamson, G., Wang, L., Moore, P. (2017). Feature-based control and information framework for adaptive and distributed manufacturing in cyber physical systems. *Journal of Manufacturing Systems*, 43, 305–315.

Anderson, C. (2012). *Makers: The New Industrial Revolution*. Random House Business Books, London.

Baader, F. and Sertkaya, B. (2009). Usability issues in description logic knowledge base completion. In *Formal Concept Analysis*, Ferré, S. and Rudolph, S. (eds). Springer, Berlin Heidelberg [Online]. Available at: http://link.springer.com/10.1007/978-3-642-01815-2_1 [Accessed 17 March 2021].

Basseville, M. (1988). Detecting changes in signals and systems – A survey. *Automatica*, 24(3), 309–326.

Chen, P.P.-S. (1976). The entity-relationship model – Toward a unified view of data. *ACM Transactions on Database Systems*, 1(1), 9–36.

Chentouf, R. and Jutten, C. (1996). Combining sigmoids and radial basis functions in evolutive neural architectures. *Undefined* [Online]. Available at: http://citeseerx.ist.psu.edu/viewdoc/download?doi=10.1.1.54.1611&rep=rep1&type=pdf.

Cybenko, G. (1989). Approximation by superpositions of a sigmoidal function. *Mathematics of Control, Signals, and Systems*, 2, 303–314.

Dasgupta, S., Kalai, A.T., Monteleoni, C. (2005). Analysis of perceptron-based active learning. In *Learning Theory*, Auer, P. and Meir, R. (eds). Springer, Berlin Heidelberg [Online]. Available at: http://link.springer.com/10.1007/11503415_17 [Accessed 17 March 2021].

Drucker, H. (2002). Effect of pruning and early stopping on performance of a boosting ensemble. *Computational Statistics & Data Analysis*, 38(4), 393–406.

Funahashi, K.-I. (1989). On the approximate realization of continuous mappings by neural networks. *Neural Networks*, 2(3), 183–192.

Ganter, B. and Wille, R. (1999). *Formal Concept Analysis*. Springer, Berlin Heidelberg [Online]. Available at: http://link.springer.com/10.1007/978-3-642-59830-2 [Accessed 17 March 2021].

Golatowski, F., Blumenthal, J., Haase, M., Burchardt, H., Timmermann, D. (2003). Service oriented software architecture for sensor networks. *Proceedings of the International Workshop on Mobile Computing IMC'03*, 93–98.

Gunes, V., Peter, S., Givargis, T., Vahid, F. (2014). A survey on concepts, applications, and challenges in cyber-physical systems. *KSII Transactions on Internet & Information Systems*, 8(12), 4242–4268.

Hampel, F.R., Ronchetti, E.M., Rousseeuw, P.J., Stahel, W.A. (2011). Robust statistics: The approach based on influence functions [Online]. Available at: https://nbn-resolving.org/urn:nbn:de:101:1-201502079115 [Accessed 17 March 2021].

Huchard, M., Roume, C., Valtchev, P. (2002). When concepts point at other concepts: The case of UML diagram reconstruction. In *Proceedings of the 2nd Workshop on Advances in Formal Concept Analysis for Knowledge Discovery in Databases (FCAKDD)*, 32–43.

Klingenberg, C.O., Borges, M.A.V., Antunes Jr., J.A.V. (2019). Industry 4.0 as a data-driven paradigm: A systematic literature review on technologies. *Journal of Manufacturing Technology Management* [Online]. Available at: https://www.emerald.com/insight/content/doi/10.1108/JMTM-09-2018-0325/full/html [Accessed 17 March 2021].

Krogel, M.-A. (2008). *Database Mining: Propositionalization for Knowledge Discovery in Relational Databases*. VDM Verlag, Saarbrücken.

Lachiche, N. (2011). Propositionalization. In *Encyclopedia of Machine Learning*, Sammut, C., Webb, G.I. (eds). Springer, Boston.

Lehtokangas, M., Saarinen, J., Kaski, K., Huuhtanen, P. (1995). Initializing weights of a multilayer perceptron network by using the orthogonal least squares algorithm. *Neural Computation*, 7(5), 982–999.

Levenberg, K. (1944). A method for the solution of certain non-linear problems in least squares. *Quarterly of Applied Mathematics*, 2(2), 164–168.

Lowrance, C.J. and Lauf, A.P. (2019). An active and incremental learning framework for the online prediction of link quality in robot networks. *Engineering Applications of Artificial Intelligence*, 77, 197–211.

Marquardt, D.W. (1963). An algorithm for least-squares estimation of nonlinear parameters. *Journal of the Society for Industrial and Applied Mathematics*, 11(2), 431–441.

Nguyen, D. and Widrow, B. (1990). Improving the learning speed of 2-layer neural networks by choosing initial values of the adaptive weights. *1990 IJCNN International Joint Conference on Neural Networks*, San Diego, USA, 17–21 June [Online]. Available at: http://ieeexplore.ieee.org/document/5726777/ [Accessed 17 March 2021].

Noyel, M., Thomas, P., Thomas, A., Charpentier, P. (2016). Reconfiguration process for neuronal classification models: Application to a quality monitoring problem. *Computers in Industry*, 83, 78–91.

Patel, M.C. and Panchal, M. (2012). A review on ensemble of diverse artificial neural networks. *International Journal of Advanced Research in Computer Engineering and Technology*, 1(10), 63–70.

Porter, M.E. and Heppelmann, J.E. (2014). How smart, connected products are transforming competition. *Harvard Business Review*, 92(11), 64–88.

Robbins, H. and Monro, S. (1951). A stochastic approximation method. *The Annals of Mathematical Statistics*, 22(3), 400–407.

Roblek, V., Meško, M., Krapež, A. (2016). A complex view of industry 4.0. *SAGE Open*, 6(2), 2158244016653987.

Rouane-Hacene, M., Huchard, M., Napoli, A., Valtchev, P. (2013). Relational concept analysis: Mining concept lattices from multi-relational data. *Annals of Mathematics and Artificial Intelligence*, 67(1), 81–108.

Rumelhart, D.E., Hinton, G.E., Williams, R.J. (1986). Learning representations by back-propagating errors. *Nature*, 323, 533–536.

de Sousa Jabbour, A.B.L., Jabbour, C.J.C., Foropon, C., Godinho Filho, M. (2018). When titans meet – Can industry 4.0 revolutionise the environmentally-sustainable manufacturing wave? The role of critical success factors. *Technological Forecasting and Social Change*, 132, 18–25.

Srinivasan, A., Muggleton, S.H., Sternberg, M.J.E., King, R.D. (1996). Theories for mutagenicity: A study in first-order and feature-based induction. *Artificial Intelligence*, 85(1), 277–299.

Tao, F., Qi, Q., Liu, A. (2018). Data-driven smart manufacturing. *Journal of Manufacturing Systems*, 48, 157–169.

Thomas, P. and Bloch, G. (1997). Initialisation of multilayer feedforward neural networks. *15th IMACS World Congress on Scientific Computation, Modelling and Applied Mathematics WC'97*, Berlin, Germany, 25–29 August [Online]. Available at: https://www.researchgate.net/publication/312297180_Initialisation_of_multilayer_feedforward_neural_networks_for_non-linear_systems_identification.

Thomas, P. and Suhner, M.-C. (2015). A new multilayer perceptron pruning algorithm for classification and regression applications. *Neural Processing Letters*, 42(2), 437–458.

Thomas, P., Suhner, M.-C., Derigent, W. (2019). Relearning procedure to adapt pollutant prediction neural model: Choice of relearning algorithm. *2019 International Joint Conference on Neural Networks (IJCNN)*, Budapest, Hungary, 14–19 July [Online]. Available at: https://ieeexplore.ieee.org/document/8852193/ [Accessed 17 March 2021].

Wille, R. (1982). Restructuring lattice theory: An approach based on hierarchies of concepts. In *Ordered Sets*, Rival, I. (ed.). Springer Netherlands, Dordrecht [Online]. Available at: http://link.springer.com/10.1007/978-94-009-7798-3_15 [Accessed 17 March 2021].

Williams, P.M. (1995). Bayesian regularization and pruning using a Laplace prior. *Neural Computation*, 7(1), 117–143.

Zimmermann, E., Bril, H., Thomas, P., Pannequin, R., Noyel, M. (2018). Using AHP process for scheduling problem based on smart lots and their quality prediction capability. *8th Workshop on Service Orientation in Holonic and Multi-agent Manufacturing, SOHOMA'18*, Bergamo, Italy, 11–13 June [Online]. Available at: https://hal.archives-ouvertes.fr/hal-01823501.

10

Human–Industrial Cyber-Physical System Integration: Design and Evaluation Methods

Marie-Pierre PACAUX-LEMOINE[1] and Frank FLEMISCH[2,3]

[1] *LAMIH UMR CNRS 8201, Université Polytechnique Hauts-de-France, Valenciennes, France*

[2] *Institute of Industrial Engineering and Ergonomics, RWTH Aachen University, Germany*

[3] *Fraunhofer Institute for Communication, Information Processing and Ergonomics, Wachtberg, Germany*

10.1. Introduction

Industry 4.0 promises to raise the levels of productivity and integration of industrial production. Integration concerns systems, whether digital or physical, and distributed at various organizational levels of the production system, but integration must also take into account the human being who will have to face new challenges. Productivity improvement seems to be mainly envisaged by introducing or increasing the number of interconnected autonomous systems as is the case with industrial cyber-physical systems (ICPS). However, the design of this type of highly autonomous production system cannot abstain from a "smart" association of human operators at any level of

---

For a color version of all figures in this book, see www.iste.co.uk/cardin/digitalization.zip.

Digitalization and Control of Industrial Cyber-Physical Systems,
coordinated by Olivier CARDIN, William DERIGENT and Damien TRENTESAUX.

activity, at the risk that they are less and less aware of the state of the processes and the control modes. The human is often considered as the element that must find the solution and make the right decision to control an unexpected situation, but they must be given the means to do so (Patrick Millot *et al.* 2015). If productivity is normally improved by the deployment of autonomous systems, it risks falling sharply if the process, due to an unexpected or unthinkable event, is in a state for which no solution has been programmed or listed. Even without talking about an accident of the type that occurred at the Fukushima nuclear power plant in 2011, unforeseen events, fortunately often much less serious than a tsunami, can creep into the process more or less visibly and quickly. These events can send the process into an unexpected state that is difficult to control without the active and properly informed presence of humans. This is not a new issue, and Figure 10.1, dated 1989, is evidence of this. It will not be enough to break the ice to free the human from their withdrawal so that they will be able to quickly understand the state of the process abandoned in a critical situation, identify the causes and consequences of this state and quickly take good decisions and actions.

Figure 10.1. *What about a highly automated industrial system based on the absence of an active and informed human presence? (source: Cheney (1989), New Yorker Magazine)*

The whole objective is therefore to take advantage of the development of new technologies, capabilities and skills that can lead to more productive and flexible ICPS, but these industrial systems must be cooperative. As stated here and in the definition proposed in Chapter 1, these industrial systems, which will be cyber-physical, will have to be cooperative among themselves and with humans. But the reciprocal is also true; it would be desirable for humans to cooperate with the systems in order to exploit their performance on certain functions. In order for humans to cooperate, they must have confidence in the capabilities and competences of the systems, without refraining from checking their operation and the resulting outputs. The cyber-physical system (CPS) as a partner, as shown in Figure 10.2, is, of course, difficult to envisage for many reasons, including ethical and technical ones, but the idea of complementarity between humans and CPS is nevertheless attractive.

Figure 10.2. *Complementarity in terms of physical capacity and competence between humans and CPS. A human and a robot are working together. The human asks the robot how its weekend was and the robot replies "so-so"*

To identify this complementarity and support cooperation, a set of information must be shared between the human and the systems, information on the physical/technical elements themselves and also information on the actors involved in the control of these elements, whether human or technical. Thus, as illustrated by Figures 1.3 and 1.4 of Chapter 1, the cooperation takes place at several levels, between the physical and cyber parts and within each part, as well as between the different systems involved in the global organization of the ICPS integrating the human. Whether it is the cooperation between the human and the digital control system of the physical part of the industrial system, or between the human and the system dedicated to data analysis, tests and learning of the cyber part, the cooperation must be built from both the human and the technological point of view.

Cooperation is indeed the basic element of the construction of the ICPS integrating the human, each agent must be cooperative. What is cooperation? *Two agents of a system are in a cooperative situation if each of the agents are aiming for goals that interfere with the goals of the other (interference management), and they try to manage these interferences in a way that facilitates the activity of the other (facilitation)* (Hoc 1996). Thus, the human and the digital control system of the physical part aim to control the physical elements to reach common objectives. Interferences can appear, for example, because of a different consideration of the performance indicators. The human, by their experience, can, in particular, favor a criterion or provide new information to the digital control system. In the same way, in the cyber part, the agents' goals, of a higher decision-making level than for the physical part, can also interfere. A human decision can be questioned following the analysis of this decision via simulation tools showing the inadequacy of the decision.

In order to identify interferences and know how to facilitate the activity of the other, and thus achieve complementarity, a cooperative agent (whether human or technical) must be endowed with two competences, Know-How-to-Operate and Know-How-to-Cooperate (Pacaux-Lemoine and Itoh 2016). The Know-How-to-Operate is the internal capacity of the agent to solve problems concerning the process, according to their skills (knowledge, rules, skills, experience, expertise) and capacities (workload, fatigue, lack of energy, downgraded mode, breakdown, etc.), completed by the external capacity of the agent to take information about the process and the environment (access to data from the process) and act on the process (access to commands). The Know-How-to-Cooperate is the internal capacity of the agent to elaborate a model of the other agent, in order to deduce its intentions, analyze the tasks/functions to be performed and organize the activity by defining a common plan. This internal capacity of Know-How-to-Cooperate is also completed by an external capacity of communication to understand the other agent and provide information to the other agent.

In order to build a cooperation accepted by humans, effective in terms of complementarity between actors, and efficient in avoiding that the cooperation overloads the global activity but, on the contrary, allows an increase in performance, the design of human industrial cyber-physical systems (HICPS) must be based on a rigorous methodological approach that takes into account all the above-mentioned capabilities. After a quick presentation of existing design methods, the following sections propose a detailed description of the different steps required to design human–cyber-physical systems.

10.2. Design methods

The use of appropriate concepts and methods can make all the difference in whether a new industrial project, or the evolution of an existing project to an ICPS, is successfully implemented or not. The choice is not trivial, especially when profound changes in the process or associated organization must be made to achieve objectives such as those of Industry 4.0. In science, the challenge is to propose relevant methods, with a recognized scientific foundation, to provide the main guidelines needed to implement the new project and the new systems it may involve. Whether it is by defining the project's objectives, issuing hypotheses on the achievement of the desired objectives, or analyzing data to judge the interest of the transformations, the method must help the HICPS designer to identify and then justify the changes to be made to the existing systems or the new directions to be taken.

In this chapter, we focus on the design and evaluation of industrial cyber-physical systems that will be interacting or even cooperating with a human operator. Since we are dealing with systems dedicated to Industry 4.0, these human operators are called Operators 4.0 (Romero 2016). There are several so-called user-centered design methods. They make it possible, in particular, to evaluate the physical and/or cognitive ergonomics of human–machine systems. These methods provide the necessary knowledge for interface design and evaluation, such as usability engineering and human–computer interaction models based on the cognitive activity of users. Nielsen (1993) defined usability as a subpart of acceptability or the extent to which a product meets user expectations. Gould and Lewis (1985) described usability engineering as a general approach with three strategies: early consideration of the user and their tasks, empirical measurement and iterative design. This approach considers user aspects in most of the project management steps and defines several standards. However, other methods exist, from different fields such as the method proposed in social acceptability by Brangier *et al.* (2010). The authors presented a comparison between the social and ergonomic approaches. They underlined the interest of exploiting the complementarity between the approaches. This is also the objective of the method proposed by Millot (1995), called the "U" method. This method takes the V-cycle (Royce 1970) as its starting point, but proposes a simpler approach to designing and evaluating systems. The V-cycle, which comes from systems engineering, builds the method on the different stages of the waterfall model. However, it is very difficult to use when the environments for which the system is designed are complex, such as the dynamic environments of Industry 4.0. In addition, the V-cycle does not take into account the human being, nor their interactions with the systems. The "U" method has this objective, as well as adjusting the involvement of the human to the involvement of the systems, and vice versa, in the control of an environment in a cooperative manner.

Based on the "U" method, Figure 10.3 presents an iterative approach based on four main features: an exploratory phase to identify systems that would be interesting to test, a refinement and development phase for systems identified as interesting, the design phases of these systems and the evaluation phases of the designed systems.

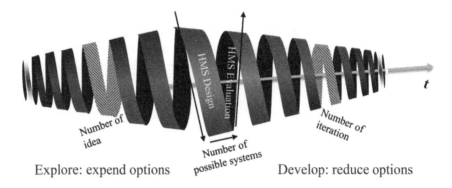

Figure 10.3. *Iterative procedure with spinal refinement, adapted from Pacaux-Lemoine and Flemisch (2015) and Pacaux-Lemoine and Flemisch (2021)*

The exploratory phase underlines the importance and time needed to choose the systems to be designed and evaluated to meet the expected objectives, which may also evolve as a result of discussions and tests. The more the designer-explorers discuss the objectives with the new project managers, future users and evaluator-explorers, the more the number of possible systems will increase. But the more the evaluator-developers exchange with the future users, as well as with the designer-developers, the more the number of possible systems will be reduced, in order to finalize the approach on the final system that will be integrated.

10.3. Method of integrating HICPS

Initially used in telerobotics (Patrick Millot and Roussillon 1991), the "U" method has been applied to other application domains such as automotive (Pacaux-Lemoine and Crévits 2010), which led to the proposal of a new version of the method presented in Figure 10.4. New steps and information have indeed been introduced to enrich the "U" model, in particular, on the representations of human operators and CPS through the description of their respective functions and roles, on their interaction through a Common Workspace and finally, on the multi-level dimension of cooperation. The method proposes a top-down step to design one or more HICPS, which are then tested during the bottom-up evaluation phase. The steps of the top-down design phase use the model of a cooperative agent, the definitions of degrees of cooperation, levels of cooperation, as well as the notion of Common Workspace, defined several years ago in the following works dealing with the design of human–machine systems. For more information on these definitions and studies, the reader can refer to the following: Pacaux-Lemoine and Flemisch (2019) and Pacaux-Lemoine (2020). However, these definitions are briefly presented to describe the interest of their use in the design and evaluation of HICPS, especially in the context of Industry 4.0.

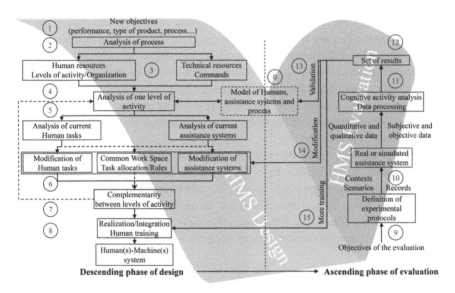

Figure 10.4. *HICPS integration method*

10.3.1. *Descending phase*

From the first step of the method, the designers must identify and understand the objectives of the HICPS they have to develop, in order to improve the process, or even invent it (see Figure 10.4 "1"). The objectives are most often related to a quest to increase the performance of a process, but performance is a word behind which there are several often interdependent sub-objectives. It can be an increase in the number of types of products produced by a manufacturing system, a decrease in the number of accidents in a manufacturing area or a decrease in the time it takes to transport these products from one point to another in the plant. However, performance can also be induced by increased safety, improved work comfort or improved capacity/competence of human operators, so that the HICPS increases its physical or cognitive capacity, or compensates for a weakness or disability. This kind of improvement is already demanded by Industry 4.0, in adapting HICPS to the skills of human operators with regard to their expertise, experience, skill, habitual or instantaneous cognitive and physical capacity, and according to the state of a process running in normal or degraded mode. All of these aspects should be discussed at this early stage with the industrial facility managers, process experts and end-users of the new systems to be developed. This analysis of the objectives is also important to carry out the second step of the method, which consists of studying the process to be improved or invented (see Figure 10.4 "2").

A process and the activity of human operators related to the control of this process are most often not new; they already exist in the industrial system. Models of the organization of these activities may therefore exist, or models of the functions and tasks to be performed by the existing human operators or HICPS. Access to these models can be very informative for the designer (see Figure 10.4 "0"). But it may happen that only human tasks exist and the designer must imagine and create an HICPS that automates some of the human tasks. The designer must then identify the limits of their intervention, defined by the set of tasks or functions whose modification has been validated by the process managers. It is, however, desirable that the designer has the agreement of the future users to facilitate the acceptance of the new systems, on the one hand, and, on the other hand, to propose the new tasks that they will have to perform. Today, it is often only operational safety and cybersecurity that define these limits, but other values such as the workload and the motivation of human operators must be considered.

The designer must then study the composition and organization of the human and technical resources (see Figure 10.4 "3"), which may lead to a different analysis than that provided by the models or process managers. The designer's objective here is not to avoid the influence of the managers, but to have a neutral approach in order to offer new and original perspectives. Specialists in ergonomics and cognitive and social psychology make it possible to carry out the analysis of human resources activities in a timely manner, in particular, by identifying the cognitive and physical constraints linked to the activity, as well as the social constraints linked to the organization. This is why the method emphasizes the interest of highlighting the degrees and levels of cooperation in the organization (see Figure 10.4 "4"). The designer must thus identify the tasks and sub-tasks of the human operators and the HICPS at each level of activity, also known as the decision-making level, such as the operational, tactical and strategic levels regularly mentioned in industrial systems organizations. Similarly, the designer must identify the information and activities that are transversal to the activity levels (see Figure 10.4 "5") to facilitate cooperation between these levels (also called layers of cooperation; Pacaux-Lemoine and Flemisch 2019). At each activity level, they suggest modifications to existing tasks or the creation of new tasks for the human operator or HICPS (see Figure 10.4 "6"). The analysis of the activity levels is an iterative procedure, level by level, but it also ensures the complementarity of the tasks or functions between the levels and their cooperation (see Figure 10.4 "7"). Indeed, these tasks or functions, depending on the type of description of the activity that is carried out, are attached to the individual activities of an agent, whether human or cyber-physical, or to its cooperative activities linked to the interaction with other agents. This is how, as presented in the introduction, the functions of Know-How-to-Operate and Know-How-to-Cooperate are defined (Hoc and Lemoine 1998). To complete the elements presented in the introduction, the Know-How-to-Operate function makes it possible for an agent to know how to control a process according to four main sub-functions, which are: taking information on the process, analyzing this information to prognose or diagnose the state of the process, making decisions to respond to an identified problem and taking action, i.e. sending commands to correct the state of the process. The Know-How-to-Operate function makes it possible for an agent to manage its interactions with other agents in a cooperative way. It is divided into four sub-functions: information gathering on the other agents, detection of interference, i.e. differences in judgment between the agents on the state of the process or of the other agent, management of these interferences to agree on a common solution and allocation of authority on the control functions to be performed. The Know-How-to-Operate and Know-How-to-Cooperate functions can be analyzed using a grid to identify and define the set of functions (Pacaux-Lemoine 2020).

After having checked the complementarity between the levels of activity, the designer can proceed with the programming, except if they are in the "exploratory" part of the method for which the functions can be simulated or played (Flemisch *et al.* 2019). If the designer is in the "implementation" part of the method, they can program the functions of the HICPS, the interface with the human operator (visual, sound, tactile, haptic, etc.), and then they train the human operators in their new functions (see Figure 10.4 "8"). The definition and organization of the functions of the human operators and the HICPS are important steps in the design process, but the design of the interface, external representation of the Common Workspace, and thus support of the cooperative activity are also a crucial step to the success of the new HICPS. However, this chapter does not address these aspects, but uses recognized references, including those that allow choosing or mixing several forms of sensory feedback (e.g. Baltzer *et al.* (2017)) and many other articles dedicated to interfaces in the context of Industry 4.0. At the end of the top-down phase, the bottom-up phase takes over to evaluate the HICPS thus designed.

10.3.2. *Ascending phase*

The "engineering" approaches often correspond (wrongly) to the "implementation" part of the design phase of the method, the bottom-up evaluation phase, most of the time "technical", starting when there is a minimum of functions of the ICPS to be implemented, on at least one activity level of the industrial process. With the approach proposed in this chapter, in addition to the technical validation of the ICPS, we propose an ergonomic validation of the latter. The objectives of the evaluation must therefore answer the questions raised by the hypotheses put forward, such as: what do we want to highlight with the evaluations? How can the new HICPS be evaluated and prove its interest? Is it well accepted by future human operators? The **experimental protocols** and **procedures** must answer these questions (see Figure 10.4 "9"). The experimenters define the **contexts** of use for which the HICPS has been developed; it concerns all or part of a process (e.g. a complete production cell or a production unit). The experimenters also define **scenarios**, making it possible to play with the interactions between the human operator and the HICPS to achieve the objectives. In a scenario, the process is in a predefined start-up state, with a set of tasks that are proposed to the participants through experiments. The participants are encouraged to perform these tasks, with or without the assistance of the HICPS, to reach the requested objectives, despite the occurrence of unexpected events triggered by the experimenters and programmed in the scenarios (machine breakdown, new products to be manufactured, raw material supply problem, etc.). It is necessary to develop several experimental scenarios if several experimental conditions are evaluated, involving, for example, different HICPS configurations and/or proposing different levels of automation (Pacaux-Lemoine *et al.* 2021). The scenarios must be different so that a participant cannot recognize a situation and thus make the same decision as before, or the same type of interaction with the ICPS. However, they should be of similar complexity and offer similar tasks so that the data from the experiments with these scenarios are comparable. The duration of a scenario depends on the type of tasks requested, from a few minutes for the control of a robot at the operational level, to several hours when the objective is to evaluate an aid to the supervision of a complete industrial process with strategic planning tasks. Most often, the same scenarios are not used for the same experimental conditions; they are crossed according to a Graeco–Latin square to erase order and learning effects. In other words, participants do not test the same HICPS configurations with the same scenarios, so the order in which the experimental conditions and scenarios are tested has no impact on the recorded data.

A reference experimental condition is usually defined; it can be the process as it was before any modifications, for example without adding HICPS or changing the organization. Comparing data from the experiment with this condition with data from the conditions implementing the modifications allows for the potential benefits of the new installation to be demonstrated.

Following the definition of the experimental protocol, it is necessary to establish the **experimental procedures**, i.e. the different stages of exchange between the experimenters and the participants. First, the experimenters present the scientific objectives of the experiment to the participants, then the experimental platform on which they are trained if they are new to the field of application, and/or if the tasks to be carried out are new, especially those related to the new HICPS. The participants must therefore understand which tasks to perform in which context, following which events, and this, without initially using the new HICPS developed to assist them. After this training, they are trained to use the new HICPS, and then practice using them through dedicated scenarios, different from the experimental scenarios, but similar in complexity.

The experimental environments are either a real process, identical or scaled down reproduction of a real installation, a simulator, a virtual environment reproducing the external environment of the process and the functionalities of the real environment, or a combination of the two (see Figure 10.4 "10"). The level of realism of simulators can vary from a very low level, when participants only perform relatively simple tasks, but many times (e.g. simple microworld on a computer), to a very high level of realism, when the simulation only concerns the external environment of the process, but the control and command systems are the real ones (e.g. fighter pilot training simulators). The most advanced simulators can combine both real and simulated environments and control systems. For experimenters, simulated environments are much easier to control than real environments that are dependent on adverse events and therefore not repeatable from participant to participant, or scenario to scenario. However, even if the experimental environment is under control, participants' behavior may not be natural. Participants are aware that their activities are being recorded and they sometimes do their best to meet the experimenters' assumed expectations.

Simulated environments make it possible to evaluate the implementation of HICPS in secure and controlled conditions, even if the HICPS are brought to their operating limits. These simulation tests are essential before transposing them into a real environment, which brings its own set of constraints. It is indeed much less controllable than a simulated environment, especially to study the cooperation between the human operator and the ICPS in detail. Moreover, technical problems can occur more often than in a simulated environment, such as disturbances or communication interruptions. Even if such problems can occur in real conditions, these uncontrolled events prevent the realization of experiments based on similar scenarios and may lead to the absence of statistically significant results. Simulated environments can also be used to collect several types of subjective data, such as verbal protocols, as well as other types of data collection, such as workload and situation awareness.

For each of the experimental steps, the designers and experimenters prepare **the data records**. The data can be recorded automatically or manually; they can be objective, subjective, quantitative, qualitative, raw, interpreted or coded, depending on the experimental environment and the established protocol (see the examples in Pacaux-Lemoine *et al.* (2021)). The definition and especially the control of the recordings are steps to be taken care of, because it is rarely easy to repeat experiments that mobilize personnel, participants, technical and financial means. The quality of the data also impacts the quality of the results. The word "data" is one of the most cited today, such as databases, "Big Data", data mining, data clouds, but experimenters must find the right compromise between recording a great deal of data but spending more time cleaning, sorting and analyzing it, and selecting the most relevant data to check the objectives to be achieved and how to analyze them.

Data recording and analysis are central to understanding activity within the HICPS, and in particular, **the cognitive activity** that emerges (see Figure 10.4 "11"). The designers can program the data collections directly on the experimental platform. Thus, concerning the HICPS, the designers can easily detect and record any activity, whether the functions concern information gathering, information analysis, decision-making or actions implemented on the process (Know-How-to-Operate); the same applies to cooperative activities with the human operator, as soon as the HICPS takes information from the latter, detects and manages interference between their respective functions and decides on the allocation of functions (Know-How-to-Cooperate). As these activities are at the very heart of the HICPS programs, they are easily trapped. Obviously, this type of collection is much more complex for humans! But there are different ways to obtain this information. The easiest and least invasive way to deploy and is obviously to record all of the commands sent by the participant via the HICPS interface, as well as the information contained in theCommon Workspace. This precoded data is valuable information for experimenters to understand the participants' decision-making with respect to process states or HICPS behavior. The precoding can be based on cooperative agent activity models, such as the one proposed in the top-down design phase, whose Know-How-to-Operate and Know-How-to-Cooperate functions are quickly recalled above.

Spontaneous verbalizations and video recordings of the participants and the control and command interfaces can support the precoded data. Spontaneous verbalizations are of particular interest when two participants are working together during the experiments (see the examples in Habib *et al.* (2021)). However, participants may use domain-specific vocabulary (e.g. professional operators) and experimenters may have to ask for explanations. Therefore, another way is to complete the experiments with a phase of confrontation of the participants with video recordings of what they have done. The aim is for them to explain their decisions and actions, not to justify themselves, but so that the experimenter can better understand the behaviors adopted.

The participants can be asked about the perceived workload at several temporal stages of the scenarios pre-established by the experimenters. The instantaneous workload is requested orally or via a scale displayed on one of the control screens of the experimental platform. Although this response task appears to be an additional task for the participant, it is nevertheless part of the cooperative tasks that the participants have to perform, i.e. to ask themselves about their own workload in order to decide on the possible sharing of this workload with a competent HICPS. The workload transmitted by participants throughout a scenario can then be compared to the performance at the same times of the entire HICPS. The workload can also be assessed at the end of each scenario. One of the most widely used methods is the one proposed by Hart and Staveland in 1988, called NASA TLX (task load index). Two series of questions are asked to the participants. They have to express their feelings on six descriptors of the workload induced by the tasks performed, by placing a cross on a 10 cm line. These descriptors are mental demand, physical demand, time demand, performance, effort and frustration level. These descriptors are then compared two by two by the participants to weight their importance in the calculation of an overall load. This type of questionnaire is very rich when the human operators are professionals, as they often have a very good representation of their work and the tasks they have to perform. They are often forced to ask themselves the same questions for self-assessments, especially when they are required to take risks.

Assessing the **situation awareness** of participants during a scenario is also a very interesting tool; it is about how participants perceive and understand the environment to be controlled, in order to make a decision. There are several methods. Endsley (1995) proposed a method associated with the three-level model of situation awareness, namely levels based on detecting information, understanding this information and projecting its state into the future to make a decision. The associated method, called SAGAT (situation awareness global assessment technique; Jones and Endsley 2004), is only used in a simulated environment since it requires freezing the evolution of the environment, displaying blank screens and asking participants to express their understanding of the current and future situation of the environment. SAGAT is a recognized method, but it has its limits because of the need to freeze the situations, and is therefore not applicable to real dynamic environments. Other methods therefore exist, such as the one that consists of asking a domain expert to "look over the shoulder" of the participant and propose a subjective evaluation (Durso *et al.* 1998). It also uses a method based on queries, but without recourse to memory, SPAM (situation present assessment method). The assessment is based on the experimenter's detection of errors made by the participants following the triggering of events programmed in the scenarios. Concerning the evaluation of situation awareness in real time and without freezing the environment, Jones and Endsley (2004) proposed a method that consists of regularly asking the participants a series of questions on the three levels previously presented. They also incorporate the response time of the participants to judge the quality of situation awareness.

Questionnaires remain the primary means of assessing the quality of interactions between participants and ICPS. As for the online coding of the activities of the ICPS and the participant's activity via the HICPS interface, the questionnaires can be built on the model of a cooperative agent; how did the participant perceive their own activity and that of the ICPS dedicated to the control of the process (i.e. their Know-How)? How did they perceive their cooperation with the ICPS (i.e. their and the ICPS's Know-How-to-Cooperate)? How do they think that the ICPS perceived their cooperative activity (its Know-How-to-Cooperate and the human operator's Know-How-to-Cooperate)? Other questionnaires are sometimes added so that the participants can evaluate the way in which the experiments were carried out (experimental environment, duration of training, training or other remarks, etc.).

The data recorded online and offline complement each other, in order to moderate overly hasty interpretations made by the experimenters from the analysis of the objective data, or overly subjective and unjustified evaluations made by the participants. Step 12 of the method (see Figure 10.4 "12") is the result of all of the previous steps. It presents the results of the experiments conducted on the developed HICPS. Three conclusions are drawn from these results, conclusions that make it possible to update the steps of the top-down design phase of the HICPS. **The first conclusion** validates the HICPS and the data updates the human operator, HICPS, and process models based on the modifications that were made to achieve the new goals (see Figure 10.4 "13"). **The second conclusion** highlights the problems with the design (see Figure 10.4 "14"). It is therefore necessary for the applicants to reconsider some objectives, or for the designers to correct some aspects of the

HICPS, i.e. the tasks of the human operator, the ICPS, the Common Workspace or the organization. If the analyses conducted are well detailed, they provide precise information on what needs to be changed. **The third conclusion** concerns the need for better training and/or coaching of the participants (see Figure 10.4 "15"), and then, if necessary, the repetition of the experiments.

10.4. Summary and conclusion

In conclusion, we propose a synthesis of all the types of experiments that can be carried out to design and evaluate HICPS in an iterative way. This synthesis is structured around three main axes that define three dimensions that can be used to characterize experiments (see Figure 10.5).

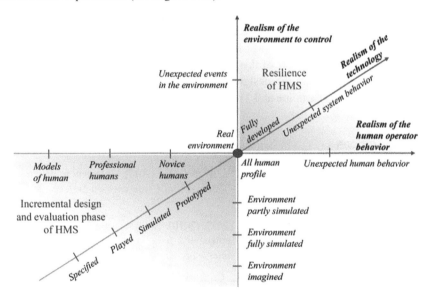

Figure 10.5. *Dimensions*

The first dimension concerns **the realism of the environment** to be controlled, such as industrial processes. It describes the realism of the experimental situations, the environment, the control and command interfaces, as well as the scenarios that are deployed. The second dimension takes into account **the realism of the HICPS** to be implemented, and in particular, the maturity of the implemented systems. Last but not least, the third dimension deals with the **realism of the human operator behaviors,** of which we can imagine that the most finalized behavior would be that of the 4.0 operator. These three dimensions can help to define the right number of experiments to be carried out to develop an HICPS that is efficient and accepted by future users, but they also help us to identify the necessary increments between the different experiments. Should we first work on a real process to test new HICPS? Should we first work with experienced operators or train new operators for new tasks? Can the ICPS be simulated, e.g. using the capabilities of the digital twin? States of realism are positioned on each axis of Figure 10.5, but they are given as examples; other intermediate states can be imagined. The figure also proposes a central point that could be considered as the final point of the experiments; the data resulting from the following steps would in fact be feedback from the human operators, following the exploitation of the ICPS that were provided to them. Indeed, several characteristics of the HICPS can evolve and destabilize the initially planned operation, modification of the behavior of the human operator for various reasons (workload, motivation, complacency with respect to the ICPS, or on the contrary, lack of confidence), or of the ICPS (automatic learning, or on the contrary, lack of adaptation to an evolving environment, etc.). The arrows in Figure 10.5 finally point to an "unknown world", in which several unexpected events may occur, whether good or bad. But part of this "unknown world" will fortunately be studied in the near future to orient the design of HICPS towards what is good for humans (Marie-Pierre Pacaux-Lemoine and Trentesaux 2019).

10.5. References

Baltzer, M.C.A., López, D., Flemisch, F., Weßel, G. (2017). Interaction patterns for cooperative guidance and control. *IEEE International Conference on Systems, Man, and Cybernetics, SMC 2017*, 870–875.

Brangier, É., Hammes-Adelé, S., Bastien, J.M.C. (2010). Analyse critique des approches de l'acceptation des technologies : de l'utilisabilité à la symbiose humain-technologie-organisation. *Revue europeenne de psychologie appliquée*, 60(2), 129–146.

Durso, F.T., Hackworth, C.A., Truit, T.R., Crutchfield, T.J., Nikolic, D. (1998). Situation awareness as a predictor of performance in en route air traffic controllers. *Air Traffic Control Quarterly*, 6(1), 1–20.

Endsley, M.R. (1995). Toward a theory of situation awareness in dynamic systems. *Human Factors*, 37(1), 32–64.

Flemisch F., Baltzer M., Sadeghian S., Meyer R., Lopez Hernandez D., Baier R. (2019) Making HSI more intelligent: Human systems exploration versus experiment for the integration of humans and artificial cognitive systems. *2nd Conference on Intelligent Human Systems Integration IHSI*, San Diego, USA.

Gould, J.D. and Lewis, C. (1985). Designing for usability: Key principles and what designers think. *Communications of the ACM*, 28(3), 300–311.

Habib, L., Pacaux-Lemoine, M.-P., Berdal, Q., Trentesaux, D. (2021). From human–human to human–machine cooperation in manufacturing 4.0. *Processes*, 9(11), 1910.

Hoc, J.M. (1996). *Supervision et contrôle de processus : la cognition en situation dynamique.* Presses Universitaires de Grenoble, Grenoble, France.

Hoc, J.M., and Lemoine, M.P. (1998). Cognitive evaluation of human–human and human–machine cooperation modes in air traffic control. *International Journal of Aviation Psychology*, 8(1), 1–32.

Jones, D.G. and Endsley, M.R. (2004). Use of real-time probes for measuring situation awareness. *International Journal of Aviation Psychology*, 14(4), 343–367.

Millot, P. (1995). La coopération homme-machine dans la superviston : les enjeux, les méthodologies, les problèmes. *Séminaire supervision et coopération homme-machine*, Paris, France.

Millot, P. and Roussillon, E. (1991). Man-machine cooperation in telerobotics: Problematic and methodologies. *Proceedings of the Second Symposium on Robotics*, Gif-sur-Yvette, France.

Millot, P., Pacaux-Lemoine, M.-P., Trentesaux, D. (2015). Une conception anthropo-centrée pour casser le mythe de l'"humain magique" En génie industriel ? *Congrès international de génie industriel*, Quebec, Canada.

Nielsen, J. (1993). *Usability Engineering.* Academic Press, London, UK.

Pacaux-Lemoine, M.-P. (2020). Human–machine cooperation: Adaptability of shared functions between humans and machines – Design and evaluation aspects. HDR, Université Polytechnique Hauts-de-France, Valenciennes, France [Online]. Available at: https://hal.archives-ouvertes.fr/tel-02959402/.

Pacaux-Lemoine, M.-P. and Crévits, I. (2010). Methodological approach and road safety system evaluation. *IFAC Conference on Analysis, Design and Evaluation of Human–Machine Systems*, Valenciennes, France.

Pacaux-Lemoine M.-P. and Flemish, F. (2015). Risk management and methodological approaches: Human-machine cooperation in car (and aircrafts). *Summer School on Risk Management, a Human Centered Approach*, UVHC, Valenciennes, France.

Pacaux-Lemoine, M.-P. and Flemisch, F. (2019). Layers of shared and cooperative control, assistance, and automation. *Cognition, Technology and Work*, 21(4), 579–591.

Pacaux-Lemoine, M.-P. and Flemisch, F. (2021). Human-cyber-physical system integration (HSI) in industry 4.0: Design and evaluation methods. *30th International Symposium on Industrial Electronics*, Kyoto, Japan.

Pacaux-Lemoine, M.-P. and Makoto, I. (2015). Towards vertical and horizontal extension of shared control concept. *IEEE International Conference on Systems, Man, and Cybernetics*, 3086–3091, doi: 10.1109/SMC.2015.536.

Pacaux-Lemoine, M.-P. and Trentesaux, D. (2019). Ethical risks of human–machine symbiosis in industry 4.0: Insights from the human–machine cooperation approach. *IFAC-PapersOnLine*, 52(19), 19–24 [Online]. Available at: https://doi.org/10.1016/j.ifacol.2019.12.077.

Pacaux-Lemoine M.-P., Berdal Q., Guérin C., Rauffet P., Chauvin C., Trentesaux D. (2021a). Designing human–system cooperation in industry 4.0 with cognitive work analysis: A first evaluation. *Cognition, Technology and Work*, 1–19 [Online]. Available at: https://doi.org/10.1007/s10111-021-00667-y.

Pacaux-Lemoine, M.-P., Habib, L., Berdal, Q., Trentesaux, D. (2021b). Cooperative patterns or how to support human-cyber-physical systems cooperation. *IEEE Systems, Man and Cybernetics 2021*, Melbourne.

Romero, D., Bernus, P., Noran, O., Stahre, J., Fast-Berglund, Å. (2016). The operator 4.0: Human cyber-physical systems & adaptive automation towards human-automation symbiosis work systems. In *Advances in Production Management Systems. Initiatives for a Sustainable World*, Nääs, I., Vendrametto, O., Reis, J.M., Gonçalves, R.F., Silva, M.T., von Cieminski, G., Kiritsis, D. (eds). Springer, Cham.

Royce, W. (1970). Managing the development of large software system. *Proceedings IEEE Western Computer Conference*, IEEE Computer Society Press, Los Almitos, USA.

PART 6

Transforming Industries with Industrial Cyber-Physical Systems

11

Impact of Industrial Cyber-Physical Systems on Reconfigurable Manufacturing Systems

Catherine DA CUNHA[1] and Nathalie KLEMENT[2]

[1] *LS2N UMR CNRS 6004, Ecole Centrale de Nantes, France*
[2] *Arts et Métiers Institute of Technology, LISPEN, HESAM University, Lille, France*

11.1. Context

A production system allows for the realization of a product so that a customer order can be fulfilled. Physical flows such as supply of raw materials or components, finished products, movement of personnel and information flows (to track production) are necessary for the successful completion of the finished product. All of these flows must interact with each other. Industrial cyber-physical systems (ICPS) can be used particularly in the context of production systems, hence the appearance of a new term: CPPS (cyber-physical production system). We can thus specify the general definition of ICPS, as illustrated in Figure 1.3. In the context of production systems, the industrial system is the production system, made up of resources (see section 11.1.2). A digital control system allows for a certain number of decisions to be made regarding production. Today, all of these elements are connected, thanks to intelligent sensors and the Internet of Things, which makes

For a color version of all figures in this book, see www.iste.co.uk/cardin/digitalization.zip.

Digitalization and Control of Industrial Cyber-Physical Systems,
coordinated by Olivier CARDIN, William DERIGENT and Damien TRENTESAUX.
© ISTE Ltd 2022.

it possible to define the CPPS and the addition of the cyber layer. The rise of CPPS has led to better management of production systems because of the data processing of physical flows and information flows. The CPPS architecture, historically based on a holonic or multi-agent version defining the physical and cyber parts, is described in more detail in Chapters 7 and 8. This chapter focuses more specifically on the potential impact of the ICPS approach in the context of goods production.

11.1.1. *Developments*

The term production system refers to a set of activities and operations that enable the manufacture of a product (Blackstone 2010). The typology of production systems has evolved considerably during the 20th century. They have adapted to market developments and have also been able to integrate technical and social progress (see Table 11.1). Thus, the technical progress of the First and Second Industrial Revolutions (especially mechanization and electrification), as well as the availability of a large workforce, made it possible to respond to the constraints of mass production via the development of dedicated production systems. The third industrial revolution relied on advances in robotization to introduce variety into the product offering via flexible production systems.

CPPS correspond to the introduction of the technical advances of the fourth industrial revolution.

Constraints	Levers	Type of production system	Specificities
– High production volume – Reduced costs	– Mechanization – Electrification – Large workforce	**Dedicated manufacturing system**	– Low product variety – Dedicated hardware – Specialized operators
– Frequent renewal of the offer	– Robotization – Skilled labor	**Flexible manufacturing system**	– Wide variety of products – Adaptive hardware – Multi-skilled operators
– Changing markets	– Digitalization – Expert and adaptive workforce	**Reconfigurable manufacturing system**	– Customization – Reconfigurable hardware – Continuing education

Table 11.1. *Evolution of production systems*

11.1.2. *Issues*

The manufacturing sector is central to Europe's sustainability, be it economic, societal or environmental. In 2018, manufacturing production accounted for 14.2% of EU GDP[1]. A total of 33 million employees work in the 2 million European manufacturing companies. The sector is responsible for 25% of waste, 23% of greenhouse gas emissions and 26% of NOx^2 emissions. Chapter 3 describes in detail the sustainability issues that are of primary importance in the context of production. It is therefore necessary to consider production as an important link in the overall value chain, which has a strong impact on sustainability. As a result, modern production issues such as energy management, control of pollutant emissions, and efficient use of resources are emerging.

11.1.3. *Resources*

According to de Pablos and Miltiadis (2008), the production system can only implement a strategy (determining the mission and objectives of the organization) if the resources are mobilized to obtain a competitive advantage. However, this advantage, which was initially economic, must now be positioned in the more global context of sustainable development (see Chapter 3).

A resource is a means necessary to carry out a task. There are several types of resources: human and material. Human resources are by definition the most capable of reacting to the unknown and the most flexible in terms of the tasks to be carried out. Human capital is made up of the knowledge and skills of employees as well as of relational capital (reputation, customer portfolio, etc.) and structural capital (processes and governance) (Edvinsson 1997).

In order to carry out an operation, one or more resources are needed, human or material, for a certain period of time. Historically, the material resources considered were essentially the production machines, fixed, dedicated to a particular activity, or a limited number of operations in order to carry out a manufacturing order established according to different operating ranges. This concept has also evolved to take into account all the technical means necessary to carry out an operation: tools, energy, raw materials, information and so on. Some resources are fixed, others are mobile (mobile robots, etc.). There are also resources that can be reconfigured and reorganized according to the production to be carried out. The ability to reconfigure

---

1. Manufacturing, value added (% of GDP) – European Union. From The World Bank: Data, 2018.
2. EIT, SIA thematic factsheet on Added-Value Manufacturing, 2017.

is a major evolution of production systems, supported by the development of CPPS, and this chapter sits within this context.

11.2. Reconfiguration

To respond to the fluctuating nature of markets, both in terms of volume and diversity of desired products, the concept of a reconfigurable manufacturing system was defined by Koren *et al.* (1999). This type of organization relies on six characteristics to guarantee cost-controlled production that is capable of responding quickly to radical market changes:

1) Scalability: adaptability to a change in production volume.

2) Convertibility: adaptability to changes in product specifications.

3) Diagnosis: identification of problems.

4) Customization: adaptability to the company's uses and processes.

5) Modularity: possibility of adding, removing or modifying functionalities.

6) Integrability: simple connection and interaction.

This concept remained utopian for a long time, but the technical and scientific advances of the Fourth Industrial Revolution have made it possible for this concept to be implemented in reality (Koren *et al.* 2018).

11.2.1. *Implementation and decision levels*

To implement reconfigurable manufacturing systems (RMS), different issues need to be addressed.

– When investment decisions are made:

- How can we imagine scenarios of market evolution?

- How can we evaluate *ex ante* the reconfigurability potential of different resources?

– When markets change:

- When should we reconfigure?

- How can we evaluate alternative reconfigurations?

The decisions that need to be made in order to manage a production system properly are classified by levels, as shown in Table 11.2.

Decision level	Time horizon	Decision
Strategic	Years to come	Sizing the system according to future demand (reconfigurable?)
Tactical	Weeks – months	Allocating resources to operations, balancing resources, planning operations
Operational	Hours – days	Scheduling operations, reacting to hazards Supply?

Table 11.2. *Decision levels*

11.2.2. *Information systems*

A CPPS is by definition connected. Taking the model historically defined by the ISA 95 standard, through the CIM (computer-integrated manufacturing) pyramid, the information flows circulate in the following way, layer after layer.

The customer order arrives via ERP (enterprise resource planning). ERP processes the demand: Can the production system meet the demand from its stocks? Does it need to launch a new production order? Does it have the components in stock and the resources available? Once the decision to start production has been made, APS (advanced planning and scheduling) can be used here to plan and schedule production in an optimized way.

This production order will be transmitted via the MES (manufacturing execution system) and the different intermediate layers (SCADA and PLC) to the workshops through the different sensors and actuators. This model can be considered as an traditional version of the information system of production systems. It represents a system where the decision is centralized. Each actor must refer to a single database to know the necessary information, which wastes time during information processing. In version 4.0 of information systems, information is decentralized, in a star configuration. Each actor is able to communicate with any other actor. Each actor knows only the information they need (see Figure 11.1). The product is an integral part of the network. The adoption of a CPPS design approach enables the implementation of version 4.0.

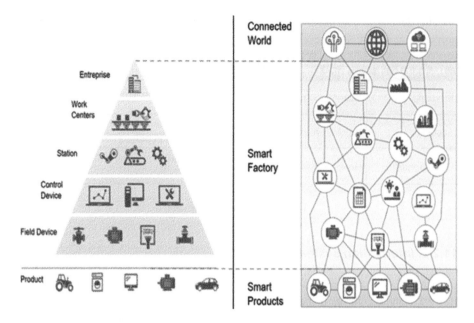

Figure 11.1. *Centralized versus decentralized information system*
(Deutsches Institut fuer Normung (DIN SPEC 91345) 2016)

A decentralized information system makes it possible for the production system to be flexible. Several means are used in this new information system: intelligent sensors, RFID (radio-frequency identification) technology and the Internet of Things. Connected to the physical part of the CPPS, they feed the cyber part where data analysis is carried out to optimize production performance more globally. These analyses, coupled with predictive techniques (sales, etc.), also allow for the optimization of stocks, energy consumption, maintenance processes and status monitoring of production resources.

11.2.3. *Adaptation in the context of CPPS/RMS*

All categories of resources must be taken into account to ensure the reconfigurability of production systems. If the six characteristics (see section 11.2.1) have been defined for machine-tool type material resources, they can be adapted to evaluate the other types. A proposal of adaptation for software is as follows:

1) **Scale**: capacity of the software to follow the evolution of a load according to the structuring factors of the company (number of employees, turnover, etc.).

2) **Convertibility**: ability to transform existing software functionality to meet new production requirements.

3) **Diagnosis**: self-diagnosis and identification of possible software problems.

4) **Customization**: ability to adapt the software to the company's uses and processes.

5) **Modularity**: ability to add, remove, replace and/or upgrade tools on the software to fit the production.

6) **Integrability**: connection and interaction with the business environment (other mechanical, information and control interfaces).

We can even add a seventh characteristic specific to this type of resource.

7) **Connectivity/IoT/mobility**: information access management (access via mobile, smartphone, tablet, from home, etc.).

New hardware resources have recently emerged, which are flexible, mobile and easily programmable. They are therefore ideal resources for reconfigurable manufacturing systems. These resources can use mobile collaborative robotics.

11.2.4. Where and when to reconfigure?

An example is illustrated in Beauville dit Eynaud *et al.* (2019): consider a site assembling two large product families. There are a number of variants per family. This site has two assembly lines, one line per product family. Each line is capable of processing all the variants in its family. Due to market fluctuations, the quantity of products to be produced in each of the two families is uncertain. Staying with the same configuration would be a risky bet: one line could be undersized and the other line oversized if the future market favors one family over the other. One reconfiguration strategy envisaged is to have a new line, capable of reconfiguring itself in real time to manufacture all the products of the two families: a fixed line using the same structure as the two previous ones with dedicated machines capable of carrying out the operations common to both families, to which mobile collaborative robots would be added. Thanks to the CPPS, these robots would move autonomously to the appropriate station to perform the operation required for the product.

11.3. Modeling

A digital shadow is a real-time representation of the state of a real system (product or production system; Schluse *et al.* 2018). This "monitoring" is possible via instrumentation that collects data through various sensors or the Internet of Things. A digital twin is a digital simulation model connected to the digital shadow of a real production system, (see Chapter 6). This digital twin can be deployed either at the physical or the cyber level of the CPPS, depending on the physical twin considered (from the equipment to the complete production system).

11.3.1. *Data collection*

Good management of production systems requires a certain number of key performance indicators (KPIs). These KPIs make it possible to monitor the proper functioning of the system in question: the overall equipment effectiveness (OEE) is traditionally the most closely monitored indicator. As introduced, these indicators are evolving in the context of sustainability and are being augmented by societal and environmental requirements beyond the usual requirements (cost, time and quality).

The CPPS allows for real-time monitoring of data; however, the amount of data in a production system is potentially huge. One problem is managing data overload (Woods *et al.* 2002) and building indicators that enable monitoring and decision-making. Leveraging and synthesis of these KPIs makes it possible to create an intelligent dashboard. Ritou *et al.* (2019) propose a multi-level aggregation approach based on business knowledge (Figure 11.2). This approach is applied to connected machine tools but can be generalized to other material resources of CPPS.

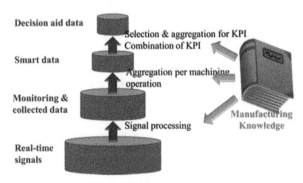

Figure 11.2. *Multi-level aggregation system (Ritou* et al. *2019)*

Aggregation operations are particularly important when KPIs are built from multiple data sources; for example, the OEE depends on the opening time (time in seconds, measured on the resources) and the quality (a number of parts or a rate from the quality department). Typically, within the workshops, interactive screens are used to show staff if the production system is working properly or, on the contrary, if corrective action is needed. For example, Beauville dit Eynaud *et al.* (2021) redefined the KPIs used for reconfigurable assembly lines.

11.3.2. *Simulation platforms*

Cyber-physical systems can be interesting levers for improving both economic performance (productivity gains and agility) and working conditions. However, the complexity of these systems makes decision-making difficult. It must therefore be based on effective feedback of actual performance as well as on simulation tools that enable the impacts of change to be anticipated. These tools, which replicate the behavior of the real system, can be digital (see the previous section) as well as take the form of physical simulation platforms.

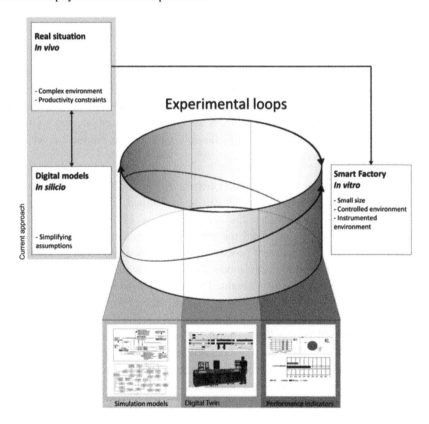

Figure 11.3. *Experimental loops (Puviyarasu and da Cunha 2021)*

These platforms are controlled and highly instrumented environments. Composed of modular elements, they meet the characteristics of reconfigurability and can replicate real production situations. Experimental loops between the industrial situation (in vivo), their digital modeling (in silico) and experimentation in a controlled environment (in vitro) can thus take place (Figure 11.3).

Solutions identified as performing well in digital models can be implemented in these platforms at low cost (time and relocation of platforms) and without any impact on real production. Deviations between the performances predicted by the digital models and those observed on the platforms make it possible to improve the digital models by identifying new parameters that were not previously taken into account. Only solutions validated in silico and in vitro will be deployed in real production systems.

11.4. Ergonomics/cognitive aspects

Collaborative robotics, by definition, is used so that humans work in direct contact with the robot. Thanks to a certain number of sensors with which it is equipped, the robot is able to detect the presence of the operator, and thus to slow down when they approach or even to stop activity. The workstation composed of a collaborative robot helps the human from an ergonomic point of view. This new resource can be used as a third hand to flexibly position the product on which the operator will have to perform their operations.

Other uses are under development (Quenehen *et al.* 2020). A given product is composed of a task list with tasks that can be performed in three modes: a 100% human mode (the operator does the entire task), a 100% robotic mode or a collaborative mode (the human and the robot work together to perform the task). Each task is defined by a different process time depending on the mode used. Quite often, the human mode is the fastest mode. However, it is also the most tiring for the operator. Hence, each task is also weighted with a cognitive factor depending on the mode used. A task performed by a human will be affected from an ergonomic point of view. If it is performed by the robot, its process time will be the longest but the ergonomic factor will be the best. The compromise is therefore the collaborative mode: similar process time but considerable ergonomic gain. However, not all operations are feasible using all modes. Current work is therefore focused on the assignment of operations between a human and a robot, with economic (related to process time) and ergonomic considerations.

The second issue addressed in the context of the integration of Human 4.0 is the cognitive aspect: how to improve the working conditions of the human. Let us first look at human as an operator. The operator must be versatile if they want to continue to be considered the most reconfigurable resource possible. This requires the human to increase their range of skills: to perform a greater diversity of tasks on a greater diversity of products. The CPPS can help people to increase their versatility. Let us imagine an assembly line composed of several manual assembly stations. This line is capable of assembling a multitude of products. If the operator wants to remain the most reconfigurable resource, they should know all the operations that can be performed on all of the products at all the stations – mission impossible. A cognitive system can help the operator in this task. Upstream, at the strategic decision level, the balancing of operations between the different stations, as well as the assignment of operators to the stations, has been decided. The scheduling of the different products has also been decided. Thanks to the information system and our connected product, we are able to display live at each workstation via a screen the operations that each operator has to perform on the product they have in their hands (determined by the given product identification, balancing, assignment and scheduling). This is the contextualized display at the workstation. We can also imagine going further thanks to a pick-to-light system that would make it possible for the components that must be assembled to be displayed to the human, or even through the use of augmented reality.

The part considering the decision-maker is dealt with in the following section.

11.5. Operation of the information system

The information system governing a production system has been described previously. Here, we will detail some situations illustrating the contributions induced by the definition of a CPPS, in particular in the management of hazards.

11.5.1. *Operational level: procurement*

Using the terminologies defined in Table 11.2, the problems classically addressed at the tactical level concern planning or resource allocation. What are the advantages of CPPS in our daily production system, at the operational level? Procurement is a good example of a decision to be made at the operational level. Components or raw materials are needed to make a product (which will be component assembly or transformation of raw materials). To improve the working conditions of the operator, these components are made available at the workstation or at the edge of the line. The connected system indicates when the line-side stock has been depleted in order to trigger a replenishment order.

An e-Kanban system can also be used. This is an adjustment tool that is based on the production carried out over a time window. By making the link with the bill of materials of the various products, it deduces the sub-components consumed over this window with a view to their replenishment (internal and external). Compared to the traditional or dematerialized Kanban, it saves having to process information on the consumption of each line-side sub-component. Combined with the knowledge of future production orders, the system is able to calculate future supply needs. This replenishment can be done autonomously by using mobile collaborative robots which would pick up the right components from the main stock at the right time and move them to the right stock on the line.

11.5.2. Responding to disruptions

Sensors are present in the system under consideration: on human or material resources, products or stocks, for example. A sensor in the field signals a failure at a given moment: a material resource that breaks down, a human resource that is absent and a lack of supply. Let us take these three cases in order:

– Broken-down material resource in breakdown: the information will be transmitted to the maintenance department, who carry out the necessary intervention as soon as possible. If a component needs to be changed on the faulty resource, the maintenance operator can check if it is in stock and plan an order if necessary. The time during which the resource is unavailable will be indicated. Thus, the planning and scheduling can be recalculated by considering this missing resource.

– Absent human resource: in a similar way as before, it will be necessary to recalculate the planning and scheduling considering that this resource is missing. Extrapolation: connection with a temping company to replace this person as soon as possible.

– Lack of supply: reaction in the emergency by quickly supplying the workstation so that production is not negatively affected. However, it will be necessary to correct this perturbation in the long term: Why was the supply not made, information not transmitted, resource dedicated to supply unavailable, stock in shortage?

The cases treated above illustrate the bottom-up case. The information (the perturbation) is noticed in the field; this information is processed by the decision-maker via the CPPS (replan, reschedule, resupply, with the least possible impact on the order book) and then goes back down to the workshops to continue production. There may also be a case of a downward perturbation: for example, a loyal customer places an urgent order. This order will have to be integrated (planned, allocated and scheduled with its impact on the scheduling) on the planned production, to satisfy this loyal customer, with the least possible impact on the initially planned production.

11.5.3. *Decision support*

Decision support methods have been proposed for decades to offer solutions to decision-makers. These tools do not aim to replace human beings but to help them in their decision-making. Klement and Silva (2020) propose a generic decision support tool that can be used for planning, allocation or scheduling problems. This tool could be extended to help the human make the best decision to manage the manufacturing system. The connectivity of the systems provided by the CPPS now allows for a better description of the real systems, thus a better parameterization of the tools of assistance to the decision and especially a transfer of the decision from the decision-maker towards the field.

The use of the information system makes it possible to create a dashboard to monitor production. This dashboard includes the indicators presented in section 11.3.1. Amzil *et al.* (2021) propose a virtual Obeya: a multi-view real-time dashboard so that each user has access only to the information pertinent to them in real time. In addition to simply monitoring production, this virtual Obeya is also a decision support tool. Thanks to the connectivity of the systems, all the available data is continuously fed into an IoT hub. Data conversion allows interoperability. The causal analysis of all of this data by a tool using neural networks and genetic algorithms not only makes it possible to detect perturbations, but also to anticipate them in order to prevent future disruption to the real system. The CPPS now makes it possible to predict the future through better data analysis to improve the management of manufacturing systems.

11.6. Illustrative example

Let us take an example of an assembly line consisting of six manual stations, arranged in a line. This line is used to assemble cylinders. A wide variety of cylinders can be assembled, depending on the different options (about a hundred configurations, total assembly times vary between one and three minutes). Thanks to preliminary load balancing studies, for each cylinder, the operations to be performed at each station are known. A visual example of this production system is shown in Figure 11.4.

Figure 11.4. *Manual assembly line developed at the Arts et Métiers
Campus in Lille, with educational and industrial transfer objectives*

Taking up various concepts detailed in this chapter, transforming this line to a CPPS has several advantages:

– Quality: thanks to the contextualized display at the workstation, the operator knows in real time which assembly operations they have to perform on the product they have in their hands, without having to learn by heart the planned schedule for the day or all the possible ranges. With the pick-to-light system, this also makes it possible to illuminate the correct component to be picked up and assembled.

– Supplies: thanks to automatic line-side replenishment via AGV, coupled with the e-Kanban system, line-side stocks are always supplied in the right quantity and with the right type of components.

– Production monitoring: thanks to the interactive dashboard, production problems can be easily visualized and corrected as soon as possible. With a virtual Obeya, the causes can also be anticipated.

Figure 11.5 shows a close-up of the line with the integration of the technologies mentioned. This line is used at the Arts et Métiers campus in Lille in an educational context to teach industrial management to engineering students. It is also a support for the research activities of the LISPEN (*Laboratoire d'Ingénierie des Systèmes Physiques et Numériques*, Physical and Digital Systems Engineering Laboratory) teachers-researchers as well as for the activities of demonstrators or industrial transfer.

Figure 11.5. *Line equipped with 4.0 technologies (collaborative robot, RFID, interactive dashboard)*

11.7. References

Amzil, K., Yahia, E., Klement, N., Roucoules, L. (2021). Causality learning approach for supervision in the context of industry 4.0. In *Advances on Mechanics, Design Engineering and Manufacturing III*, Roucoules, L., Paredes, M., Eynard, B., Morer Camo, P., Rizzi, C. (eds). Springer, Cham.

Beauville dit Eynaud, A., Klement, N., Gibaru, O., Roucoules, L., Durville, L. (2019). Identification of reconfigurability enablers and weighting of reconfigurability characteristics based on a case study. *Procedia Manufacturing*, 28, 96–101.

Beauville dit Eynaud, A., Klement, N., Roucoules, L., Gibaru, O., Durville, L. (2021). Framework for the design and evaluation of a reconfigurable production system based on movable robot integration. *International Journal of Advanced Manufacturing Technology*, 118, 2373–2389.

Blackstone Jr., J.H. (ed.) (2010). *APICS Dictionary*, 13th edition. APICS, Chicago.

Deutsches Institut fuer Normung (DIN SPEC 91345) (2016). Reference architecture model Industry 4.0 (rami4.0).

Edvinsson, L. (1997). *Intellectual Capital: Realizing your Company's True Value by Finding its Hidden Brainpower*. Harper Business, New York.

European Commision (2017). Factories of the future. Manufacturing Horizon 2020 and Beyond. Roadmap, EFFRA, Brussels.

Klement, N. and Silva, C. (2020). A generic decision support tool to planning and assignment problems: Industrial applications and Industry 4.0. In *Scheduling in Industry 4.0 and Cloud Manufacturing*, Sokoliv, B., Ivanov, D., Dolgui, A. (eds). Springer, Cham.

Koren, Y., Heisel, U., Jovane, F., Moriwaki, T., Pritschow, G., Ulsoy, G., Van Brussel, H. (1999). Reconfigurable manufacturing systems. *CIRP Annals*, 48(2), 527–540.

Koren, Y., Gu, X., Guo, W. (2018). Reconfigurable manufacturing systems: Principles, design, and future trends. *Frontiers of Mechanical Engineering*, 13(2), 121–136.

de Pablos, P. and Miltiadis, L. (2008). Competencies and human resource management: Implications for organizational competitive advantage. *Journal of Knowledge Management*, 12(6), 48–55.

Puviyarasu, S.A. and da Cunha, C. (2021). Smart factory: From concepts to operational sustainable outcomes using test-beds. *Logforum*, 17(1), 7–23.

Quenehen, A., Thiery, S., Klement, N., Roucoules, L., Gibaru, O. (2020). Assembly process design: Performance evaluation under ergonomics consideration using several robot collaboration modes. *Proceedings of the IFIP International Conference on Advances in Production Management Systems*, Novi Sad, Serbia, 477–484.

Ritou, M., Belkadi, F., Yahouni, Z., Da Cunha, C., Laroche, F., Furet, B. (2019). Knowledge-based multi-level aggregation for decision aid in the machining industry. *CIRP Annals*, 68(1), 475–478.

Schluse, M., Priggemeyer, M., Atorf, L., Rossmann, J. (2018). Experimentable digital twins – Streamlining simulation-based systems engineering for industry 4.0. *IEEE Transactions on Industrial Informatics*, 14(4), 1722–1731.

Woods, D.D., Patterson, E.S., Roth, E.M. (2002). Can we ever escape from data overload? A cognitive systems diagnosis. *Cognition, Technology & Work*, 4(1), 22–36.

12

Impact of Industrial Cyber-Physical Systems on Global and Interconnected Logistics

Shenle PAN, Mariam LAFKIHI and Eric BALLOT
Physical Internet Chair, MINES ParisTech, PSL Research University,
Centre de gestion scientifique, i3 UMR CNRS 9217, Paris, France

12.1. Logistics and its challenges

While logistics specialists have always been aware of the importance of their activity, for the general public it is more like the silent engine of our economies, whose functioning we willingly forget as long as it works. In 2020, the health crisis caused by Covid-19 shed light on the importance of supply chains. Whether it was masks, vaccines or even food during lockdown, the importance of transporting goods, of supplies and of inventory management reappeared. The paralysis experienced by European industry due to the lack of supplies of some materials and components from other continents can be attributed both to logistical failures in the transportation of goods by sea and air and to the nature of the current supply chain organization.

From a more theoretical point of view, the health crisis has highlighted, first, our dependence on global supply chains and second, their expected properties. The first concerns the robustness of these networks in the face of demand shock (e.g. demand

For a color version of all figures in this book, see www.iste.co.uk/cardin/digitalization.zip.

Digitalization and Control of Industrial Cyber-Physical Systems,
coordinated by Olivier CARDIN, William DERIGENT and Damien TRENTESAUX.
© ISTE Ltd 2022.

multiplied by 10 in a few days) even though the logistics networks are impacted (closure of a site or even a geographical area and so on). The second concerns their environmental footprint, which cannot be reduced to the energy transition given the current low efficiency of logistics operations (McKinnon 2018).

A logistics chain must be able to coordinate mobilizable resources (products, means of transport, warehouses, etc.) and associated logistics services, and it must also be able to cope with demand shock while respecting environmental constraints and the requirements of sustainable development. This can be done by working on two main concepts: *organization models* and *optimization approaches*.

In recent decades, the organizational models of logistics have undergone a remarkable evolution. Initially, logistics was studied in the form of vertically coordinated "chains". Nowadays, logistics organization tends more towards horizontal collaborative models (i.e. inter-chain pooling) or models of shared mesh networks (such as the Physical Internet) (Pan *et al.* 2019). This trend of change in the organization models of logistics can be seen in both global logistics and urban logistics, which involve many innovations.

The evolution of logistics organizations towards more shared and collaborative models is challenging traditional optimization approaches where logistics operations were managed by models that assumed independent decision-making by players in a static and often certain environment. The change in the nature of decision-making within the shared logistics network, by independent players operating at multiple levels, has contributed to the transformation of supply chain optimization approaches.

Today, logistics benefits from all the advances linked to the progress of information and communication technologies that support the change in logistics organizations towards more collaborative, shared and communicative models. The availability of real-time information leads to a more dynamic decision-making environment. In this context, an industrial cyber-physical system (ICPS) is one of the key solutions to meeting the new trends and challenges in logistics.

This chapter aims to address the impacts of new technological paradigms and, more specifically, of ICPS on the evolution of contemporary and modern logistics and supply chains at the organizational, decision-making and operational levels.

12.2. Contemporary logistics systems and organizations

The organization of contemporary logistics and supply chains is characterized by globalization, specification and outsourcing of activities. Today's supply chains are fragmented and composed of several segments and systems. At each level of the chain, logistics service providers intervene to offer specific services and add value to the different players in the chain. The purpose of this section is to present and characterize three main components of contemporary logistics chains, illustrated in Figure 12.1: intra-site logistics, urban logistics and inter-site inter-city logistics, and to study the application of ICPS to each component.

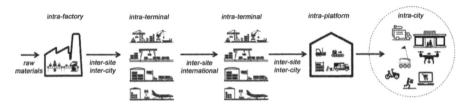

Figure 12.1. *Logistics systems and organizations*

12.2.1. *Intra-site logistics*

The aim of the intra-site logistics system, also known as "facility logistics" or "intra-logistics", is to improve the performance and productivity of a site (warehouse, sorting center, production site, cross-docking platform, terminal, point of sale, etc.) by optimizing the management of operations and the management of physical flows (raw materials, equipment, resources, etc.) and internal information flows.

In terms of activities, the intra-site logistics system mainly concerns the handling and management of internal flows (i.e. receiving, internal transport, warehousing and storage, sorting, picking, packaging, dispatching, etc.).

Over the decades, intra-site logistics has undergone profound upheavals, steadily reshaping itself in line with innovations and the Industry 4.0 paradigm (see Fragapane *et al.* (2021) for a state of the art). In this context of strong change, due mainly to digitalization and robotization, ICPS have had remarkable contributions to improveing not only site productivity but also flexibility, re-configurability and resilience to internal disruptions (Panetto *et al.* 2019).

Specifically, ICPS can play a key role in managing digitalization and robotization in a logistics site effectively and efficiently. They rely on real-time data, information transmission and human collaboration for effective analysis of decentralized decision-making and control (Rajkumar *et al.* 2010; Lee *et al.* 2015). Thus, they can contribute to the improvement of data and information communication between different internal systems of sites, and, in the end, to the improvement of real-time decision-making and control. ICPS can provide real-time dynamic information communication, which ensures that internal systems are responsive to various disturbances. Thus, internal systems become more flexible and resilient as they are constantly looking for alternative and proactive solutions (i.e. conveyor congestion, maintenance, etc.).

In order to highlight the contribution of ICPS to intra-site logistics, Lee *et al.* (2015) studied the example of applying ICPS in a digital factory to ensure the just-in-time maintenance policy. In their paper, Kong *et al.* (2020) gave another example of application in e-commerce picking platforms, using wearable technologies and modeling them by ICPS.

12.2.2. Intra-urban logistics

Intra-urban logistics, which may also be referred to as "urban or city logistics" or "urban freight transport", is the last leg in the logistics chain, that is, the leg between the last storage point (regional platforms, warehouses, urban micro-hubs, shops, etc.) and the final customer delivery point (points of sale, private homes, automatic lockers, etc.) within the confines of urban areas (Taniguchi and Thompson 2014).

Today, intra-urban logistics is one of the most important issues for supply chain professionals and local authorities. Dealing with the flow of goods in already congested cities, it involves and concerns a wide range of players. In the context of strong mutation, intra-urban logistics is turned upside down by new challenges and stakes linked to the change in customers' demands and requirements.

In their article, Pan *et al.* (2021b) introduced five main challenges that call into question the current models and management of intra-urban logistics: (1) the exponential growth of flows in megacities, (2) the increase in the frequency of on-demand deliveries by service providers such as *Deliveroo* and *Amazon Prime Now*, (3) the emergence of omnichannel logistics with speed and flexibility requirements and the need to manage returns, (4) the restriction of municipal regulations (i.e. imposition of delivery hours, expansion of low-emission zones, etc.) and (5) consumer behavior with regard to sustainable development. In this context where demand has become as strong as constraints, several levers of action deserve to be highlighted and further developed to reduce the negative externalities of intra-urban logistics and to streamline logistics actions in cities.

Some solutions are already considered on the basis of mutualization, intelligent management of urban spaces dedicated to logistics activity and the *Smart City* (Harrison *et al.* 2010), in order to satisfy logistics demands in a smart, more efficient and sustainable way (Pan *et al.* 2021b). These new solutions are based on new technologies such as the Internet of Things, ICPS or digital twins in order to focus on the interconnection of smart city infrastructures (i.e. physical, information technology, social, commercial infrastructures, etc.) and logistics facilities. New technologies allow for the transmission of data and information in real time between different physical systems (companies, logistics, inhabitants, etc.) and enable dynamic planning and decision-making.

12.2.3. *Inter-site inter-city logistics*

Inter-site inter-city logistics covers the entire logistics chain between sites in national and international areas (hereafter inter-site logistics, for short). Referring to Figure 12.1, inter-site logistics is composed of three main sections: (1) an upstream section that constitutes the part between production sites and terminals (i.e. maritime, rail, air, multimodal, etc.). (2) A downstream section that constitutes the part between the terminals and the platforms or urban regional warehouses. These two sections are provided by national or regional transport, often road or rail–road multimodal transport. (3) An intermediate section, which constitutes the part between the various international terminals. This section is generally provided by international transport.

Inter-site logistics has several characteristics that differentiate it from the other two logistics segments, for example, the wide perimeter of the multi-company and multi-nation, the length of the planning horizon due to transport and storage time (especially for maritime), the multi-types of goods and the multi-modality of transport. Due to its large size and the multiplicity of players, inter-site logistics presents barriers to the management of logistics actions as well as to the management of relationships and interactions between different players.

First, at the physical level, the non-standardization, or existence of a multiplicity of logistics standards, is one of the obstacles that generates many inefficiencies in inter-site logistics. Contrary to the example of maritime containers that are globally standardized (i.e. 20' or 40' feet), logistics loading units for storage or land transport are subject to numerous packaging unit standards (cartons, parcels, bags, etc.) and handling equipment (pallets, rolls, cages, etc.).

Second, at the information technology level, industrial digitalization has certainly led to a significant improvement in logistics performance. However, the interoperability and inter-connectivity of different digital solutions of players or systems in inter-site logistics still poses real problems, for example, data or information formats, reliability of communication channels, data privacy (Pan *et al.* 2021a).

Third, at the organizational level, the lack of trust, the search for a relevant governance model, the synchronization of decisions and actions are the main issues related to the management of inter-site logistics.

Due to the different barriers to the management of inter-site logistics, it is plausible that the characteristics of the ICPS defined in this way can contribute significantly to the management of logistics actions within this logistics part. ICPS can improve logistic cooperation, and also improve digital and organizational interoperability within inter-site logistics.

Today, contemporary logistics is trapped by fragmented and environmentally-unfriendly organizations. To break this deadlock, innovative solutions are beginning to take hold in people's minds: the interconnection of large-scale logistics networks, for example, the Physical Internet.

12.3. The Physical Internet as a modern and promising logistics organization

12.3.1. *Concept and definition*

Since the 2000s, the concept of the "Physical Internet" has become a new paradigm for managing logistics and supply chains for sustainable development. This new paradigm has been introduced to reduce inefficiencies and ineffectiveness due to the fragmentation of current logistics flows, services and systems (Montreuil 2011; Ballot *et al.* 2014). Based on mutual collaboration, the concept of the Physical Internet aims to interconnect logistics systems on a large scale in order to take advantage of synergies between different systems. Interconnection allows for an opening of logistics networks and a sharing of means and services (transport, handling, storage, delivery, etc.) and infrastructures (platforms, hubs, routes, etc.) in a collaborative and mutual way between the different systems and players. All of this comes with the aim of improving the quality of service, efficiency and sustainability of logistics systems.

To design and deploy this new paradigm, several projects are underway at both the European and global levels. In Europe, the technology platform *ALICE* (www.etp-logistics.eu) proposes a coordinated roadmap for a full deployment of the Physical Internet by 2040. In particular, this platform introduces the concept of the Physical Internet as an efficient solution to achieve the European Union's greenhouse gas emission reduction targets (ALICE 2020).

The paradigm of the Physical Internet reflects the desire to move towards a more open, dynamic, decentralized and interconnected management model of logistics flows with more comprehensive decision-making mechanisms. This new management model will call into question several concepts of current logistics and will require a radically different design of the current organization of logistics systems. This section is intended to present one of the key elements of the Physical Internet network design, which is the network topology.

12.3.2. *Topologies of networks of networks*

The Physical Internet can be considered as a network of logistics service networks based on interconnection or hyper-connection (Oger *et al.* 2018; Ballot *et al.* 2014). Having been inspired by the concept of the digital Internet, computer network topologies can be used as a reference for the design of Physical Internet networks. Figure 12.2 illustrates some examples.

The Physical Internet network has often been presented as an *interconnected, mesh network*, that is, a network that allows for peer-to-peer connection without a central hierarchy. The Physical Internet network has drawn heavily on the mesh network that represents a common topology in computer networks (Sarraj *et al.* 2014b). This network topology is particularly relevant for the inter-site logistics in the Physical Internet network, as it provides flow transfer that reduces stockouts and copes with various disruptions (Yang *et al.* 2017). However, the nature of the infrastructure and players present in the Physical Internet network necessitates the presence of other network topologies.

The *tree network* corresponds to one of the classic distribution patterns in contemporary logistics (e.g. the distribution of consumer products from a factory to warehouses and distribution centers, and then to the points of sale and end-consumers). This type of topology can be perfectly integrated into a Physical Internet network, using shared platforms instead of dedicated platforms for a given supply chain.

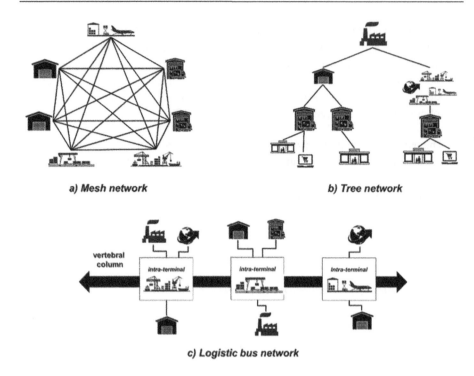

a) Mesh network   *b) Tree network*

c) Logistic bus network

Figure 12.2. *Examples of logistics network topologies*

Today, practical solutions for using this network topology in a context of logistics sharing and pooling are emerging. The startup *CRC Services* (Collaborative Routing Centers, www.crc-services.com) offers a regional consolidation service for multi-supplier and multi-distributor flows. This service offers a good opportunity to consolidate flows both upstream and downstream, without radically changing current logistics practices.

The *bus topology* can be used where the Physical Internet network is designed around terminals and large transport infrastructures. An example of the use of this topology in a shared network is the Trans-European Transport Network (TEN-T[1]). This network is the backbone of a multimodal European transport network. It is made up of main terminals (maritime, rail, air, multimodal, etc.), priority logistics corridors and major infrastructures linking European countries. The objective of this

---

1. https://ec.europa.eu/transport/themes/infrastructure/ten-t_en.

bus network is to speed-up the consolidated flows between terminals using multimodal transport.

In order to integrate this topology into the interconnected network of the Physical Internet, it is necessary to develop local connections that allow flows from factories or platforms to be linked to this bus network. For this purpose, there is a European project, Clusters 2.0 (www.clusters20.eu), which aims to create a cooperation of multi-industry flows around the terminals.

12.4. Perspectives of ICPS applications in interconnected logistics: the example of the Physical Internet

According to the definitions in Chapter 1 of this book, ICPS are characterized as collaborative systems of systems bridging the physical real world and the digital (virtual) world. The characteristics of ICPS thus defined can be consistent and useful for modeling the systems of virtual multi-player systems such as the network of the Physical Internet.

In the physical world, the concept of the Physical Internet allows for the exchange of physical flows between logistics players or networks based on physical interoperability, while in the virtual world, the ICPS of the Physical Internet (i.e. ICPS-PI) allows for the exchange of data and information between systems of different players based on digital interoperability. The ICPS-PI will thus enable digital interoperability, ensure communication and transfer of data and information in the network (online or offline) and ensure control and traceability throughout the network.

This section is intended to discuss a concrete example of the contribution of ICPS to address an important issue in the implementation of the Physical Internet network: *routing protocols*. The potential contributions of ICPS to the modeling and implementation of routing protocols in the Physical Internet network will be discussed first. A discussion on the exploitation of ICPS-PI will then be conducted around two main axes which are data-driven and digital twin-driven.

Indeed, ICPS-PI modeling will foster interdisciplinary approaches around data science and intelligence, as illustrated in Figure 12.3.

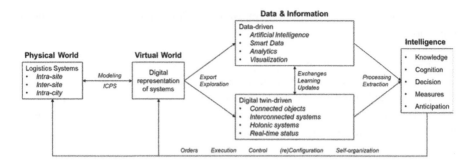

Figure 12.3. *Interdisciplinary approaches in ICPS-PI modeling*

12.4.1. *Modeling the Physical Internet by ICPS: the example of routing*

In computer science, the term *routing* is used to describe the process of directing data packets from a subnetwork node to a destination node that may be located on another subnetwork. This routing is accomplished by seeking the shortest or fastest path between a sender address and a receiver address.

The routing protocol is thus an important protocol in the Physical Internet network, in order to ensure optimal routing of goods between senders and receivers in different subnetworks. In the literature, there are very few studies on the routing problem in the Physical Internet network. For example, Sarraj *et al.* (2014a) and Dong and Franklin (2020) use, respectively, the multi-agent simulation method and graph theory to study routing protocol, taking the shortest transport path as the only metric. However, considering transport as the only determinant for optimal path selection may be insufficient for the routing protocol in the Physical Internet network.

The routing protocol in a network of interconnected logistics networks must ensure several properties that are necessary for proper functioning. A routing protocol must be accurate, simple and robust. It must be able to provide tolerance to failures that may occur during the lifetime of the network (i.e. hardware and software failures, topology changes, etc.), and accommodate topology and traffic changes without having to shut down all systems and reset the network. Moreover, it must also be stable and converge towards a balance. It must be fair to users and optimal at the global level. The last properties can be contradictory: the routing protocol must therefore ensure a compromise between fairness for each individual connection (i.e. minimizing the average resource delivery time) and global efficiency (maximizing the total network flow).

Modeling routing protocols in the Physical Internet network can be complicated for several reasons. First, the routing criteria are not homogeneous for all players in the network. Thus, the conceptualization of "Class of Service" in logistics must be evoked for the parameter setting of routing protocols.

Second, in the Physical Internet, there is no central authority to coordinate the interactions between the various interconnected systems. Each system has its own set of rules and protocols depending on the context in which it is located, that is, an autonomous system. The decision-making process can therefore be complex because in order to make a decision, a system must take into account the constraints and specificities of its partners. The difficulty of choosing a relevant protocol lies in the fact that each system does not master all the specificities of the other systems in the network. One of the difficulties in this network is to guarantee the coherence of the decisions taken by coordinating the different actions of the interconnected systems.

Due to the different issues mentioned, ICPS-PI modeling will be able to contribute to the control and coordination of routing protocols in a Physical Internet network, as well as to the consistency of decision-making between different subnetworks of the global network.

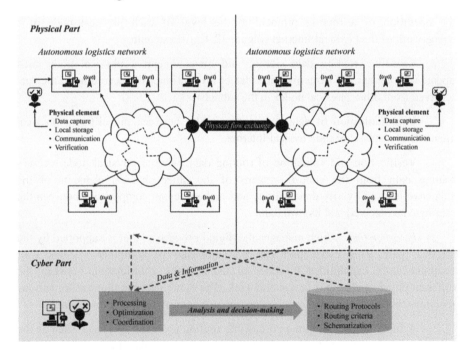

Figure 12.4. *Simplified diagram of an ICPS-PI for routing protocol control*

Figure 12.4 shows an example of an ICPS-PI that enables the coordination and control of routing protocols in the Physical Internet network. Referring to Figure 2.3 in Chapter 2, the ICPS-PI thus presented is composed of two parts as follows:

1) *The physical part*, where the main focus is on the elements that must be controlled in the end. In a subnetwork (i.e. an autonomous network) of the Physical Internet, these elements contain all the logistic nodes (warehouse, distribution center, point of sale, etc.), logistic resources (goods, trucks, etc.) and humans (operators, users, etc.) who are considered to be elements contributing to the operational management of the physical part. These physical elements have a considerable role in the management of routing protocols. Through sensors or data inputs, for example, these physical elements send routing data (the metrics for updating the node's routing table, the routing algorithm, etc.) to a control system. The control system allows for the storage, verification and validation of routing data at the level of each physical element. This control system generally establishes an interaction with human supervisors and reflects the data to the physical elements in order to make decisions that make it possible to reach the desired objectives. Through this interaction, and from different indicators observed on the physical elements, a supervisor can also impose or modify the routing tables through the control system. The physical part can thus perform various functions necessary for the operation of a routing protocol at the level of each physical node of a subnetwork of the Physical Internet (Figure 12.4), for example:

– Real-time routing data storage and management: a physical node must update its routing table (as a historical database) continuously, according to the data received from other physical nodes in the subnetwork.

– Communication of data and routing tables between the different physical elements of a subnet of the Physical Internet.

– Verification and validation of routing data: when a physical node receives routing data from the control systems of the other physical elements of the subnetwork, it will verify their validity and make relevant comparisons between the routing data received and its own data.

2) *The cyber part*, which manages the digital processing that is supported by the physical part. This cyber part can be composed of computer systems with communication capabilities in order to manage the coordination between the different physical elements in a subnetwork. The cyber part can thus ensure various functions that are necessary for the operation of a routing protocol, for example:

– A function providing the core of the routing protocol operation, such as the type of the protocol used by the subnet, the metrics to be taken into account and the class of service proposed.

– A communication function to interact with other subnetworks in the network, whether they are close or distant, in the same subnetwork or in an external subnetwork.

– A function for calling remote services, for example, a web service being capable of performing a multi-criteria analysis or a web service being capable of finding a route according to the selected metrics.

The combination of the physical and cyber parts of the ICPS-PI thus defined will enable better management and coordination of routing protocols in a Physical Internet network.

12.4.2. *Exploiting ICPS: the data-driven approach and the digital twin-driven approach*

12.4.2.1. *Data-driven approach*

While ICPS modeling collects data from objects and stores it in a historical database, it is then important to process and analyze this data to gain the desired information and knowledge. For example, Lee *et al.* (2015) applied this process in a digital factory to solve a machine maintenance problem. They developed the "Time Machine" concept, consisting of three sections: (i) collection of snapshots for each significant change of objects or systems, (ii) comparison of snapshots for verification of data and status of objects or systems and (iii) data analysis, forecasting and planning. Each step is combined with methods and tools from data science or other fields such as Big Data analytics, learning algorithms and optimization or simulation methods.

This process, introduced by Lee *et al.* (2015), as well as all related approaches, can be applied to logistics systems like intra-site logistics. Nevertheless, their application to systems with a wider scope may have some limitations, such as inter-site logistics, intra-urban logistics or the network of the Physical Internet.

In this context, several issues need to be studied beforehand – for example, the issue of data privacy when collecting snapshots at the level of a multi-player and multi-supply chain network. Despite the development of sophisticated algorithms, the complexity and dynamics of these systems make it difficult to diagnose or check the status of the systems, and to predict and plan for future changes.

In a large-scale network such as the Physical Internet, the planning horizon of each player varies considerably (i.e. in the range of hours, days, weeks or months). Therefore, the synchronization of planning becomes a major problem for real practices.

Although ICPS-PIs offer an opportunity to decentralize logistics decisions and planning, this decentralization may give rise to new problems related to cooperation and the coordination of decisions for better mutual and collective optimization.

In the literature, some emerging approaches seem to be promising to overcome these difficulties. For example, Federated Learning, which is a technique designed by Google in 2017. Its objective is to respect data privacy through learning (Yang *et al.* 2019). This technique proposes a method of learning on the distributed and locally stored data samples (i.e. agents) without the need to consolidate them in a central server. Only the learning results, such as parameter settings, are sent to the central optimization model, following a predefined coordination mechanism based on a data privacy preservation algorithm. Thus, the protection of sensitive company data is ensured.

Nevertheless, this technique may have some vulnerabilities related to data corruption, agent failure or data communications and so on. Several recent studies seek to apply the federated learning technique to ICPS (Lu *et al.* 2020). Initial results encourage more research on the topic (especially in the context of cooperative logistics).

12.4.2.2. *Digital twin-driven approach*

A digital twin is a concept often studied for product design and lifecycle management (Lim *et al.* 2020). In the field of logistics, the digital twin is already studied and applied to certain sectors and logistics systems. For example, in intra-site logistics, Derigent *et al.* (2020) studied a smart factory simulated by a holonic multi-agent system, and Greif *et al.* (2020) also used digital twins to simulate construction sites.

However, very few studies address the application of digital twins to inter-site systems or intra-urban logistics. In this context, digital twins can be an important research avenue to investigate the ICPS-PI of large-scale systems. The concept offers a way to examine ICPS-PIs from a comprehensive and holistic view, and to study the relationship between systems containing hierarchical systems.

Digital twins are therefore essential in the design, engineering, and modeling of logistics networks such as the Physical Internet that seek real-time interconnection of networks and services. The status of the digital twins is regularly updated in accordance with the status of the physical part, enabling real-time control and traceability of objects, as well as rapid reaction to system disruptions and even reconfiguration of systems for long-term resilience.

Furthermore, in order to model objects and their relationships, digital twins are associated with semantic and ontological information. The modeling by digital twins makes it possible to build a reasoning system based on information and knowledge in the virtual world, as well as a creation of new knowledge. Contrary to what one might think, this modeling could be even more detailed than the actual physical world.

Digital twin modeling is increasingly being studied for context-sensitive systems and services. The use of digital twins is therefore interesting and useful for urban logistics and, more specifically, for Smart Cities and smart logistics services. For example, in the case of city delivery by autonomous vehicles, they need to be sensitive to the urban context in order to respect safety constraints and interactions with inhabitants, as well as environmental requirements (Liu *et al.* 2020). The recent European project LEAD is another concrete example of such research (www.leadproject.eu).

Finally, by coupling the data-driven approach and the digital twin-driven approach, the objective is to create an intelligence of systems, whether they are human systems or objects (i.e. a self-organization of systems).

In the broadest sense of the term, this intelligence in ICPS must be collective between the different systems. It must be involved in the design and engineering of systems, in decision-making and in the execution of orders, with the aim of systemic continuous improvement.

Moreover, this intelligence must also have a knowledge creation capacity that will accompany the development of human intelligence and cognition for a reengineering of systems.

12.5. Conclusion

From the discussions in this chapter, it is clear that ICPS can help address an important issue in modern logistics that is related to the interconnection of logistics networks and services, whether local or global.

Through the example of the concept of the Physical Internet, which is a network of interconnected networks, this chapter has highlighted the contributions of ICPS for the conceptualization, modeling and design of an interconnected network. By proposing a modeling of routing protocols in a network of networks (ICPS-IP) and exploiting this modeling according to data-driven and digital twin-driven approaches, the discussions in this chapter allow us to open new research perspectives in these areas.

12.6. References

ALICE (2020). Roadmap to Physical Internet. Report [Online]. Available at: www.etp-logistics.eu/wp-content/uploads/2020/11/Roadmap-to-Physical-Intenet-Executive-Version_Final.pdf.

Ballot, E., Montreuil, B., Meller, R. (2014). *The Physical Internet: The Network of Logistics Networks*. La Documentation française, Paris, France.

Derigent, W., Cardin, O., Trentesaux, D. (2021). Industry 4.0: Contributions of holonic manufacturing control architectures and future challenges. *Journal of Intelligent Manufacturing*, 32, 1797–1818 [Online]. Available at: https://doi.org/10.1007/s10845-020-01532-x.

Dong, C. and Franklin, R. (2021). From the digital internet to the physical internet: A conceptual framework with a stylized network model. *Journal of Business Logistics*, 42, 108–119 [Online]. Available at: https://doi.org/10.1111/jbl.12253.

Fragapane, G., de Koster, R., Sgarbossa, F., Strandhagen, J.O. (2021). Planning and control of autonomous mobile robots for intralogistics: Literature review and research agenda. *European Journal of Operational Research*, 294, 405–426 [Online]. Available at: https://doi.org/10.1016/j.ejor.2021.01.019.

Greif, T., Stein, N., Flath, C.M. (2020). Peeking into the void: Digital twins for construction site logistics. *Comput. Ind.*, 121, 103264 [Online]. Available at: https://doi.org/10.1016/j.compind.2020.103264.

Harrison, C., Eckman, B., Hamilton, R., Hartswick, P., Kalagnanam, J., Paraszczak, J., Williams, P. (2010). Foundations for smarter cities. *IBM J. Res. Dev.*, 54, 1–16 [Online]. Available at: https://doi.org/10.1147/JRD.2010.2048257.

Kong, X.T.R., Yang, X., Peng, K.L., Li, C.Z. (2020). Cyber physical system-enabled synchronization mechanism for pick-and-sort ecommerce order fulfilment. *Comput. Ind.*, 118, 103220 [Online]. Available at: https://doi.org/10.1016/j.compind.2020.103220.

Lee, J., Bagheri, B., Kao, H.-A. (2015). A cyber-physical systems architecture for industry 4.0-based manufacturing systems. *Manuf. Lett.*, 3, 18–23 [Online]. Available at: https://doi.org/10.1016/j.mfglet.2014.12.001.

Lim, K.Y.H., Zheng, P., Chen, C.-H. (2020). A state-of-the-art survey of Digital twin: Techniques, engineering product lifecycle management and business innovation perspectives. *J. Intell. Manuf.*, 31, 1313–1337 [Online]. Available at: https://doi.org/10.1007/s10845-019-01512-w.

Liu, Y., Pan, S., Ballot, E. (2020). Digital twin platform for smart city logistics: Conceptualization and ontology-based modeling. *7th International Physical Internet Conference (IPIC 2020)*, Shenzhen, China, 18–20 November.

Lu, Y., Huang, X., Dai, Y., Maharjan, S., Zhang, Y. (2020). Federated learning for data privacy preservation in vehicular cyber-physical systems. *IEEE Netw.*, 34, 50–56 [Online]. Available at: https://doi.org/10.1109/MNET.011.1900317.

McKinnon, A. (2018). *Decarbonizing Logistics: Distributing Goods in a Low Carbon World*. Kogan Page, London, UK.

Montreuil, B. (2011). Toward a physical internet: Meeting the global logistics sustainability grand challenge. *Logist. Res.*, 3, 71–87 [Online]. Available at: https://doi.org/10.1007/s12159-011-0045-x.

Oger, R., Montreuil, B., Lauras, M., Benaben, F. (2018). Towards hyperconnected supply chain capability planning: Conceptual framework proposal. *5th International Physical Internet Conference (IPIC 2018)*, Groningen, Netherlands, 18–22 June.

Pan, S., Trentesaux, D., Ballot, E., Huang, G.Q. (2019). Horizontal collaborative transport: Survey of solutions and practical implementation issues. *Int. J. Prod. Res.*, 57, 5340–5361 [Online]. Available at: https://doi.org/10.1080/00207543.2019.1574040.

Pan, S., Trentesaux, D., McFarlane, D., Montreuil, B., Ballot, E., Huang, G.Q. (2021a). Digital interoperability in logistics and supply chain management: State-of-the-art and research avenues towards physical internet. *Comput. Ind.*, 128, 103435 [Online]. Available at: https://doi.org/10.1016/j.compind.2021.103435.

Pan, S., Zhou, W., Piramuthu, S., Giannikas, V., Chen, C. (2021b). Smart city for sustainable urban freight logistics. *Int. J. Prod. Res.*, 59, 2079–2088 [Online]. Available at: https://doi.org/10.1080/00207543.2021.1893970.

Panetto, H., Iung, B., Ivanov, D., Weichhart, G., Wang, X. (2019). Challenges for the cyber-physical manufacturing enterprises of the future. *Annu. Rev. Control*, 47, 200–213 [Online]. Available at: https://doi.org/10.1016/j.arcontrol.2019.02.002.

Rajkumar, R., Lee, I., Sha, L., Stankovic, J. (2010). Cyber-physical systems: The next computing revolution. *47th ACM/IEEE Design Automation Conference*, Anaheim, CA, USA, 13–18 June [Online]. Available at: https://doi.org/10.1145/1837274.1837461.

Sarraj, R., Ballot, E., Pan, S., Hakimi, D., Montreuil, B. (2014a). Interconnected logistic networks and protocols: Simulation-based efficiency assessment. *Int. J. Prod. Res.*, 52, 3185–3208.

Sarraj, R., Ballot, E., Pan, S., Montreuil, B. (2014b). Analogies between internet network and logistics service networks: Challenges involved in the interconnection. *J. Intell. Manuf.*, 25, 1207–1219 [Online]. Available at: https://doi.org/10.1007/s10845-012-0697-7.

Taniguchi, E. and Thompson, R.G. (2014). *City Logistics: Mapping the Future*. CRC Press, Boca Raton, FL, USA.

Yang, Y., Pan, S., Ballot, E. (2017). Mitigating supply chain disruptions through interconnected logistics services in the physical internet. *Int. J. Prod. Res.*, 55, 3970–3983 [Online]. Available at: https://doi.org/10.1080/00207543.2016.1223379.

Yang, Q., Liu, Y., Chen, T., Tong, Y. (2019). Federated machine learning: Concept and applications. *ACM Transactions on Intelligent Systems and Technology*, 10(2) [Online]. Available at: https://doi.org/10.1145/3298981.

13

Impact of Industrial Cyber-Physical Systems on Transportation

John MBULI[1] and Damien TRENTESAUX[2]

[1] Bombardier Transport France, Alstom Group, Saint-Ouen, France
[2] LAMIH UMR CNRS 8201, Université Polytechnique Hauts-de-France, Valenciennes, France

13.1. Introduction

This chapter deals with the impact of industrial cyber-physical systems (ICPS) on transportation systems, such as rail and road, and the way the performance of these transportation systems can be improved using ICPS. Transportation is an important application field of the concept of CPS (Mohanty 2020). The impact of ICPS on transportation systems is illustrated in Figure 13.1 (adapted from Trentesaux and Branger (2018)). It mainly concerns freights, passengers and logistics (e.g. cyber logistics systems (Kong *et al.* 2021), see Chapter 12). The scope of this chapter concerns the production of *passenger transportation services*, not the production of the transportation system itself (see Chapter 11 for this aspect). Regardless of the transportation mode, the sector is characterized by push–pull forces and complexity factors, which drive the evolution of constructors' products and condition their competitiveness, as well as those of the fleet operators.

For a color version of all figures in this book, see www.iste.co.uk/cardin/digitalization.zip.

Digitalization and Control of Industrial Cyber-Physical Systems,
coordinated by Olivier CARDIN, William DERIGENT and Damien TRENTESAUX.
© ISTE Ltd 2022.

13.1.1. *Pull forces*

"Pull forces" translate to evolution by demands. From this point of view, at national (e.g. regulatory politics and national operators) and local (logistics operators, etc.) levels, we can face new economical, societal and environmental expectations, federating numerous key-performances indicators (KPIs) expressed in various terms.

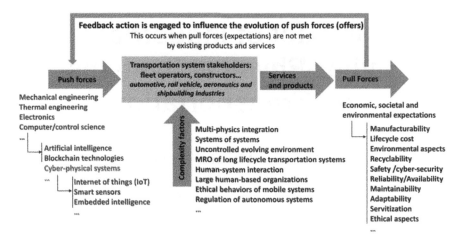

Figure 13.1. *Forces and complexity factors in the transportation sector*

Regarding environmental expectations, it is a consensus that climate change is one of the most concerning existential threats to mankind. There is indeed a direct correlation between energy consumption and climate change, as explored by several discussions (Akhmat *et al.* 2014). According to the Geography of Transport Systems project[1], the contribution of the transportation sector to energy consumption rose from 24.2% in 1971 to 33.7% in 2016 in OECD countries. Globally, the transportation sector contributes to more than half of the global oil demands, with the current trends expected to double by 2050[2]. For example, as far as the energy efficiency in the transportation sector is concerned, rail transport is the most energy efficient, with 2% total energy demand while serving 8% and 7% of global passengers and freight respectively. Therefore, the rail transport industry should typically be an integral part of the energy transition discussion.

---

1. See: https://transportgeography.org/.
2. See: https://www.https://www.iea.org/futureofrail/.org/futureofrail/.

Other pull forces translate to the need for an increased mobility for goods and people, coupled with the need for an improved adaptability, availability and reliability of transportation systems and fleets. For example, the guarantee of a high level of dependability of a railway truck or a train in urban transportation systems is a critical stake because urban infrastructures are saturated and quite often impossible to extend because of the dense nature of these areas.

Moreover, fleet operators, users and passengers do not only require available systems and fleets, but also advanced exploitation services. This leads to constructors and operators selling more and more transportation services instead of physical transportation systems.

13.1.2. *Complexity factors of the transportation sector*

Different factors make it hard for the constructors to meet these new expectations expressed by these "pull forces". These factors are denoted here as "complexity factors". A non-exhaustive list of some of the main ones is provided hereinafter:

– First, transportation systems are complex engineered systems that embed various integrated, multi-physics equipment. Equipment behaviors and data generated from sensors are diversified, hardening their complete and exhaustive control. These transportation systems are loosely coupled; thus, an entire fleet of transportation systems can be considered as a "system of systems", which is known to be reactively and proactively managed with difficulty.

– Second, transportation systems are mobile and communicating elements evolving in uncontrolled and open environments. The reactive optimization of their behavior and their maintenance processes are typically complicated tasks. The cost of negative user perception in case of unavailability of a transportation system or the financial penalties involved when a given level of reliability or availability are of great importance.

– Third, transportation systems, and especially trains, planes and ships are long-lasting systems compared to the rapid evolution of the introduced "pull forces" coupled with one of the technological offers (see the push forces hereinafter). Fleets are constantly aging, implying the rise of the importance of Maintenance, Repair and Overhaul (MRO) operations, stakes and costs. Moreover, with time, these long-lasting transportation systems are subjected to different MRO operations coupled with different use rates and usage, depending on the type of climate and the geography where the mobile system evolves. The warranty conditions also evolve with time (constructors' guarantees are provided for a limited amount of time) for each element of a fleet, strongly influencing policies and stakeholders', operators' and users' decisions.

– Moreover, the human aspect is of great importance. The variety of Human-ICPS types and level of interaction and cooperation (e.g. driving assistances) is also a source of complexity. In addition, various human based organizations interact in the transportation sector: operators, constructor, user and consumer communities are fundamentally human-based and often scattered at a regional or a national level, based on dedicated or highly specialized skills.

– And finally, the emergence of an autonomous system immersed in human society leads to regulation and liability issues, which are still unsolved. This complexity factor is hardened when considering the integration of AI learning models into robotic mobile systems and their possible unethical behavior (Trentesaux and Karnouskos 2020).

13.1.3. *Push forces*

The second kind of forces, denoted as "push forces", translate the existence of disruptive recent technological developments. These forces enable researchers, engineers and constructors to satisfy "pull forces" while at the same time handling the "complexity factors" (see Figure 13.1). This technological offer finds its origin in recent advances in various scientific fields, such as mechanical engineering (e.g. lightweight car), thermal engineering (e.g. low energy train) or in the information and communication technologies (ICT) field encompassing electronics, computer science and control science. Specifically, and relevant to ICT, two kinds of contributions are currently highly studied by researchers in the field of ICPS:

– The first one is related to the recent development of innovative models and methods in artificial intelligence (AI) technology. Relevant contributions include, for example, recent advances in supervised or unsupervised learning capabilities, such as neural networks, deep learning and deep belief, image recognition and pattern clustering to name a few.

– The second one is related to contributions in innovative new ICPS architectures, based on the integration of the previously introduced AI tools with Internet of Things (IoT), smart sensors, embedded intelligence and cloud, fog or edge technologies and so on.

In Figure 13.1, a feedback loop is suggested, closing the loop from the "pull forces" when expectations are not met by transportation products and services, to influence the evolution of "push forces". This loop fosters the development of new solutions to be put on the market, or the adaption of existing ones.

13.2. The impact of ICPS on transportation

There are different ways to apply the concept of ICPS on transportation. We can identify infrastructure-based ICPS, vehicle–infrastructure-based ICPS and vehicle-based ICPS (Deka et al. 2018). Table 13.1 provides some illustrations of these three types.

	Physical component	Cyber component	Applications
Infrastructure-based transportation ICPS	Infrastructure, traffic sensors (signal, cameras) and actuators (red lights, lane access)	Traffic, infrastructure-related data management systems	Traffic monitoring and control Infrastructure maintenance and production center
Vehicle–infrastructure-based transportation ICPS	Infrastructure, vehicles, traffic sensors and actuators, vehicles and associated sensors (GPS) and actuators (brake)	Traffic, infrastructure, vehicle-related data management systems	Traffic warning (jamming), queues, smart parking, Infrastructure maintenance and production center Vehicle/fleet maintenance and production center
Vehicle-based transportation ICPS	Vehicles and associated sensors and actuators	Vehicle-related data management systems	Lane control, proximity warning Vehicle/fleet maintenance and production center

Table 13.1. *Types of transportation ICPS (adapted from Deka* et al. *(2018))*

The deployment of an ICPS architecture for a transportation service (see Figure 13.2) is often justified by the need to deploy an autonomous sensing and actuation system (e.g. autonomous cars) to interact with its infrastructure and supervision centers, to counterbalance and handle the different complexity factors introduced.

Such a supervision is also intended to enable the deployment of advanced, reactive and cost-effective exploitation and maintenance planning and operations to ease the way some of the pulling forces are taken into account. In that context, using an ICPS-based approach typically seeks to optimize the availability of the systems (self-monitoring), the safety of passengers (advanced sensing and reaction systems), the use of the infrastructure (smart parking, congestion reduction, etc.) and the saving of energy (Rawat et al. 2015). Developing ICPS is also intended to ease the use of renewable energy (e.g. electric autonomous cars connected to the smart grid). Recyclability (circular economy) is also emerging as a potential benefit of the use of ICPS because of its ability to ease the historization of system activities to determine which equipment could be reused as spare equipment, remanufactured or recycled.

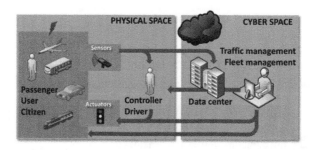

Figure 13.2. *A general view of an ICPS for transportation service*

Let us consider different examples illustrating the development of some transportation service ICPS. Wan *et al.* (2018) applied the concept of ICPS to the automotive sector (see Figure 13.3a). The authors specifically focused on the development of a secure wireless communication process among cars (vehicle-to-vehicle V2V communication). Yang *et al.* (2016) applied the concept of ICPS to the maritime sector (see Figure 13.3b). The authors proposed a cooperative cognitive maritime cyber-physical system, and their paper focuses on the development of high-speed and low-cost communication services. Fleet MRO operations are a typical application field of ICPS. In Andreacchio *et al.* (2019), a cyber-physical based identification of airplane assets (seat covers) was proposed to facilitate the balancing of maintenance replacement policies to optimize long-run average costs per unit time. In Trentesaux *et al.* (2015), an ICPS architecture for cooperative MRO task planning and control was specified. Cooperation is realized among equipment, tools, maintenance centers and planes upon an accurate management of the health status of the systems (diagnosis and prognostics).

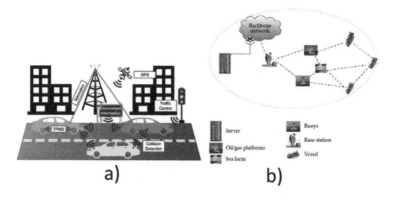

Figure 13.3. *a) Automotive (Wan* et al. *2018)*
and b) maritime (Yang et al. *2016) ICPS*

Obviously, applying an ICPS approach in transportation raises several new challenges to be handled that are not specific to the transportation sector. Typically, cybersecurity of data, communication and control, for example (Sun and Song 2017). Another issue concerns the return on investment, since deploying a large ICPS is costly when there is no clear guarantee that adding a cyber space, for example, will generate sufficient financial, societal and environmental savings.

13.3. Rail transportation service: an illustrative example

Using ICPS and multi-agent systems (MASs) approaches, a reactive cyber-physical maintenance and operational decision support system, named SUPERFLO, is provided as an illustrative example (see Figure 13.4). SUPERFLO addresses the above discussed pull forces, namely, the availability, reliability and the decision-making reactivity in the rail transport industry at the fleet level. SUPERFLO considers the integration of trains and infrastructures as an ICPS. As an ICPS itself, SUPERFLO consists of a physical space and a cyber space. A MAS model is integrated in the physical space of the global ICPS framework introduced in Chapter 1.

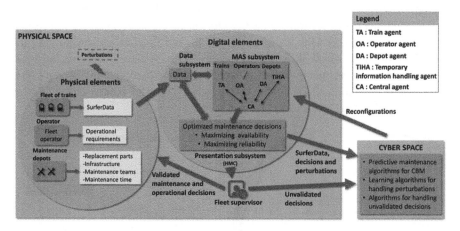

Figure 13.4. *ICPS architecture of SUPERFLO*

SUPERFLO dynamically provides maintenance and operational decision support to a human fleet supervisor. Concretely, the referred decision support is intended to not only improve the availability and reliability of the fleet of trains, but also to improve the whole decision-making process under perturbations. In the course of this work, the fleet availability is defined as the minimum number of trains required to meet the operational requirements within a specified horizon, as defined by the fleet operator (Kozanidis *et al.* 2010; Feng *et al.* 2012; Mbuli *et al.* 2019). Hence, in this case, increasing the number of mission ready trains eventually increases the fleet availability. The fleet reliability is addressed through shifting the maintenance intervention strategy towards prediction and prevention philosophy (Iung 2012). As shown by various research works, predictive maintenance, specifically when done through condition monitoring, also known as condition-based maintenance (CBM), does not only reduce the related operational costs, but also increases the assets' reliability (Dragomir *et al.* 2009; Ali *et al.* 2015). Hence, in the context of this chapter, increasing CBM interventions in the fleet of trains will consequently increase the reliability of the fleet. Prior works on the fleet's health status have been carried out at Surferlab[3], with a specific focus on the train monitoring architecture (Fadil *et al.* 2019) and the train data management (Trentesaux and Branger 2018). Such works are a key condition to the development of large ICPS, where stamped data from mobile equipment is required in quantity and quality, wherever the equipment is (Le Mortellec *et al.* 2013). The SUPERFLO fleet data management system is based on this approach and the corresponding patented *Surfer data management system* (Branger *et al.* 2017). This system enables the development of interoperable and standardized SurferData concerning different integrated levels of mobile equipment. This information is used for supervision purposes, but is also sent to the cyberspace to feed the learning algorithms, and finetune and reconfigure the control of the fleet availability and reliability. This system is constructed on a generic holonic model (composed of a digital agent for each system), along with a standardized formatting and stamping of equipment data and events sensed through *ad hoc* networks (see Figure 13.5).

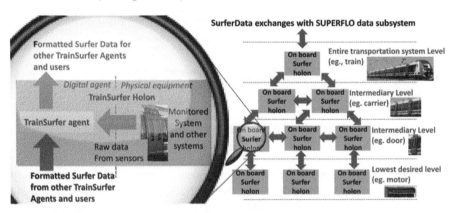

Figure 13.5. *The TrainSurfer Holon and the TrainSurfer architecture*

---

3. See: http://www.surferlab.fr/.

SUPERFLO is able to adapt the maintenance and operational decisions following perturbations. In this context, the perturbations are considered to be the events which were not anticipated or the disruptions within anticipated events (Hajibabai and Ouyang 2016; Mbuli *et al.* 2020). Concretely, in the fleet of trains, such disruptions might be unanticipated delays in the delivery of the replacement parts, bad estimations of the time needed for repairs and unanticipated breakdowns which directly affect the fleet availability (planned trains' missions). SUPERFLO dynamically mitigates the effects of such disruptions and hence maintains the acceptable levels of the fleet availability and reliability. SUPERFLO helps the human fleet supervisor in maintenance and operational decision-making by maximizing the fleet's reliability and satisfying the fleet's availability requirements, while mitigating the effects of disruptions after the decisions have been adopted.

13.3.1. *The physical space of SUPERFLO*

The physical space of SUPERFLO hosts the real-world physical elements and the digital elements that control them. The physical elements provide data to the digital elements and are the targets of the maintenance and operational decisions provided by the latter through the human fleet supervisor. The fleet of trains, the operator and the maintenance depots are the elements hosted by the physical space and in turn, a multi-agent system (MAS) makes up the digital part of the physical space.

13.3.1.1. *Physical elements in the physical space*

The physical space is composed of three types of elements. The first one is the trains, which are considered as vehicle-CPS embedded with sensors in their various systems, such as the breaks, traction and door systems. The second one is the fleet operators, who are responsible for the operational requirements of the fleet of trains. This translates to the minimum number of trains required to carry out the planned missions within an established horizon (Feng *et al.* 2012). The third one is the maintenance depots, which carry out maintenance operations. The maintenance depots consist of important elements, such as the inventory of the replacement parts, maintenance hangars with the required resources, such as the rails with proper supply catenary voltage, and different maintenance teams with proper maintenance skills.

13.3.1.2. *Digital elements in the physical space*

The digital elements in the physical space of SUPERFLO contain the data and computational systems through which the maintenance and operational decision support is provided to the human fleet supervisor for the maintenance of the fleet of trains, under various constraints such as the fleet operational requirements and maintenance resources. The computational system in the digital elements takes into account the perturbations that the physical elements are subjected to. In order to mitigate the effects of such perturbations, the computational system adapts the maintenance and operational decisions. The cyber space hosts the data subsystem, the MAS subsystem and the presentation subsystem.

The **data subsystem** first manages the SurferData received from the physical elements in the physical space, the fleet operational requirements from the operator and the data from the maintenance depots. This information is sent to the model subsystem that contains the computational entities in the cyber space. Moreover, the data subsystem manages and handles the data from the cyber space. For example, the maintenance and operational decisions proposed by the MAS model, and which are not validated by the human fleet supervisor, are sent to the learning algorithms in the cyber space for reconfigurations. In turn, this data is sent again to the digital elements in the physical space for consideration in the next computations.

The **MAS subsystem** is made up of five agents, namely the train agent (TA), operator agent (OA), depots agent (DA), temporary information handling agent (TIHA) and central agent (CA) (see Figure 13.6).

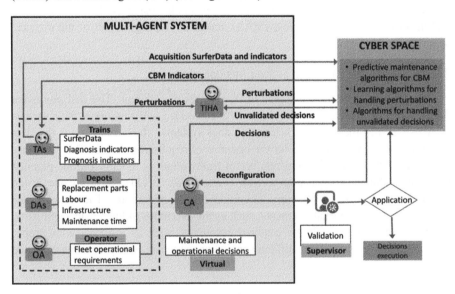

Figure 13.6. *Architecture of the MAS model integrated in the digital part of SUPERFLO*

The TAs are the agents that are intertwined with the trains in the fleet from the physical space. Therefore, there are as many TAs as there are trains in the fleet. Each TA receives the SurferData sent by the TrainSurfer Holons embedded in the corresponding train and generates health status indicators of the trains for corrective interventions. TAs will also communicate the SurferData to the predictive maintenance algorithms in the cyber space for prognosis, in order to determine the future health status of the trains for CBM interventions. Finally, the diagnosis and prognosis (corrective and CBM) indicators of each TA are communicated to the central agent (CA). The OA is the agent that mirrors the fleet operator. Through this agent the fleet operational requirements are defined. This means the OA establishes the minimum number of trains required to satisfy the planned fleet missions within a specified horizon. The DAs are the agents that mirror and receive data from the maintenance depots in the physical elements of the physical space (one for each depot). Each DA establishes the availability of the replacement parts, maintenance teams with the required skills and maintenance rail tracks. This information is then communicated to the central agent (CA). The CA agent receives the data and computes and provides maintenance decision support to the human fleet supervisor. The TIHA agent has two important roles. First, the maintenance decisions that have not been validated by the human fleet supervisor are sent to the learning algorithms in the cyber space. These decisions are analyzed to determine the reasons that they have not been confirmed. The adjustments made to these decisions are fed to the TIHA agent for consideration in the next computations. Second, the TIHA agent is responsible for feeding the perturbations experienced by the physical elements to the cyber space.

The **presentation subsystem** consists of the human–machine interface (HMI) (Töniges *et al.* 2017), through which the maintenance and operational decisions by the MAS model are communicated to the human fleet supervisor for their validation and application to the physical elements.

13.3.2. *The human fleet supervisor*

The fleet supervisor is the human charged with reporting the fleet's key performance indicators (KPIs) to the fleet operators and managing the fleet's maintenance plans dynamically (Mbuli *et al.* 2020). In the context of this chapter, fleet maintenance and operational decision support is provided to the fleet supervisor by the MAS model in the digital part of the physical space. In turn, the fleet supervisor is charged with the validation of these decisions and their application to the fleet of trains in the physical space of SUPERFLO.

13.3.3. *The cyber space of SUPERFLO*

The cyber space of SUPERFLO hosts the learning and reconfiguration algorithms. It consists of the predictive maintenance algorithms for the computations of the CBM indicators (Mbuli *et al.* 2019), reconfiguration algorithms for handling perturbations, and algorithms for handling unvalidated maintenance and operational decisions by the human fleet supervisor. Using the Surfer data management architecture, the TAs send the SurferData to the cyberspace for prognosis; in turn, the predictive maintenance algorithms in the cyber space compute the CBM indicators and communicate them to the respective TA agents. Moreover, as far as unvalidated maintenance and operational decisions by the human fleet supervisor are concerned, they are sent to specific handling algorithms in the cyber space. Once the reasons for their rejections have been established and the adjustments have been made, these decisions are fed to the TIHA agent who in turn communicates them to the CA for their consideration in the next computations. Finally, whenever there are perturbations facing the physical elements in the physical space, for example, breakdowns after operational planning and delays in replacement parts delivery, the maintenance and operational decisions, as well as the perturbations are fed to specific algorithms in the cyber space by the CA and TIHA, respectively. These algorithms, which are responsible for handling and mitigating disturbances, will propagate the necessary readjustments and adaptations to the maintenance and operational decisions, before these reconfigurations are fed to the CA for communication and eventual application by the fleet supervisor.

13.3.4. *Evaluation of the proposed model and industrial expectations*

An evaluation of SUPERFLO based on the Regio2N Omneo fleet of trains at Bombardier Transport France has been made. The challenge with the Regio2N fleet was not only to increase the fleet availability and reliability, but also to mitigate the costly effects of perturbations as far as the maintenance and operational decisions are concerned. First, as far as the economic aspects are concerned, the major contributors to the perturbations are the unanticipated breakdowns, which are grouped into three categories. The type A breakdowns are the immobilizing breakdowns that correspond to long delays of the planned operations, and they typically cost between 200,000 and 300,000 euros, depending on the fleet type. The type B breakdowns correspond to operational delays between one and five hours, and they cost between 40,000 and 60,000 euros in penalties. The type C breakdowns correspond to the breakdowns which have no impact on the planned operations, and they cost between 1000 and 2000 euros in penalties. From the records, the losses from the Omneo Regio2N fleet from January 2017 to November 2017 due to type

A, B and C breakdowns register at 17 million euros. The losses are not only due to the lack of reliable predictive maintenance algorithms for breakdown anticipation, but also the inability to quickly adapt the maintenance and operational decisions, causing major operational delays and hence penalties. The authors estimate a saving of 9 million euros between the same period (January–November 2017) if SUPERFLO mitigates 80% of type A and B breakdowns.

For this fleet, the major problems lay within the cancellation and delays of the planned train trips. From the operational records, for example, the average rate of delays was 10% in 2016, with 25% of delays exceeding 20 minutes. Moreover, in the same year, 3.4% of these trains were cancelled. The stakes are indeed very high as these problems do not inspire confidence in the passengers of the rail transport industry. This is confirmed by the overall decline in the usage of regional and intercity trains in France by 5% from 2012 to 2016[4]. Through its ability to satisfy the availability and reliability requirements in a disruptive environment, SUPERFLO proposes reducing the cancellation to nearly 0%, by delaying and reprogramming the trips to be cancelled (as laid out in the computational mechanisms by the agents in the MAS model), and cutting down the delays by 80%. For illustration purposes, let us consider the following event: the alarm of a coach door motor, a critical system, has been triggered as a result of the application of prognosis and diagnosis rules to the fleet data. The door is suspected to fail soon. SUPERFLO gathers SurferData relevant to the current, voltage and localization of the door's motor. Consequently, the supervisor, supported by SUPERFLO, analyzed the availability of spare motor equipment (in different maintenance depots) and planned an opportunistic maintenance operation on this train in a depot with this spare equipment (see Figure 13.7). This information is transferred to the cyber space to enrich the learning algorithms, and finetune the corresponding alarm triggering and rules.

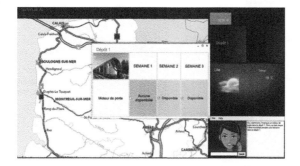

Figure 13.7. *Supervisor's HMI (equipment availability analysis)*

---

4. See: https://www.assemblee-nationale.fr/dyn/15/rapports/cion-eco/l15b0842_rapport-avis.

Regarding the evaluation of the impact of the cyberspace on the fleet of trains, several experiments have been carried out. In Mbuli *et al.* (2019), a method for root cause identification and fault prediction has been developed using the coupling of unsupervised machine learning techniques with supervised ones, with application in the same equipment (a door). Historical data from embedded sensors were first analyzed to identify different root causes of the same types of faults. The results of this first stage were then used for training, in order to generate rules suggested to the fleet supervisor. The experiments showed the efficiency of the method and its usefulness in the cyberspace: it prevents some of the introduced penalties incurred by Bombardier for trains under guarantee. In addition, the results from root cause identification should be used to improve predictive maintenance at the fleet level.

13.4. Concluding remarks

The development of ICPS in the transportation sector is fostered by several pull forces relevant to sustainability. For this purpose, transportation ICPS are obviously linked to the smart grid, smart cities and other large-scale ICPS. Aligned with Figure 2.4, Figure 13.8 depicts how the transportation system can be viewed as a CPS-intelligent product (see Chapter 4) that crosses the different ICPS involved in its lifecycle, such as production ICPS (see Chapter 11) or operation and maintenance (this chapter). The transportation systems can thus be viewed as the spinal column that articulates all of these ICPS (Barbosa *et al.* 2016): it enables information exchange about their life (health status and performances) to optimize, for example, the design of future generation of transportation systems or the overhaul of existing ones (see the feedback loop in Figure 13.1).

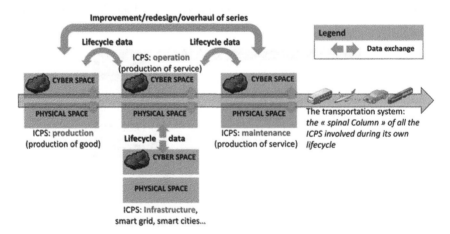

Figure 13.8. *The transportation system as the spinal column of a series of ICPS*

13.5. Acknowledgments

Surferlab was founded by Bombardier Transport, Prosyst and the UVHC/UPHF. It is scientifically supported by the CNRS and partially funded by the ERDF (European Regional Development Fund), Hauts-de-France.

13.6. References

Akhmat, G., Zaman, K., Shukui, T., Sajjad, F. (2014). Does energy consumption contribute to climate change? Evidence from major regions of the world. *Renewable and Sustainable Energy Reviews*, 36, 123–134.

Ali, S., Qaisar, S.B., Saeed, H., Khan, M.F., Naeem, M., Anpalagan, A. (2015). Network challenges for cyber physical systems with tiny wireless devices: A case study on reliable pipeline condition monitoring. *Sensors*, 15, 7172–7205.

Andreacchio, M., Bekrar, A., Benmansour, R., Trentesaux, D. (2019). Assessing cyber-physical systems to balance maintenance replacement policies and optimize long-run average costs for aircraft assets. *IET Cyber-Physical Systems: Theory & Applications*, 4, 148–155.

Barbosa, J., Leitão, P., Trentesaux, D., Colombo, A.W., Karnouskos, S. (2016). Cross benefits from cyber-physical systems and intelligent products for future smart industries. *2016 IEEE INDIN*, 504–509.

Branger, G., Le Mortellec, A., Clarhaut, J., Sallez, Y., Berger, T., El Sanwar, K., Grzesiak, F., Asse, A., Trentesaux, D. (2017). System and method for the asset management of railway trains. Patent, WO2017211593.

Deka, L., Khan, S.M., Chowdhury, M., Ayres, N. (2018). Transportation cyber-physical system and its importance for future mobility. *Transportation Cyber-Physical Systems*. Elsevier, Amsterdam, The Netherlands.

Dragomir, O.E., Gouriveau, R., Dragomir, F., Minca, E., Zerhouni, N. (2009). Review of prognostic problem in condition-based maintenance. *2009 European Control Conference (ECC)*, 1587–1592.

Fadil, A., Trentesaux, D., Branger, G. (2019). Event management architecture for the monitoring and diagnosis of a fleet of trains: A case study. *Journal of Modern Transportation*, 27, 169–187.

Feng, Q., Li, S., Sun, B. (2012). An intelligent fleet condition-based maintenance decision making method based on multi-agent. *International Journal of Prognostics and Health Management*, 3, 1–11.

Hajibabai, L. and Ouyang, Y. (2016). Dynamic snow plow fleet management under uncertain demand and service disruption. *IEEE Transactions on Intelligent Transportation Systems*, 17, 2574–2582.

Iung, B. (2012). Overview on E-maintenance facilities addressing PHM vs. CBM+ requirements. *International Conference on Prognostics and Health Management*. IEEE PHM, Beijing, China.

Kong, X.T.R., Kang, K., Zhong, R.Y., Luo, H., Xu, S.X. (2021). Cyber physical system-enabled on-demand logistics trading. *International Journal of Production Economics*, 233, 108005.

Kozanidis, G., Liberopoulos, G., Pitsilkas, C. (2010). Flight and maintenance planning of military aircraft for maximum fleet availability. *Military Operations Research*, 15, 53–73.

Le Mortellec, A., Clarhaut, J., Sallez, Y., Berger, T., Trentesaux, D. (2013). Embedded holonic fault diagnosis of complex transportation systems. *Engineering Applications of Artificial Intelligence*, 26, 227–240.

Mbuli, J., Nouiri, M., Trentesaux, D., Baert, D. (2019). Root causes analysis and fault prediction in intelligent transportation systems: Coupling unsupervised and supervised learning techniques. *2019 International Conference on Control, Automation and Diagnosis (ICCAD)*, 1–6.

Mbuli, J., Chargui, T., Trentesaux, D., Bekrar, A., Dailly, T. (2020). Multi-agent system for the reactive fleet maintenance support planning of a fleet of mobile cyber-physical systems. *IET Cyber-Physical Systems: Theory & Applications*, 5, 376–387.

Mohanty, S.P. (2020). Advances in transportation cyber-physical system (T-CPS). *IEEE Consumer Electronics Magazine*, 9, 4–6.

Rawat, D.B., Bajracharya, C., Yan, G. (2015). Towards intelligent transportation cyber-physical systems: Real-time computing and communications perspectives. *Southeast Con*, 1–6.

Sun, Y. and Song, H. (eds) (2017). Secure and Trustworthy Transportation Cyber-physical Systems. Springer, Singapore.

Töniges, T., Ötting, S.K., Wrede, B., Maier, G.W., Sagerer, G. (2017). An emerging decision authority: Adaptive cyber-physical system design for fair human-machine interaction and decision processes. *Cyber-Physical Systems, Intelligent Data-Centric Systems*. Academic Press, Amsterdam, The Netherlands.

Trentesaux, D. and Branger, G. (2018). Foundation of the surfer data management architecture and its application to train transportation. *Service Orientation in Holonic and Multi-Agent Manufacturing, Studies in Computational Intelligence*. Springer, Cham, Switzerland.

Trentesaux, D. and Karnouskos, S. (2020). Ethical behaviour aspects of autonomous intelligent cyber-physical systems. *Service Oriented, Holonic and Multi-Agent Manufacturing Systems for Industry of the Future, Studies in Computational Intelligence*. Springer, Cham, Switzerland.

Trentesaux, D., Knothe, T., Branger, G., Fischer, K. (2015). Planning and control of maintenance, repair and overhaul operations of a fleet of complex transportation systems: A cyber-physical system approach. *Service Orientation in Holonic and Multi-Agent Manufacturing, Studies in Computational Intelligence*. Springer, Cham, Switzerland.

Wan, J., Lopez, A., Faruque, M.A.A. (2018). Physical layer key generation: Securing wireless communication in automotive cyber-physical systems. *ACM Transactions on Cyber-Physical Systems*, 3, 13:1–13:26.

Yang, T., Feng, H., Yang, C., Sun, Z., Yang, J., Sun, F., Deng, R., Su, Z. (2016). Cooperative networking towards maritime cyber physical systems. *International Journal of Distributed Sensor Networks*, 12, 3906549.

14

Impacts of Industrial Cyber-Physical Systems on the Building Trades

William DERIGENT[1] and Laurent JOBLOT[2]

[1] *CRAN CNRS UMR 7039, University of Lorraine, Nancy, France*
[2] *Arts et Metiers Institute of Technology, LISPEN, HESAM University, UBFC, Chalon-Sur-Saône, France*

14.1. General introduction

The construction industry plays a decisive role in the world economy. Despite its importance (1,502,500 workers in France for 148 billion euros (excluding VAT) of work per year[1]), it is still described as less productive and innovative than other sectors. A 2020 study even revealed that the added value of a worker on a building site in France has fallen by about 20% over the last 20 years (Beddiar 2020). In response, many actors recognize the need to innovate in order to reverse this trend. New forms of work are emerging thanks to the introduction of technologies or principles such as building information modeling (BIM), virtual and augmented reality, prefabrication, the Internet of Things (IoT), additive manufacturing and robotization. All over the world, large companies are already experimenting with some of these technologies, but their implementation is still in its infancy, especially

---

For a color version of all figures in this book, see www.iste.co.uk/cardin/digitalization.zip.

1. https://www.ffbatiment.fr/federation-francaise-du-batiment/le-batiment-et-vous/en_chiffres/les-chiffres-en-france.html.

Digitalization and Control of Industrial Cyber-Physical Systems,
coordinated by Olivier CARDIN, William DERIGENT and Damien TRENTESAUX.
© ISTE Ltd 2022.

in small companies. This is indeed the major difficulty of this sector of activity. In 2020, small companies (fewer than 20 employees) represent about 99% of French construction companies and 59% of the sector's salaried employees. On a European scale, the situation is the same, with 92% of companies having fewer than 10 employees[2]. It is also an extremely diversified and fragmented sector with, for example, 24% of companies specializing in general masonry and 11% in electricity or painting. A total of 650,000 companies (+45% in 10 years) in the sector are ultimately spread over more than 20 different trades in France[3].

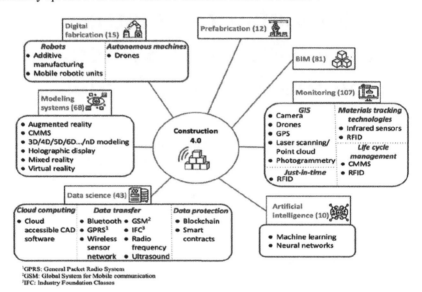

Figure 14.1. *Distribution of 4.0 technologies used in construction according to seven technology groups from Perrier et al. (2020)*

This overview, though very brief, may at first glance seem rather bleak. The definition proposed in this book for industrial cyber-physical systems (ICPS) seems to be rather far from the construction activities and the picture presented here. The means and size of the companies involved are more reminiscent of craftsmanship than of systems that operate autonomously and interact. However, the situation is not fixed, and we see it as a unique opportunity for cooperation between researchers and industrialists to work on numerous projects with significant scope and impact. The significant margins of progress that remain make construction a very stimulating and worthy sector. This chapter therefore provides a non-exhaustive

2. https://www.capeb.fr/les-chiffres-de-lartisanat [accessed November 2021].

3. https://dataviz.metiers-btp.fr/entreprises [accessed November 2021].

picture of the opportunities, experiences and transformations that have taken place over the last 10 years. Many of these have been, and increasingly will be, supported by the emergence of "new" technologies originally developed for the manufacturing sector.

A study aimed at providing a comprehensive classification of the 4.0 technologies currently studied and applied in the construction industry (Perrier *et al.* 2020) reveals, indeed, that these technologies are finally managing to spread within this sector. This literature review, based on 2,041 documents from the Scopus database, clarifies in particular the main actions and the most common applications in construction. As summarized in Figure 14.1 by the authors, it turns out that seven technological "bricks" are under consideration and are very regularly cited and applied by different authors, namely: digital manufacturing, prefabrication, BIM, artificial intelligence (AI), modeling (AR/VR, nD modeling), dimensional or geographic survey technologies (laser scanning, drones, unmanned aerial vehicles (UAVs), photogrammetry, GPS) and material tracking (RFID tags, wireless sensor networks). Some of the most promising advances are presented in the following sections.

Thus, through these numerous studies and with regard to Figure 1.5 in Chapter 1, we can see that technologies already exist in the building sector to complete the various functionalities of ICPS. Some solutions allow for the **capture and distribution** of information to report more precisely and more quickly the situations encountered on site by the interveners. Some blocks of technology will contribute perfectly to the activity of **digitalization of the building sites** then facilitating the activities of piloting and decision-making. As we will emphasize later on, routines and autonomous solutions are currently being studied, in particular to enrich and accelerate this digitalization phase. Finally, just like the manufacturing sector's infatuation with digital twins, data science or AI reinforces the potential of BIM models during the construction and operation phases through increased **learning and interaction** capacities. In this sense, Construction 4.0 systems are ICPS (or parts of ICPS). Even if there is not yet a widely-used ICPS in construction that includes all of these functions, initiatives are appearing in the form of proofs of concept (POC). An example of an ICPS prototype under construction is presented in section 14.4.

14.2. The place of BIM in Construction 4.0

Following in the footsteps of the major groups, and in order to finally change the paradigm, the construction sector is stepping up its efforts and attempting to embark on the digital path. The best example of this is the digital mock-up (DM) and more specifically BIM. In agreement with the French-speaking association buildingSMART France[4] and a large majority of the actors in the construction industry, BIM is commonly the acronym for "building information model" and corresponds to the digital representation of the physical and functional characteristics of a building. The BIM is then used as a shared database to capitalize on the information related to the building, and to exchange it. This exchange process (interoperability) is facilitated by the industry foundation classes (IFC) exchange standard[5] (International Organization for Standardization 2016). BIM can also be "building information modeling" as a business process of generating and using building data during its entire lifecycle. It is then a process of exchange around the DM for collaborative work between professionals. With these different functionalities, BIM is thus seen as a decision-making tool during the lifecycle of a project. We can even mention 4D or 5D if the modeling takes into account time and cost, respectively. To be more precise, 4D BIM, for example, is a process that makes it possible to associate a 3D digital model with information relating to the planning of a project, which provides precise visual planning for all phases of the project and can go as far as the simulation of the movements of materials (movements of cranes, for example, to check the accessibility on site). 4D can be implemented through tools such as Synchro 4D[6] or Navisworks[7]. Many therefore see BIM as "the cornerstone of Construction 4.0" (Bourgault *et al.* 2021). These authors rely on studies conducted by the construction industry in Quebec which have highlighted more than 30 opportunities made possible by the use of BIM[8]. In addition to the improvement of the quality of the works and the information exchanged, the five elements most often mentioned by the experts are the importance of efficiency gains (35% of the experts), the reduction of risks on the construction site (33%), the possibility of prefabrication and integration of manufacturers (25%), the reduction of waste (23%), as well as the improvement of the transfer of construction data to the management of the assets (20%). Many of these gains seem to be tenfold if BIM is accompanied by a lean approach and digitalization of the company[9]. It would thus be possible to move from a plan completion rate (in the sense of planned activities) of 50 to over 70%. The use of BIM thus acts as a catalyst for improvements and

---

4. https://www.buildingsmartfrance-mediaconstruct.fr/.

5. ISO 16739:2013.

6. https://www.bentley.com/fr/products/product-line/construction-software/synchro-modeler [accessed November 2021].

7. https://www.autodesk.fr/products/navisworks/overview [accessed November 2021].

8. https://espace2.etsmtl.ca/id/eprint/20928/2/Poirier%20E%202018%2020928.pdf [accessed November 2021].

9. https://www.bcg.com/publications/2018/boosting-productivity-construction-digital-lean [accessed November 2021].

changes that go far beyond the functions of modeling, sharing and information exchange.

It is still difficult to propose a consensus definition of the term "Construction 4.0". We have just mentioned the fact that many 4.0 technologies are already benefiting a few precursors in the sector. The question could then be raised as to whether these "new" technologies are in some way **"redundancies"** or **complements** to BIM alone. By looking at the intentions of different studies on the subject, some answers can be proposed. The analysis of articles published since 2011 and the appearance of the notion of Industry 4.0 confirms that not only are the *raisons d'être* of BIM reinforced, but that they are, in fact, enriched (Joblot *et al.* 2020). By *"raison d'être"*, the authors mean, for example, improving productivity, collaboration, data quality and dissemination, or reducing costs or environmental impacts in construction projects. Beyond that, other improvements have been noted, generally driven by technologies such as the IoT, the use of drones, 3D printing (used, for example, in prefabrication), AI and cloud computing (to improve feedback or to enable the automation of choices). The synthesis proposed by the authors makes it possible, in fact, to highlight the appearance of new functionalities that allow, *in fine*, new industrial perspectives. Indeed, it is regularly about real-time monitoring of objects and/or stakeholders, now making possible simulations and real-time optimization (e.g. to optimize flows, time or resources; Laurini *et al.* (2019), Favier *et al.* (2019)). The monitoring of planning and the creation of knowledge and experience databases are also being tested and could then become widespread and again facilitate planning, risk or cost management (Tibaut and Zazula 2018).

All of these elements and this rapprochement to the ICPS bring new sources of interest or questions for industrialists, as we detail in the following sections, yet BIM was still only occasionally exploited by less than 1/3 of French companies in 2018[10].

14.3. Examples of transformations in the construction sector

ICPS can be the source of important transformations in the construction sector. In the following section, several examples of the use of technologies and principles are detailed, according to the four functions of an ICPS, i.e. control, learn and interact, sense and distribute information, and digitalize.

---

10. https://axeobim.fr/observatoire-du-bim/.

14.3.1. *Control: real-time site management*

ICPS, given their ability to control complex systems, could be applied to the control of construction sites. Indeed, academics and construction professionals agree on the fact that construction projects are becoming increasingly difficult to manage due to the increasing complexity of the projects. To understand this complexity, several works have recommended and demonstrated the usefulness of tools such as BIM 4D. Tserng *et al.* (2014) suggest, for example, that BIM 4D could be used for construction site monitoring, with adaptations. Indeed, if this approach makes it possible to have a visualization of the theoretical progress of the construction site, it remains, in practice, not very suited to monitoring of construction sites and to the control (in the sense of the management of the construction site) of possible deviations from the initial plans. To remedy this, it is therefore necessary to couple BIM 4D with data collected on the construction site in order to compare the planned state ("as-planned") with the actual state ("as-built") of the building. The information collected for the monitoring can be either directly related to the tasks (i.e. percentage of task completed) or to the products or resources of these same tasks (i.e. product status, product location). In the latter case, measurement of the planned/actual variance is not direct and it is then necessary to define metrics, making it possible to calculate it from the collected information. The collection method can vary: it can be manual, semi-automatic or even automatic. This process can be illustrated by the work of Matthews *et al.* (2015) who present an architecture based on BIM 4D, where the percentage of completion of each planned task is updated daily either by the contractors or by the site manager, via mobile applications.

In order to automate this update, Han *et al.* (2015) propose a 4D object recognition system that combines 3D object recognition, based on site surveys, with planning information. By determining the geometric differences between the actual 4D model and the planned 4D model, it becomes possible to identify deviations. The Internet of Things can also be used to capture information from the construction site where 4D BIM models are updated with product information collected by RFID readers. In terms of performance improvements, some studies suggest a reduction in the overall construction time of approximately 17% following the adoption of a system that combines RFID and BIM 4D. However, these systems require implementation efforts, including careful management of resistance to change and training of site personnel. The information collection method chosen can create time-consuming steps in the construction process, due to the manual reading of information, for example.

This quick overview of the objectives and constraints related to real-time site management actually reveals that the barriers between the academic and industrial sectors must be as porous as possible. It is in this way, and by constantly integrating or experimenting with new technologies and organizational models, that the obstacles resulting from increased productivity or expectations can be overcome. It is possible to go even further by bringing more immersive experiences to the construction actors to visualize in real time this well-known information coming from the field or more simply to better define the contours of a project, to anticipate or prepare more upstream evolutions or certain interventions.

14.3.2. *Learning and interacting: virtual reality and machine learning*

The concepts of virtual (VR), augmented (AR) or mixed reality (MR) are not new and are gradually being introduced in the manufacturing industry. Their use in construction, however, is more limited. VR is, for example, a set of technologies that allows a user to be immersed in a virtual environment in real time and with "realistic" interactions, involving sensory receptors such as sight, hearing and touch. It is an experience, if visual, that can be exercised on computers, tablets, VR headsets, or through much weightier solutions such as CAVE (Cave Automatic Virtual Environment). The study by Perrier *et al.* (2020) specifies that there are many scientific or industrial experiments in VR or AR in the construction sector to date. This article on the construction trades made it possible for the authors to classify the 4.0 technologies present according to:

– their ability to meet 10 target actions (automate, communicate, distribute, localize, model, optimize, reconstruct, simulate, normalize and visualize);

– the phase of the construction project lifecycle during which the experiment took place (the columns);

– the project management process that the technology impacts (communication management, costs, health and safety, human resources, procurement, quality, risks, project scope or duration).

The prospects for VR/AR techniques in a construction project are summarized in Table 14.1.

The chosen angle of analysis, however, did not allow any particular advances to be identified in "Operation and Maintenance" activities. For many years, however, VR/AR applications have been aimed at investigating how to improve facility management, another important issue related to building operating costs. Indeed, it has been noted that "80% of the costs of operating, maintaining, and replacing a building are determined in the first 20% of the design process"[11]. In other words, the maintenance and renovation of a building is four times its initial cost over its lifecycle. The monitoring of equipment and the facilitation of these stages via VR-type applications has therefore become a priority for companies and start-ups in recent years, such as the HORUS solution[12] proposed by the IARA team of developers. The functionalities proposed via these applications are thus multiple and AR/VR support can improve guidance on the intervention site, the visualization of hidden elements, interaction and quick access to information (technical data sheets, plans, etc.).

	Design and engineering	Construction
Communications	**Visualizing** – 3D visualization of digital models and texture – (AR/VR/nD modeling) – 3D visualization of building information (VR) – Communicate Improvement of customer understanding in the design phase (VR)	**Visualizing** – 3D visualization of digital models and texture (AR/VR/nD modeling)
Health and safety	**Simulating** – Safety training (VR)	**Locating** – Capture of hand movements (VR/camera) **Communicating** – Safety training (VR)
Risk	**Simulating** – Safety training (VR)	

Table 14.1. *Prospects for VR/AR technologies.*
Based on the review by Perrier et al. (2020)

Bridges are also tending to develop between VR/AR and other solutions such as building management systems (BMS), CMMS and IoT. The ultimate challenge is to enable and generalize the use of the BIM as-built documentation. These prospects justify the current enthusiasm of publishers such as BENTLEY[13] and Unity (world leader in free game engines) who seek to orient their products to make them "BIM compatible". For example, the latter offers "Unity Reflect"[14] to facilitate VR

11. ISO 15686-5:2008.

12. https://www.horus-bim.com/ [accessed November 2021].

13. https://www.bentley.com/fr/about-us/news/2017/october/09/pna-06-microstation-lumenrt [accessed November 2021].

14. https://unity.com/products/unity-reflect [accessed November 2021].

experimentation and development while maintaining real-time updates and project imports from Revit, BIM 360, Navisworks, SketchUp or Rhino. Interoperability and compatibility with these leading vendors is likely to be the primary requirement for widespread use of these new features.

14.3.3. *Capturing and distributing: use of wireless technologies (RFID and WSN)*

The Internet of Things has developed significantly since the early 2000s leading to a number of initiatives in the construction field. Two main types of microelectronic technologies are used: passive, semi-active or active chips (RFID and NFC) and wireless sensor networks (WSNs) using various types of communications (LORA, SigFox, BLE, etc.), powered by energy or autonomous. The major application remains to capture and send back information coming from construction products (i.e. prefabricated beams) or from resources used during construction (i.e. cranes, trucks, etc.) for management or maintenance needs. For example, in the field of lifting, the Potain company monitors crane activities based on different data and conditions of use, obtained through sensors placed on the structure. The data collected in this way can be used to supplement a maintenance logbook and is used by rental companies to optimize their maintenance and repairs (see Chapter 3). They are also offered in the field of operator training to personalize the educational content proposed[15].

On a completely different note, many research works have highlighted the benefits of integrating Internet of Things technologies in prefabricated construction products, which are increasingly used for cost and time reasons. As proof, Li and Becerik-Gerber (2011) already presented an extensive review of research works or industrial initiatives in the construction field, using RFID technologies. These have thus been tested and can generate significant economic gains in all phases of the precast concrete lifecycle, for example, in the quality management of precast products or for the construction supply chain, by providing product information to stakeholders. WSN are used when active monitoring of the structure is required, such as for early inspection of concrete or for structural health monitoring (Jiang and Georgakopoulos 2012). There are also some industrial initiatives. For example, the Lafarge company embedded RFID tags directly into the concrete of the D2 tower for a traceability application. Companies such as 360 SmartConnect (www.360sc.io) are using these NFC technologies to offer innovative services related to the universal and intelligent traceability of products, materials and construction sites. These

---

15. http://www.chantiersdefrance.fr/reseaux/constructeurs-potain-digital-transforme-lentretien-grues-a-tour/ [accessed November 2021].

long-lasting devices can be integrated directly into the material. However, this can be accompanied by problems of accessibility of the chip and storage memory. To solve these problems, research work has focused on "communicating materials" (Kubler *et al.* 2010), materials capable of communicating with their environment, processing, exchanging information and storing data in their own structure.

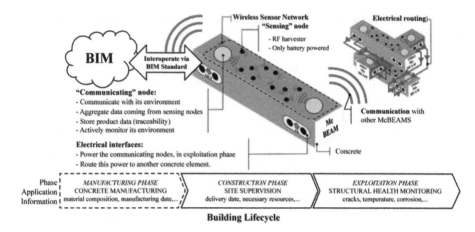

Figure 14.2. *Description of the ANR McBIM project*

In addition, these materials also have the ability to measure the state of their environment and to measure their own internal physical parameters. Mekki *et al.* (2016) propose to apply this principle to construction by integrating wireless sensor networks into concrete. However, while the application seems interesting, it needs to overcome technological and scientific limitations currently studied in the framework of the McBIM project (communicating materials for BIM) labeled by the ANR (French National Research Agency) in 2018, ongoing until 2022 (http://mcbim. cran.univ-lorraine.fr), as presented in Figure 14.2.

14.3.4. *Digitalizing: digitalizing technologies for BIM*

For an old or existing building, the concept of a digital mock-up is too recent to be available. For a renovation project in BIM, it will therefore be necessary to make this model in the image of the building as built. Hence, it is called an "As-Built" model. This is a complex task due to the imperfections of the real building, and this often time-consuming rendering implements various digitalization solutions (Landrieu *et al.* 2013; Volk *et al.* 2015). To improve the accuracy and speed of this acquisition, many solutions have been developed over several years, allowing for object recognition and automatic insertion/prediction of invisible objects (Tang *et al.* 2010). With the help of 4.0 technologies, professionals are also proposing increasingly innovative means of surveying, which they praise for their performance, ergonomics and accuracy. In addition to digitalizing buildings using drones, Geoslam is now offering the original Zeb Go[16] acquisition process, which can obtain 43,200 points per second. The announced accuracy is +/- 0.1% or 1 cm, and this product only requires a simple movement, camera in hand, inside the building to transcribe the existing into a point cloud. The growing use of tablets is pushing developers to innovate and solutions such as ARtoBuild[17] can now generate 2D plans in PDF format and 3D plans in IFC format from tablets of 10 inches or more.

Figure 14.3. *Spot®, Bostondynamic's robot dog*

Steps are therefore gradually being taken and many construction companies throughout the world (Bouygues Construction in France, Pomerleau in Canada, etc.) are also experimenting with "robot dog" type solutions (Spot®[18]) from Bostondynamics (Figure 14.3) to inspect the progress of worksites autonomously or to carry out scanning or surveillance of potentially dangerous sites. Equipped with a camera or laser scanner (compatible with FARO and Trimble), Spot® helps to identify deviations and rework more quickly and is capable of routinely and safely scanning a workspace in the event of coactivity (cobotics). It then contributes, as recently for the FORD plant in Van Dyke, to the creation of digital twins of construction sites or production sites.

16. https://geoslam.com/solutions/zeb-go/ [accessed November 2021].

17. https://www.bimeo.fr/artobuild [accessed November 2021].

18. https://www.bostondynamics.com/spot [accessed November 2021].

14.4. Example of ICPS in construction

Once again, it is necessary to distinguish between the construction phase and the building operation phase. Future constructions and the emergence of smart cities suggest "over" exploitation of 4.0 technology to make buildings more intelligent, comfortable, economical and secure (Beddiar *et al.* 2019). It is, however, still rare to combine all or part of the digital developments presented in this chapter for construction purposes to thus develop and exploit an ICPS in construction. Some experiments are, however, undertaken in this direction and are the subject of publications or POCs (Furet *et al.* 2019; You and Feng 2020). The solutions implemented in this last publication to "**print**" a 95 m² social housing and named Yhnova are, for example, based on a technology named Batiprint3D[19] and developed by teams from the University of Nantes (LS2N, GeM). This work, which was launched in 2017, required the development of a set of processes centered around a specific "autonomous" robotic machine rolling directly on a concrete slab, the base of the future building. This ICPS consisted of a poly-articulated arm (PAA) to print the walls ("standard" robot, branded Staübli[20]) and the automatic guided vehicle (AGV) came from the company BA Systèmes[21].

Figure 14.4. *Implementation of the Yhnova project*

Thus constituted, the PAA allows for, initially and by successive layers, the realization of the polyurethane foam formworks (two "parallel" boards forming a complete wall, as presented in Figure 14.4). The AGV ensures the positioning/movement of the arm between different positions according to trajectories defined from the BIM model. Positioning errors caused by slab flatness defects are corrected in real time by measuring the spatial position of the AGV via a set of 11 fixed targets/laser beams. The information transmitted by two on-board inclinometers further improves the knowledge and digital representation of the

19. https://www.batiprint3d.com/en [accessed November 2021].

20. https://www.staubli.com/en-us/ [accessed November 2021].

21. https://alstefgroup.com/ [accessed November 2021].

"physical" assembly. Thus, by successive processing of the data and reconfiguration of the models, the position of the 3D printing nozzle is corrected in real time, allowing for positioning to within +/ − 0.5 mm of the future installations. Thanks to BIM, all the reservations of the pre-equipment (fluid inlets and outlets, energy and network inlets, windows and doors, etc.) and the reinforcement steels of the construction are, in the same way, positioned with precision. These foam structures are then used as formwork in which the concrete is poured by the same robotic 3D printer for a house built in less than 54 hours.

14.5. Achieving the digital transformation of businesses

The previous points have highlighted how the four functions of an ICPS (control, learn and interact, sense and distribute, and digitalize) can be used, step by step, to make up for the delay in the construction sector. If properly mastered, these functions will help to erase the image of a craft sector that has become obsolete or uninteresting for the new generations. The building and public works sectors are in turn caught up in the wave of digitalization which they must learn to overcome. This digitalization and the major changes that accompany it will be all the more accepted and rapid if companies know how to be critical and organized during the deployment of new digital solutions and technologies. It will also be necessary to reduce the compartmentalization of activities, companies between them and solutions implemented. The scientific literature reveals that these last challenges can be overcome thanks to the deployment of indicators making it possible to quantify the maturity of companies relative to these technologies. It will also be necessary for publishers and solution providers to make these new technologies simple, adaptable and interoperable, and thus to facilitate links between the multitude of players and businesses involved in projects.

Faced with the process of adopting these new technologies, and in particular BIM, many argue that without internal (individuals, teams, organizations, projects) or sometimes external (subcontractors or stakeholders) measurements and evaluations, different partners are unable to regularly quantify their successes, failures, strengths and weaknesses. It would even be impossible for them to be effective and critical of their investments (Proença and Borbinha 2016). However, to remedy this, they could rely on the use of maturity models (MM). The latter are described as tools that help characterize, throughout the process of implementing an information system, fragilities and/or progress. In the scientific literature, the underlying concepts are defined as follows: capacity (BIM or not) is the ability to perform a task, deliver a service or generate a product; maturity is the degree of excellence or mastery in the execution of this task. MM thus make it possible from matrices of situations or from successions of questions to restore in the form of visuals and indicators the levels of mastery of the entity facing, for example, the imperatives of BIM – but not only this (Azzouz *et al.* 2016). These MM represent an essential basis for the continuous improvement process. They may focus on risk management during a construction project, the involvement of stakeholders, the safety culture and so on (Eadie *et al.* 2012) counted 10 years ago about 53 MMs for the construction sector to "characterize" its maturity with regard to information and communication technology (ICT). Even today, such solid and well-constructed sets of BIM-oriented metrics can really help companies to optimize the performance of their workforce and can alleviate some of the reluctance related to the implementation of BIM (by including aspects such as training and education). They are also important supports when stakeholders develop roadmaps or identify future business goals and projects. Even though they are still not widely used by industry, more and more targeted models are being developed to best meet the needs and specificities of companies. Without being exhaustive, let us note, for example, the recent appearance of the "IDEAL" maturity model aimed to evaluate and analyze the performance of projects that implement both BIM and Lean (Mollasalehi *et al.* 2018). This integrated BIM and lean MM thus aim to evaluate and monitor the performance of projects that implement these two organizational supports. The authors proposed a maturity evolution according to five main levels, from *Initial* to *Optimized in the long run.*

In another way, the BIM maturity model for renovation (BiM²FR) supports the evolution of small companies involved more particularly in renovation. This MM is based on good practices and principles that should be addressed during the implementation of BIM (Joblot *et al.* 2019). The structure of BiM²FR and its use make it possible, among other things, to question and focus on key success factors, organizational and managerial approaches such as Lean Construction, project management, the Integrated Project Delivery Approach[22] (The American Institute of Architects 2007) or the contents of BIM Agreements[23], all elements that facilitate the implementation of BIM. This MM is available via a free web platform (www.BiM2FR.eu), making it possible for each company to obtain in a few minutes objective feedback on the situation in which it finds itself on the path of BIM. Finally, other studies have recently focused on the correlation between the maturity of a BIM model and the ability to collaborate to develop a low environmental impact construction (Mohammed 2020). Based on already existing governmental[24] and

---

22. http://www.aia.org/contractdocs/AIAS077630 [accessed November 2021].

23. https://buildingsmartfrance-mediaconstruct.fr/memos-pratiques-BIM/#sample-convention [accessed November 2021].

24. http://www.aia.org/contractdocs/AIAS077630 [accessed November 2021].

scientific models (BIS 2011; Succar *et al.* 2012) and through a validation by the Delphi survey technique, the author proposes an organizational framework to regulate and optimize the collaboration and maturity level of a BIM model and thus facilitate the execution and final characteristics of the developed green buildings.

Beyond the consulting companies, many supports are available to accompany companies in these important digital and organizational changes. This "4.0 migration" is to be expected in the years to come within the construction sector and its multitude of players. This migration is integrated or can be articulated around the digital model and BIM. The main challenge that remains to be overcome is that of interoperability and the ability of all the players and solutions mentioned to communicate and interact. As recognized by industrialists and scientists, the generalization of BIM practices alone, although irremediable and irreversible, is still slow and hampered by the lack of interoperability between solutions (Sattler *et al.* 2020). Fortunately, this point is evolving, step by step, thanks to numerous works based on the neutral IFC exchange format. However, the task has become even more complex with the appearance of all the new technologies and functionalities mentioned in this chapter. In addition to the problems of interoperability "of the" digital models, there are also those resulting from the desire to enrich and interact with a multitude of "means" with very different languages and temporalities. However, it is through this last integration effort that the systems resulting from Construction 4.0 will become fully-fledged ICPS.

14.6. References

American Institute of Architects (2007). Integrated project delivery: A guide [Online]. Available at: http://www.aia.org/contractdocs/AIAS077630 [Accessed 12 December 2020].

Azzouz, A., Shepherd, P., Copping, A. (2016). The emergence of building information modelling assessment methods (BIM-AMs). *Proceedings of the Integrated Design Conference*, University of Bath, UK.

Beddiar, K. (2020). Bâtiment 4.0 – Enjeux, concepts et technologies [Online]. Available at: https://www.techniques-ingenieur.fr/base-documentaire/innovation-th10/innovations-en-electronique-et-tic-42257210/batiment-4-0-c3207/ [Accessed 2 June 2021].

Beddiar, K., Grellier, C., Woods, E. (2019). *Construction 4.0 : reinventer le bâtiment grâce au numérique : BIM, DfMA, Lean Management...* Dunod, Paris, France.

BIS (2011). A report for the government construction client group building information modelling (BIM) working party strategy paper. Report, Department for Business Innovation & Skills (BIS) [Online] Available at: https://www.cdbb.cam.ac.uk/Resources/ResoucePublications/BISBIMstrategyReport.pdf [Accessed 25 June 2018].

Bourgault, M., Danjou, C., Pellerin, R., Perrier, N., Boton, C., Forgues, D., Iordanova, I., Poirier, É., Rivest, L., Joblot, L. (2021). *Le Québec économique 9 – Chapitre 17 – Transformer le secteur de la construction par le numérique : un chantier ambitieux et nécessaire.* CIRANO, Quebec, Canada.

Eadie, R., Perera, S., Heaney, G. (2012). Capturing maturity of ICT applications in construction processes. *Journal of Financial Management of Property and Construction,* 17, 176–194.

Favier, A., Scrivener, K., Habert, G. (2019). Decarbonizing the cement and concrete sector: Integration of the full value chain to reach net zero emissions in Europe. *IOP Conference Series: Earth and Environmental Science,* 225(1).

Furet, B., Poullain, P., Garnier, S. (2019). 3D printing for construction based on a complex wall of polymer-foam and concrete. *Additive Manufacturing,* 28, 58–64.

Han, K.K., Cline, D., Golparvar-Fard, M. (2015). Formalized knowledge of construction sequencing for visual monitoring of work-in-progress via incomplete point clouds and low-LoD 4D BIMs. *Advanced Engineering Informatics,* 29(4), 889–901.

International Organization for Standardization (2016). Classes de fondation d'industrie (IFC) pour le partage des données dans le secteur de la construction et de la gestion des installations – ISO 16739:2013 [Online]. Available at: https://www.iso.org/fr/standard/51622.html [Accessed 2 June 2021].

Jiang, S. and Georgakopoulos, S.V. (2012). Optimum wireless powering of sensors embedded in concrete. *IEEE Transactions on Antennas and Propagation,* 60(2 Part 2), 1106–1113.

Joblot, L., Paviot, T., Deneux, D., Lamouri, S. (2019). Building information maturity model specific to the renovation sector. *Automation in Construction,* 101, 140–159.

Joblot, L., Danjou, C., Pellerin, R., Lamouri, S. (2020). Industry 4.0 and BIM: Do they share the same objectives? *Proceedings of the International Joint Conference on Mechanics, Design Engineering & Advanced Manufacturing,* June 2–4, 412–418.

Kubler, S., Derigent, W., Thomas, A., Rondeau, É. (2010). Problem definition methodology for the Communicating Material paradigm. *IFAC Proceedings,* 43(4), 198–203.

Landrieu, J., Père, C., Nugraha Bahar, Y., Nicolas, G. (2013). Représentation hybride du modèle numérique pour la gestion d'un patrimoine bâti dit ancien. Conference proceedings, Biarritz, France.

Laurini, E., Rotilio, M., Lucarelli, M., De Berardinis, P. (2019). Technology 4.0 for buildings management: From building site to the interactive building book. *ISPRS Annals of the Photogrammetry, Remote Sensing and Spatial Information Sciences,* 707–714.

Li, N. and Becerik-Gerber, B. (2011). Life-cycle approach for implementing RFID technology in construction: Learning from academic and industry use cases. *Journal of Construction Engineering and Management,* 137, 1089–1098.

Matthews, J., Love, P.E.D., Heinemann, S., Chandler, R., Rumsey, C., Olatunj, O. (2015). Real time progress management: Re-engineering processes for cloud-based BIM in construction. *Automation in Construction,* 58, 38–47.

Mekki, K., Zouinkhi, A., Derigent, W., Rondeau, E., Thomas, A., Abdelkrim, M.N. (2016). USEE: A uniform data dissemination and energy efficient protocol for communicating materials. *Future Generation Computer Systems*, 56.

Mohammed, A.B. (2020). Collaboration and BIM model maturity to produce green buildings as an organizational strategy. *HBRC Journal*, 16(1), 243–268.

Mollasalehi, S., Aboumoemen, A.A., Rathnayake, A., Fleming, A.J., Underwood, J. (2018). Development of an integrated BIM and lean maturity model. *Proceedings of the 26th Annual Conference of the International Group for Lean Construction*, IGLC, Chennai, India, 1217–1228.

Perrier, N., Bled, A., Bourgault, M., Cousin, N., Danjou, C., Pellerin, R., Roland, T. (2020). Construction 4.0: A survey of research trends. *Journal of Information Technology in Construction (ITcon)*, 25(24), 416–437.

Proença, D. and Borbinha, J. (2016). Maturity models for information systems – A state of the art. *Procedia Computer Science*, 100, 1042–1049.

Sattler, L., Lamouri, S., Larabi, M., Pellerin, R., Maigne, T. (2020). L'interopérabilité BIM multi-métier : la collaboration par la requête. In *Le BIM et l'évolution des pratiques : ingénierie et architecture, enseignement et recherche*, Teulier, R. and Marquès, S. (eds). Eyrolles, Paris, France.

Succar, B., Sher, W., Williams, A. (2012). Measuring BIM performance: Five metrics. *Architectural Engineering and Design Management*, 8(2), 120–142.

Tang, P., Huber, D., Akinci, B., Lipman, R., Lytle, A. (2010). Automatic reconstruction of as-built building information models from laser-scanned point clouds: A review of related techniques. *Automation in Construction*, 19(7), 829–843.

Tibaut, A. and Zazula, D. (2018). Sustainable management of construction site big visual data. *Sustainability Science*, 13(5), 1311–1322.

Tserng, H.-P., Ho, S.-P., Jan, S.-H. (2014). Developing BIM-assisted as-built schedule management system for general contractors. *Journal of Civil Engineering and Management*, 20(1), 47–58.

Volk, R. and Sevilmis, S.F. (2015). Deconstruction project planning based on automatic acquisition and reconstruction of building information for existing buildings. *Proceedings of the SASBE2015*. Pretoria, South Africa, 47–56.

You, Z. and Feng, L. (2020). Integration of industry 4.0 related technologies in construction industry: A framework of cyber-physical system. *IEEE Access*, 8, 122908–122922.

15

Impact of Industrial Cyber-Physical Systems on the Health System

Franck FONTANILI[1] and Maria DI MASCOLO[2]

[1] Université de Toulouse – IMT Mines Albi,
Industrial Engineering Department (CGI), Albi, France
[2] Université Grenoble Alpes, CNRS, Grenoble INP, G-SCOP, France

15.1. Introduction

15.1.1. *The health system and its specificities*

As in the industrial field, though arguably far less mature, health cyber-physical systems (HCPS) are a key element in the evolution and modernization of the health system. However, it is tricky and risky to imagine a direct transposition of industrial cyber-physical systems (ICPS) without taking into account the specificities of the health system, presented in this section. The term "health system" refers to all of the organizations, institutions, resources and people whose main objective is to identify and satisfy the health needs of the population (WHO 2021). It is made up of three main classes of actors: (1) the producers of care, (2) the institutions in charge of administrative and financial organization and (3) the population as users. In this chapter, we are mainly interested in the production of care. This takes place in healthcare structures (public and private health establishments), home care networks, private practices and preventive structures (maternal and child protection,

For a color version of all figures in this book, see www.iste.co.uk/cardin/digitalization.zip.

Digitalization and Control of Industrial Cyber-Physical Systems,
coordinated by Olivier CARDIN, William DERIGENT and Damien TRENTESAUX.
© ISTE Ltd 2022.

school medicine, occupational health services), including pharmaceutical industries and analysis laboratories. These different care production environments participate, in a coordinated manner where possible, in the reception and care of patients based on care paths. A care pathway is a sequence of activities carried out by a range of professionals (medical, paramedical, administrative and technical) using material resources (equipment), linked directly or indirectly to care: consultations, technical or biological procedures; medicinal and non-medicinal treatment; management of acute episodes (decompensation, exacerbation); and other care (in particular, medico-social care, as well as social care) (HAS 2021). We can therefore see that a care pathway can be assimilated to a process, in accordance with the ISO 9000:2015 standard and business process management (BPM), bearing in mind that these approaches and techniques are still rarely used in healthcare, as highlighted by Andellini *et al.* (2017). Going beyond the care pathway, the health pathway is the set of stages and the pathway followed by a subject in an organized health and social system, in a given time and space. It provides a response to preventive, social and medico-social needs. As for the life path, it integrates the care and health paths. It is a response to the needs of the person in their environment. It thus integrates all the players in the societal sphere and, in particular, interactions with education and employment. It is thus comprehensive care for the user, taking into account their choices, in coordination with all actors (ARS 2016).

We are particularly interested here in the production of hospital care, which today occupies a predominant place in the consumption of care and medical goods: 47% in France in 2019, i.e. 97 billion euros, +2.4% compared to 2018 (DREES 2020). This very important evolution in the production of care began in the 1970s. Indeed, the public hospital has undergone a profound transformation and has moved from a function of receiving the most destitute to a real function of producing care, with the development of technical platforms (operating theatres, anesthetic and surgical techniques, diagnostic techniques, etc.) and hospital professionalism (Fargeon 2014).

The hospital is thus a real, very complex production system in which a huge number of patient flows, at the heart of the system, intermingle with flows of information, visitors, drugs, medical devices, consultants, staff, waste, meals and so on. But unlike a manufacturing system, in which a production error affects the product but does not affect the customer themselves, in a healthcare production system, the patient is directly affected by medical errors or organizational malfunctions. As medical errors are fortunately extremely rare, we are mainly interested here in the organizational dimension of the healthcare system, which is often relegated to the background, but whose impact is nonetheless not negligible on healthcare expenditure, as well as on the overall perception of the quality of care by patients (Millien *et al.* 2018). To make the organization effective and efficient, it is not enough to have a distribution of resources adapted to the need in a qualitative and quantitative way. It is also necessary to coordinate and use them rationally (Germain 2012). This last aspect is not only crucial, but it also makes the production of healthcare much more complex than the production of goods. Indeed, producing healthcare implies an action, a medical or paramedical act performed by a doctor or nurse on a patient. It is therefore an essentially human process, which consequently has two specific features: (1) a much greater variability than that of a mechanized or automated industrial process and (2) a multitude of unpredictable events with essentially human causes. Both require frequent medical and organizational decisions to be taken very often in "real time".

15.1.2. *The digital evolution of healthcare production and health*

Recently, a digital transformation of the healthcare production system has made it possible to encourage and promote the evolution of medical devices, medical practices and engineering in the organization of flows. At the institutional level, the French Ministry of Solidarity and Health, for example, has launched several programs (MaSanté 2022, HOP'EN, e-Parcours, etc.) to develop e-health, telehealth and telemedicine. The Covid-19 health crisis has certainly enabled a cultural and organizational level to be reached, making it possible for these new practices to be known, accepted and even approved by the youngest segment of the population. Moreover, medicine is evolving and transforming with the concept of the 4 P's (predictive, preventive, personalized and participatory health; Hood (2013)). Several extensions have even been proposed to go beyond the 4 P's: relevant, healthcare pathway, patient-centered, precise, pervasive and so on. This evolution is being driven by data, often generated by patients themselves. At the academic and industrial level, Hospital 4.0 (or Health 4.0), inspired by the Industry 4.0 concept, integrates several fields, including e-Health, connected objects, artificial intelligence and CPS (Afferni *et al.* 2018).

In the rest of this chapter, we look at how HCPS are used in the literature (section 15.2), before focusing on the contribution of a digital twin-based HCPS of patient pathways in the hospital (section 15.3).

15.2. HCPS in the literature

Health cyber-physical systems combine the use of smart biosensors and various connected objects, with access to data from patient health records, to facilitate decision support, whether medical or organizational. Haque *et al.* (2014) propose a taxonomy of HCPS presented as a tree with eight main branches: (1) applications, (2) architecture, (3) data capture, (4) data management, (5) data processing, (6) communication, (7) security and (8) control action. In this taxonomy, it is branches (1), (3) and (8) in particular which present specificities that are significantly different from the ICPS. For applications, the authors, as well as Dey *et al.* (2018), distinguish two broad categories: (1) assistive or remote monitoring applications. These allow for the real-time acquisition of physiological data, collected through sensors or biosensors associated with the consideration of medical needs of people leading a normal life at home or in service residences. Such applications facilitate the monitoring and care of independent elderly people whose homes have been transformed into smart homes, referred to in the literature as Ambient Assisted Living (AAL) (Rodrigues *et al.* 2018; Elmurabet *et al.* 2020). (2) Applications in "controlled" environments, such as a hospital intensive care unit, where medical support is available at all times. Data from multiple sources – such as monitoring systems, biosensors and clinical observations – are combined to provide hospital practitioners with information to make informed decisions about possible interventions. In Haque *et al.* (2014), the authors describe a mapping of HCPS based on the proposed taxonomy. In particular, they identify about 20 references presenting different applications of HCPS, such as an application designed to automatically feed the computerized patient record with data from a wireless sensor network to collect vital signs; or another with an algorithm for detecting eight types of falls while being able to identify seven types of activity (walking, jumping, running, etc.). This mapping also identifies several secure architectures for collecting health data "at home" (smart living) as well as storing them in the cloud to facilitate telemedicine, for example. The use and combination of assisted and controlled applications is progressively transforming the healthcare system into a complex, extensive and potentially security-critical cyber-physical system but with many benefits and challenges (Insup Lee *et al.* 2012).

We now turn to branches (3) and (8) of the taxonomy presented above: data capture and control action. As in industry, the basic premise of HCPS is a connection between the physical world and the cyber or virtual world. Figure 15.1 from Pang *et al.* (2018) presents an overview of HCPS. As in Figures 1.3 and 1.4 presenting ICPS, we find the physical and cyber elements, connected by a communication network, with CPS positioned in a collaborative environment. It should be noted that here we mainly find CPS oriented towards medical monitoring, well-being and prevention.

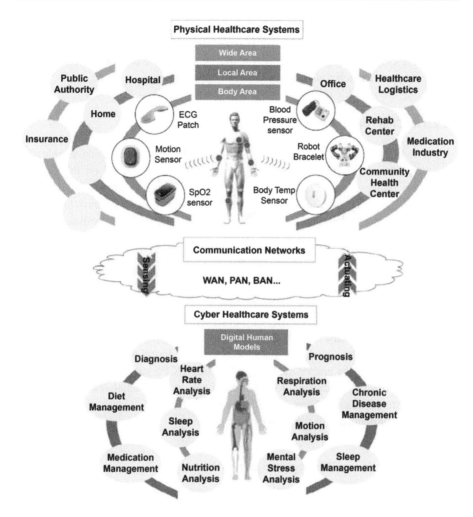

Figure 15.1. *Overview of HCPS for health monitoring,*
prevention and well-being (from Pang et al. 2018))

In the field of healthcare production, the physical world is populated by patients who evolve in different environments: hospital, home, pharmacy and so on. As we will now see, HCPS are applied, either separately or in an integrated manner (system of systems), to the patient alone, to their environment alone, or to both combined, for purposes that are most often medical, and more rarely organizational. In the rest of this section, we first present the HCPS intended for the medical follow-up of a patient, or for the well-being and prevention of a healthy individual. Then, we take a closer look at a class of HCPS that allow for the monitoring and management of care or health paths. Although it is based more on the ICPS used for the production of goods, this class is currently much less widespread than the previous one and is not yet the subject of much research work or many publications.

15.2.1. HCPS for medical monitoring

For medical monitoring of patients, the physical components that enable this connection from the physical to the cyber can be sensors placed on the skin, or sometimes under the skin, in order to measure biological markers (blood sugar levels, for example) or physiological signals: heartbeat, state of muscle tension, brain waves, electrical response of excited photoreceptors, galvanic resistance of the skin and so on. Biosensors that can be implanted in the human body, so-called in vivo, are undoubtedly the most disruptive and promising devices, but they still raise many questions, particularly in terms of their intrusive nature and the invasion of privacy if the right to "disconnect" is not possible. Based on the capture of physiological signals transmitted by biological sources (cell, enzyme, etc.), they allow for the continuous monitoring of biomarkers associated with serious forms of chronic or acute diseases: diabetes, cardiovascular diseases, cancers and so on (Montrose 2013). By associating these sensors with digital applications accessible by patients themselves and/or medical staff, these HCPS can thus intervene in the optimization of drug treatments, for example thanks to a personalized adjustment of the administered dosage. They can also play a preventive or early detection role, particularly for people with risk factors for a disease.

15.2.2. HCPS for well-being and prevention

The rise of connected objects for well-being and health ("smart objects") is the most noticeable aspect today. A multitude of "wearable" sensors integrated into bracelets, watches, glasses, clothing and shoes make it possible for everyone to monitor constants such as heart rate, blood pressure, oxygen level in the blood, or more basic physical activity (motion sensors, fall sensors, pedometer and accelerometer) (Rodrigues *et al.* 2018). Other sensors, for more preventive uses and whose data require analysis by a doctor, can be used: electrocardiograms, electroencephalograms and so on. As for the cyber or virtual components, they are most often in the form of computer applications, mobile or fixed, capable of visualizing, processing and analyzing the data transmitted by the sensors implanted on the physical part. The HCPS are therefore for individuals who are equipped with them as well as for the actors of the health system (caregivers), an innovative solution for medical decision support for care or prevention.

Figure 15.2 illustrates the data transmission chain between the physical part (here a patient) and the cyber part of an HCPS for remote medical monitoring and prevention.

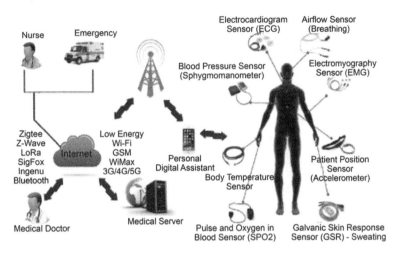

Figure 15.2. *Data transmission chain between the physical and the cyber part (from Rodrigues et al. 2018))*

15.2.3. *HCPS for organizational monitoring of patient pathways*

Real-time organizational monitoring of patient pathways in one or more environments (hospital, home, etc.) is currently the weak link in the healthcare system. One of the priority objectives is to make care pathways more fluid by controlling their scheduling and, as far as possible, reducing unnecessary waiting time or redundant activities for patients. For a variety of reasons, including privacy concerns and the technical and economic investment involved, very few solutions are currently deployed. Some information technology (IT) applications, used, for example, in a hospital information system (HIS), require the collection of data that can be used to track patient pathways after the fact. But this is most often done by manual or assisted entry: for example, a nurse who scans a barcode with a reader to indicate that they have completed a patient sample. This creates the risk of a time gap between the real-world event and its recording in the virtual world. Other examples of computer applications that track and trace patients' journeys are hospital emergency room or operating room (OR) management software, often not in real time since, again, the entry of milestones to mark key steps is not automated. This leads to human errors in data entry, or forgotten data entry. Combined with time differences that can sometimes be several hours long, the data is ultimately not very consistent and representative of the real world.

As a result, few healthcare production environments, such as hospitals, are today able to pilot their patient flows in real time with a reliable picture of the current situation. Just like an airplane pilot who, despite disruption, is able to follow a route thanks to instruments, the director of a hospital, or the head of a hospital department, should have a dashboard showing them in real time: (1) the number of patients on the premises, (2) the time spent by each patient in the waiting room or examination room, (3) the location of each patient, (4) the length of stay of each patient, (5) the availability or occupation of resources, and other indicators useful for managing patient flows. It is easy to imagine the daily difficulties that this involves for doctors, nurses, technical and administrative staff, particularly in terms of lost time, energy and stress. And indirectly, it is health expenditure that is impacted in the medium and long term by a short-term investment saving. Not to mention, and rightly so, the feeling of disorder and poor organization that this can cause among patients. However, solutions do exist in industry for the production of goods, with tools such as SCADA (supervisory control and data acquisition) or MES (manufacturing execution system). But in the hospital, or in other environments of the health system, while the production of care is particularly complex to control, as we have already seen, the solutions for monitoring the patient pathways in real time, which could be described by analogy with the MES as "hospital (or healthcare) execution system" (HES) are embryonic and sparse, even on a global scale. A few hospitals in North America (nine listed in 2020 by the School of Medicine & Health Science (SMHS, 2020)) are forerunners in this field as in others, no doubt thanks to a culture of innovation and change as well as privacy legislation that is much less restrictive than in France and Europe. In HealthSpaces (2020), the concept of a "hospital command center" is presented in four dimensions: (1) incident response, (2) security management, (3) building management and (4) the one of most interest to us in this chapter, capacity management and care monitoring. In this last dimension, the command center provides real-time information from different systems: bed management, emergency management, operating room management, admissions and discharge management and so on. Johns Hopkins Hospital in Baltimore, Maryland, is particularly advanced, as this institution is behind the creation of the first command center (Kane *et al.* 2019) that uses GE Healthcare solutions (GE Healthcare 2018).

15.2.4. *Sensors for monitoring patients and resources*

HCPS for the organizational monitoring of patient pathways requires data on patient flows, which is a real technological challenge. Extracting, merging and validating the data available in the HIS databases constitute the first difficulty. Indeed, the HIS does not record all the data that could be useful for monitoring patient pathways. Many activities in the patient pathway, particularly those that are neither automated nor instrumented, are not always tracked or recorded in the form of time-stamped data. For example, in an emergency department, apart from the registration of patients on their arrival at the registration desk, it is common to have only partial or unreliable data that do not allow for accurate tracking of the different pathways. It is therefore very difficult to have an overview of the location of patients in the hospital, for example, to predict bottlenecks or anticipate arrivals in downstream departments.

The acquisition or deduction of data complementary to those existing in the HIS – making it possible to finely trace a patient's journey, particularly waiting times (sitting, standing and lying down) in or outside waiting rooms, as well as movements – is the second difficulty, both technological and scientific. This can be achieved by using sensors to collect non-identifying data (e.g. counting the number of patients in a waiting room), or to know the progress of each patient in a care or preventive pathway, which requires identifying each of them. Several types of sensors can be used: cameras, microphones with or without facial recognition or voice recognition, presence detectors, motion detectors, "tag" wristbands and radio frequency readers (RFID, BLE, ZigBee and UWB), sensors integrated into smartphones (magnetometer, accelerometer and GPS) and so on (see Chapter 3 for more information on this topic). Indoor geolocation (real-time location system or RTLS) or, in a more basic way, geofencing makes it possible for data from radio frequency sensors to be processed in order to track routes in real time or to reconstruct them afterwards. The RTLS works with beacons, placed at judiciously chosen locations on the premises, which pick up signals emitted by radio frequency tags worn by the patients. The primary function of indoor positioning is the same as that of an outdoor global positioning system (GPS): to track a person on a map of the premises using different positioning algorithms based on signal triangulation. Geofencing events (a patient enters or exits a room) can be inferred from RTLS data and the layout of rooms in the hospital (Araghi et al. 2018). The same technologies can also be used for mobile technical resources needed at certain stages of a pathway. Thus, it is possible to easily and quickly locate wheelchairs, infusion stands and syringe pumps, which are often lost or stolen because they cannot be located. In addition, the very important partitioning of a hospital (many rooms) makes it difficult to locate them visually, which means time is wasted searching for them. These technologies can also be used to help guide each patient along a predefined route, like a GPS, but inside the premises. Today, indoor geolocation solutions are numerous, but apart from the economic aspect, the aspects related to acceptability and privacy are an obstacle, both for patients and staff.

We have just reviewed the many ways in which CPS can be used in a health system, some of which are more widespread in the literature than others. In the following, we will focus on a class of HCPS that is still under-studied in the literature, but which is very promising: HCPS that enable the monitoring and management of care or healthcare pathways through the use of a digital twin.

15.3. The contribution of a digital twin in an HCPS

The concept of a digital twin can be considered as one of the key elements of a cyber-physical system, provided that one of its basic principles is respected, namely a real-time interaction between the virtual and the physical world. Indeed, a digital twin is a virtual and dynamic model, fully consistent with its physical counterpart in the real world. It can simulate the behavior of its physical counterpart over a desired period of time (Zhuang *et al.* 2018). However, the term "digital twin" is sometimes used – in the scientific literature as well as by solution editors – as an "offline" simulation model, in other words without synchronization of events with the real world, even though its dynamic behavior is very close to it, as is the case in GE Healthcare (2021) for a digital twin of a hospital or Lanner (2021) for a digital twin of industrial processes. Without claiming to give a univocal and consensual definition of a digital twin, we suggest a distinction between: (1) "offline" digital twins which are able to simulate the real world asynchronously and to serve as a real digital model to conduct experiments quickly, safely and at a lower cost and (2) "online" or "DT-based CPS" digital twins, which have the same simulation capabilities but are synchronized with the real world (monitoring). The latter make it possible to have a faithful, synchronous, dynamic and realistic image of the real world. We will see later on a general approach of a CPS combining the use of an online digital twin with one or several offline digital twins, resulting in a decision support tool to drive, predict and optimize patient flows in a hospital.

In this final section, we mainly focus on digital twin-based HCPS (Tao and Zhang 2019), integrating different interacting layers and enabling both control, prediction and optimization.

15.3.1. *General principle of digital twins in health*

In the field of health, whether the digital twin is that of a patient, or simply that of an organ or one of the major systems of the human body, or even that of the environment in which patients are cared for (e.g. a hospital with its human and technical resources), it is in all cases a digital and dynamic model of the physical world that it represents. It must be able to simulate its states and behavior as faithfully as possible. This gives it the capacity to predict future behavior, for example, to test a treatment before administering it to a patient ("in silico" testing) and also to predict the short-term effects of a disturbing event on the real world. It interacts with the physical world thanks to the control, calculation and communication layers that characterize CPS in general. For this purpose, sensor networks of varying degrees of sophistication must be installed in the real world in order to collect data that will be transmitted and processed by the digital twin for its synchronization, if possible in real time. If necessary, actuators can act on the physical system at the end of a feedback loop in order to provide a correction calculated by the CPS control layer.

In the healthcare world, this correction is most often performed by the patients themselves, their doctor or a flow manager, through a manual and therefore human action (human-in-the-loop concept) on one or more physical system control variables: patient-controlled analgesia (nurse and patient) according to the level of oxygen saturation in the blood (see Li *et al.* (2015) which illustrates the feedback loop well), adjusting the flow rate of an insulin pump according to the blood glucose level in the blood (patient), adjusting the atrial or ventricular output rate and current of an external pacemaker (cardiologist), adjusting the number of windows to be opened at the hospital admissions desk according to the patient arrivals (flow manager) and so on.

15.3.2. *A proposal for an HCPS based on a digital twin of patient pathways in the hospital*

As we have seen above, the lack of real-time management of patient flows in hospitals is a real weakness in the healthcare system. If they manage to attract the interest of hospitals and develop command centers, with their "capacity management and care monitoring" dimension, which can be likened to real control towers, they constitute a suitable and highly effective HCPS solution. In this section, we present the contribution that one or even several online and offline digital twins could make to these control centers, thanks to three complementary functions: (1) a monitoring and control function by visualizing the flows in real time, (2) a prediction function and (3) an optimization function. The HCPS can thus become a real decision support tool for real-time and predictive management of patient flows. These different digital twins are based on discrete event simulators. Figure 15.3 illustrates this HCPS based on digital twins, online and offline, to ensure these three functions.

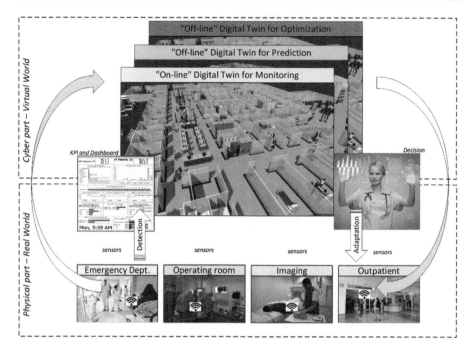

Figure 15.3. *Proposal for an HCPS based on digital twins of patient pathways in the hospital*

An online digital twin to ensure the real-time control function: the online digital twin must be a real digital and dynamic replica making it possible to visualize in real-time patients in the whole building, or at the level of a floor, a department or a particular room. This visualization, which is therefore similar to supervision, must be sufficiently realistic for the nursing or management staff to establish the link with the real world without difficulty of interpretation. Having a simulator to ensure this function, rather than a supervisor, will not only make it possible to streamline the visualization of patient flows between two events captured in the real world, but also serve as an initial model for the offline digital twins used for the prediction and optimization functions. Indeed, this online digital twin is supposed to be in a state similar to that of the real world at any time, so it can be cloned and desynchronized at any time for accelerated predictive simulations. The main technical and scientific challenges of the discrete-event simulator-based online digital twin are of two types, as highlighted by Karakra *et al.* (2020): (1) upon activation, being able to initialize to the current real-world state as fast as possible. This can be achieved through communication and computational layers that will not only collect events from sensors installed in the real world but also compute or infer flow and activity information. For example, a calculation must make it possible to know the number of patients present in a waiting room at a given time thanks to a sensor that detects the entrances and exits of this same room, or to deduce that a patient is being taken care of by a doctor in a treatment cubicle thanks to a sensor placed at the entrance of the cubicle that has detected the simultaneous presence of this patient and a doctor. Once the digital twin is in the same state as the real world, the simulation clock must be synchronized with real time. The digital twin therefore moves at the speed of the real world. (2) To be able to synchronize with time-stamped events coming from the real world and coming, for example, from patient location or geofencing sensors. For example, a sensor will detect that a patient in the real world enters or exits a waiting room, and this event will synchronize the entry or exit of the same virtual patient in the same waiting room of the digital twin. During operation, discrepancies will therefore appear between the dynamic and simulated behavior of the digital twin and the real behavior. For example, the time a patient spends in a waiting room is calculated according to a probability law at the level of the digital twin, and even though this law is able to model with a high degree of accuracy this time for a significant number of patients, it is impossible to predict the exact waiting time of each patient individually. It is therefore necessary to provide a mechanism for synchronizing and correcting the digital twin for each new event brought back from the real world.

An offline digital twin to ensure the prediction function: the purpose of this new function is to very quickly assess the consequences of unexpected events or deviations (arrival of an unscheduled patient in a consultation department, longer than expected operating time in the OR, unfinished biological analysis, etc.) on the operational short term (a few hours at most). It is therefore triggered on the occurrence of certain events that have been previously categorized as critical events. It can also be triggered periodically, at regular intervals, to allow for a projection and an anticipation of the future situation starting from the current situation. To do this, a cloning of the online digital twin makes it possible to have a simulation model whose initial state corresponds to that of the real world. It is this model that will constitute the offline digital twin, i.e. disconnected and asynchronous from the real world, since it is now a question of simulating in accelerated mode up to the targeted horizon in order to have as good a prediction as possible of the near future. This offline digital twin is therefore comparable to a conventional simulator, with the notable difference that it is initialized on the current state of the real world and not on an initial empty state or one obtained after a ramp-up period. Another important distinction is that the random behavior laws and flow management rules of this simulation model must be updated dynamically so that the predictive simulation is based not only on a large amount of historical data but also on much more recent events that may influence short-term behavior. Several replications can therefore be simulated in order to provide results that take into account variability and random events over the target horizon. The results of the simulations are therefore presented in the form of a confidence or prediction interval (e.g. in 2 hours, we can be 90% sure that there will be between 13 and 15 patients in the waiting room, which may be interesting to know since the waiting room only has 14 places). At the end of these replications, this digital twin can therefore predict the state of the real world in the near future or anticipate the effects of an unexpected event that has just occurred. If the results do not show any undesirable effect, there is no need to make any immediate decision to correct anything. If, on the contrary, the results show an effect on an indicator, there may still be time to act to try to counter and mitigate that effect. This is what the optimization or adaptation function will allow.

An offline digital twin to ensure the optimization function: the purpose of this last function is to virtually test different scenarios, making it possible to mitigate, as much as possible the undesirable effects at the targeted horizon, either of an unforeseen event or the evolution of the situation compared to the current state. For this, we will again use an offline digital twin with the same characteristics as the one used for the prediction, namely an initialization on the current state of the real world and a dynamic update of the random distribution laws. But here, the digital twin will be interconnected with an optimization module in order to very quickly simulate different scenarios to try to minimize the undesirable effects detected by the prediction function. Several optimization techniques can be used, from the most basic ones, such as complete experimental designs, to the most advanced ones such as machine learning. Even more than for the prediction function, the main technical and scientific challenge to be met concerns the speed of finding and virtually testing different solutions on the digital twin. The best ones can be proposed to a human "decision-maker" who will choose to apply one of them to the real world. It is therefore not a question of automating such a decision-making process but rather of involving a human in the correction loop. Finally, this optimization function provided by the offline digital twin will make it possible to act in the immediate future to avoid or minimize problems that could occur in the near future.

15.4. Conclusion

This chapter has provided an overview of the main applications of CPS in the health domain (which we have described as HCPS), and more specifically in the production of healthcare. Compared to an industrial system, the healthcare system has the particularity of being extremely sensitive in every sense of the word, since it concerns patients cared for by human actors. This means that its general behavior can be subject to significant variability, and also that it is subject to random events with a strong human factor, which makes CPS particularly relevant. We have highlighted that a very large proportion of HCPS applications concern the medical domain, and that it seems interesting to us to emphasize that, on the contrary, the organization and management of care or healthcare pathways is a dimension that is still relatively unexplored, from both an industrial and a scientific research point of view. From our point of view, this is an area that we encourage young researchers to explore as there are many possibilities. Among these, we have chosen to open up the possibility of an HCPS based on digital twins of patient pathways in hospitals. Such a CPS is intended to provide a true virtual replica of patient flows in a hospital in real time. Numerous technical and scientific obstacles need to be overcome, such as automatic or assisted construction and configuration, as well as the initialization and synchronization of the online digital twin, and decision support for the correction of control variables using optimization and automatic learning algorithms.

15.5. References

Afferni, P., Merone, M., Soda, P. (2018). Hospital 4.0 and its innovation in methodologies and technologies. *2018 IEEE 31st International Symposium on Computer-Based Medical Systems (CBMS)*, Karlstad, Sweden, 333–338, doi: 10.1109/CBMS.2018.00065.

Andellini, M., Fernandez Riesgo, S., Morolli, F., Ritrovato, M., Cosoli, P., Petruzzellis, S., Rosso, N. (2017). Experimental application of business process management technology to manage clinical pathways: A pediatric kidney transplantation follow up case. *BMC Medical Informatics and Decision Making*, 17, 151.

Araghi, S.N., Fontanili, F., Lamine, E., Tancerel, L., Benaben, F. (2018). Monitoring and analyzing patients' pathways by the application of Process Mining, SPC, and I-RTLS. *IFAC-PapersOnLine*, 51(11), 980–985.

ARS (2016). Agence régionale de santé : lexique des parcours de A à Z [Online]. Available at: https://solidarites-sante.gouv.fr/IMG/pdf/2016-01-11_lexique_vf.pdf.

Dey, N., Ashour, A.S., Shi, F., Fong, S.J., Tavares, J.M.R.S. (2018). Medical cyber-physical systems: A survey. *Journal of Medical Systems*, 42, 74.

DREES (2020). Direction de la recherche, des études, de l'évaluation et des statistiques : les dépenses de santé en 2019 en France et perspectives internationales [Online]. Available at: https://drees.solidarites-sante.gouv.fr/publications-documents-de-reference/panoramas-de-la-drees/les-depenses-de-sante-en-2019-resultats.

El Murabet, A., Abtoy, A., Touhafi, A., Tahiri, A. (2020). Ambient assisted living system's models and architectures: A survey of the state of the art. *Journal of King Saud University – Computer and Information Sciences*, 32, 1–10.

Fargeon, V. (2014). La production publique de soins : le secteur hospitalier en mutations. In *Introduction à l'économie de la santé*, Fargeon, V. (ed.). Presses universitaires de Grenoble, Grenoble, France.

GE Healthcare (2018). Command centers in healthcare [Online]. Available at: https://www. gehealthcare.com/feature-article/command-centers-in-healthcare.

GE Healthcare (2021). Command centers: Digital twin [Online]. Available at: https://www.gehccommandcenter.com/digital-twin.

Germain, N. (2012). Contribution à l'ingénierie des systèmes de production de soins dans les pays en voie de développement : vers un système sans murs en Haïti. PhD Thesis, Paul Verlaine University – Metz, France.

Haque, S.A., Aziz, S.M., Rahman, M. (2014). Review of cyber-physical system in healthcare. *International Journal of Distributed Sensor Networks*, 10, 217415.

HAS (2021). Haute autorité de Santé : parcours de soins, questions/réponses [Online]. Available at: https://www.has-sante.fr/upload/docs/application/pdf/2012-05/quest-rep_parcours_de_soins.pdf.

HealthSpaces (2020). The evolution of the healthcare command center [Online]. Available at https://info.healthspacesevent.com/blog/the-evolution-of-the-healthcare-command-center.

Hood, L. (2013). Systems biology and p4 medicine: Past, present, and future. *Rambam Maimonides Medical Journal*, 4(2), e0012. [Online]. Available at: https://doi.org/10.5041/RMMJ.10112.

Insup, L., Sokolsky, O., Sanjian, C., Hatcliff, J., Eunkyoung, J., BaekGyu, K., King, A., Mullen-Fortino, M., Soojin, P., Roederer, A., Venkatasubramanian, K.K. (2012). Challenges and research directions in medical cyber-physical systems. *Proceedings of the IEEE*, 100, 75–90.

Kane, E.M., Scheulen, J.J., Püttgen, A., Martinez, D., Levin, S., Bush, B.A., Huffman, L., Jacobs, M.M., Rupani, H.T., Efron, D. (2019). Use of systems engineering to design a hospital command center. *The Joint Commission Journal on Quality and Patient Safety*, 45, 370–379.

Karakra A., Lamine E., Fontanili F., Lamothe J. (2020). HospiT'Win: A digital twin framework for patients' pathways real-time monitoring and hospital organizational resilience capacity enhancement. *Proceedings of the 9th International Workshop on Innovative Simulation for Healthcare (IWISH 2020)*, 62–71. [Online]. Available at: https://doi.org/10.46354/i3m.2020.iwish.012.

Lanner (2021). Digital twins [Online]. Available at: https://www.lanner.com/en-us/solutions/digital-twin.html.

Li, T., Cao, J., Liang, J., Zheng, J. (2015). Towards context-aware medical cyber-physical systems: Design methodology and a case study. *Cyber-Physical Systems*, 1, 5–23.

Millien, C., Chaput, H., Cavillon, M. (2018). La moitié des rendez-vous sont obtenus en 2 jours chez le généraliste, en 52 jours chez l'ophtalmologiste, Études et Résultats, DREES no. 1085, October [Online]. Available at: https://drees.solidarites-sante.gouv.fr/publications/etudes-et-resultats/la-moitie-des-rendez-vous-sont-obtenus-en-2-jours-chez-le.

Montrose, A. (2013). Développement d'un immunocapteur impédimétrique pour la détection et la quantification d'une sous-population cellulaire : application au diagnostic précoce des infections. PhD Thesis, University of Toulouse, France.

Pang, Z., Yang, G., Khedri, R., Zhang, Y.-T. (2018). Introduction to the special section: Convergence of automation technology, Biomedical Engineering, and Health Informatics Toward the Healthcare 4.0. *IEEE Reviews in Biomedical Engineering*, 11, 249–259.

Rodrigues, J.J.P.C., De Rezende Segundo, D.B., Junqueira, H.A., Sabino, M.H., Prince, R.M., Al-Muhtadi, J., De Albuquerque, V.H.C. (2018). Enabling technologies for the internet of health things. *IEEE Access*, 6, 13129–13141.

SMHS (2020). Hospital command centers [Online]. Available at: https://smhs.gwu.edu/urgentmatters/news/hospital-command-centers.

Tao, F. and Zhang, M. (2019). *Digital Twin Driven Smart Manufacturing*. Academic Press, London [Online]. Available at: https://www.sciencedirect.com/science/article/pii/B9780128176306000138.

WHO (2021). Organisation mondiale de la santé : à propos des systèmes de santé [Online]. Available at: https://www.who.int/healthsystems/about/fr/.

Zhuang, C., Liu, J., Xiong, H. (2018). Digital twin-based smart production management and control framework for the complex product assembly shop-floor. *The International Journal of Advanced Manufacturing Technology*, 96(1–4), 1149–1163.

PART 7

Envisioning the Industrial Cyber-Physical Systems of the Future

PART 7

Envisioning the Industrial
Cyber-Physical Systems
of the Future

16

Ethics and Responsibility of Industrial Cyber-Physical Systems

Sylvie JONAS[1] **and Françoise LAMNABHI-LAGARRIGUE**[2]

[1] Partner Cabinet AGIL'IT, Paris, France
[2] CNRS Emeritus Research Director, Signals and Systems Laboratory,
CentraleSupelec, Université Paris-Saclay, France

16.1. Introduction

A specific legal and ethical approach to cyber-physical systems, *a fortiori* to industrial cyber-physical systems (ICPS), is not yet widespread. However, we note that, on the one hand, the characteristics of these systems allow for parallels with more commonly discussed subjects, such as artificial intelligence (AI), the Internet of Things and robots, and, on the other hand, the new research field of cyber-physical and human systems (CPHS), encompassing ICPS for their social impact, is beginning to address these issues.

First, cyber-physical systems are characterized by, among other things, the collection of a large amount of data via sensors and connectors, strong connectivity and the autonomy of their control systems (see Chapter 1). AI is defined by the European Commission as:

For a color version of all figures in this book, see www.iste.co.uk/cardin/digitalization.zip.

Digitalization and Control of Industrial Cyber-Physical Systems,
coordinated by Olivier CARDIN, William DERIGENT and Damien TRENTESAUX.
© ISTE Ltd 2022.

[...] systems that display intelligent behaviour by analysing their environment and taking actions – with some degree of autonomy – to achieve specific goals.

AI-based systems can be purely software-based, acting in the virtual world (e.g. voice assistants, image analysis software, search engines, speech and face recognition systems) or AI can be embedded in hardware devices (e.g. advanced robots, autonomous cars, drones or Internet of Things applications) (European Commission 2018).

Moreover, the European Commission, in its report of February 19, 2020 (European Commission 2020a), identified the specificities of artificial intelligence, the Internet of Things and robotics, namely: connectivity, autonomy, opacity, complexity of products and systems, and complex value chains. These apply perfectly to ICPS.

Therefore, the use of the term AI in this chapter, as well as references to robotics and related technologies, will be intended to refer to all potential activities of the cyber part of ICPS as defined in Chapter 1.

The resolutions adopted by the European Parliament on October 20, 2020[1] are in line with the above-mentioned report, and the Commission's White Paper of the same day (European Commission 2020b). One of the resolutions aims to recommend a specific civil liability regime for artificial intelligence to the Commission (European Commission 2020a). Another aspect of the resolutions envisages the establishment of a framework for the ethical aspects of artificial intelligence, robotics and related technologies (European Parliament 2020b). Thus, accountability and ethics are at the heart of the Commission's concerns with regard to the growing impact of AI, robotics and related technologies.

Furthermore, in the context of CPHS (Khargonekar and Sampath 2020), the authors introduce a conceptual framework to consider and study the problems related to ethics, from basic research and design to product development and deployment. With the emergence of these new technologies, as an extension of the management and protection of personal data, which is more a political matter with the enactment of laws such as the General Data Protection Regulation

---

1. The third resolution adopted on the same day, on intellectual property rights, will not be considered here.

(GDPR)^2, it is necessary to address these issues from a technical point of view, by proposing robust and secure algorithms. We can note this wish, for example, in Casilli (2020):

> Most current research on the social, political, and economic impacts of artificial intelligences focuses only on the deployment side. In other words, we consider AI 1) assuming it exists, 2) assuming it works, 3) assuming it is already deployed and operational in markets populated by humans. As a result, we sometimes reproduce bad reflexes inherited from the sociology of uses, which lead us to analyze the acceptability of an innovation, without asking ourselves the basic question of its origin.

In order to analyze the problems encountered in more detail, first, the question of ethics will be examined in greater detail (section 16.2), before exploring the question of responsibility more specifically (section 16.3).

16.2. Ethics and ICPS

The European Commission begins its White Paper with a list of the benefits associated with the development of AI, but quickly reminds us that it "also comes with a number of risks, such as opacity of decision-making, discrimination on gender or other grounds, intrusion into our private lives, or use for criminal purposes" (European Commission 2020b, p. 1). In its October 2020 resolution, the Parliament stated that "AI, robotics, and related technologies […] have the potential […] to directly affect all aspects of our societies, including fundamental rights and basic social and economic principles" (European Parliament 2020b). ICPS, which are related AI-enabling technologies, are affected by these concerns.

At the national level, in France the 2018 Villani report "Giving meaning to artificial intelligence" (Villani *et al.* 2018) proposed five pillars on which to build an ethical framework for the development of AI:

– increasing the transparency and audibility of autonomous systems;

– adapting the protection of rights and freedoms with regard to potential abuses linked to the use of machine learning systems;

---

2. Regulation (EU) 2016/679 of the European Parliament and the Council of April 27, 2016, on the protection of individuals with regard to the processing of personal data and on the free movement of such data.

– ensuring that the organizations that deploy and use these systems remain legally responsible for any damage caused by them;

– creating a forum for debate that is plural and open to society, in order to determine what kind of AI we want for our society in a democratic way;

– politicizing issues that are related to technology in general and AI in particular.

These five pillars coincide with the issues identified at the European level. Indeed, European institutions are particularly concerned with issues related to personal data and privacy (section 16.2.1) as well as the design modalities of AI systems (section 16.2.2). These pillars also underlie the conceptual framework introduced by Khargonekar and Sampath (2020) that is summarized in Figure 16.1. This framework has two dimensions: the stage of development, from basic research to mature technologies, and the locus of decision-making, whether individual, corporate or governmental.

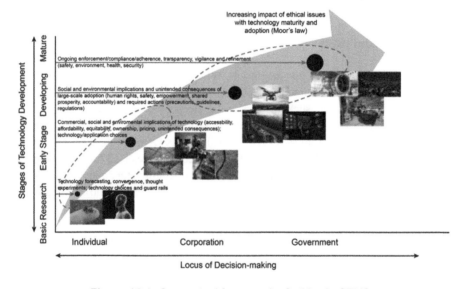

Figure 16.1. *Conceptual framework of ethics in CPHS
(Khargonekar and Sampath 2020)*

16.2.1. *Data management and protection*

The issue of data is central. AI systems require a large amount of data to give satisfactory results. This is particularly the case for ICPS, since their operation is based on capturing data through sensors and connectors and using this data to optimize the operation of the system on an industrial scale. More generally, the European Commission states that "the volume of data produced worldwide is growing rapidly and is expected to increase from 33 zettabytes in 2018 to 175 zettabytes in 2025" (European Commission 2020b, p. 5). However, not all data is necessarily personal. Does this increase in volume necessarily pose a risk to the rights and freedoms of individuals?

On this issue, the Commission first reiterated that "EU fundamental rights legislation (personal data protection, privacy and non-discrimination) [was] intended to apply to AI developers and [...] deployers" (European Commission 2020b, p. 11). The European data protection board (EDPB)[3] has also stated that "the European data protection legal framework is technology neutral and does not hinder the successful adoption of new technologies" (CEPD 2020, Recital 16). However, "data protection legislation only frames artificial intelligence algorithms to the extent that they are based on personal data and their results are directly applicable to individuals" (Villani et al. 2018).

Some authors note that "algorithmic rationality opposes the confinement of personal data to predetermined and fixed purposes, on the one hand, and can lead to 're-identifying' a person from data that taken in isolation are not identifying" (Forest 2017). This raises "the question of the compatibility of data protection regulations with inherently dynamic algorithmic processes" (Forest 2017). The Villani report also identified this issue, considering that "current legislation which is focused on the protection of the individual is not in phase with the logic introduced by these systems, the analysis of a considerable mass of information in order to identify trends and hidden behaviors" (Villani et al. 2018).

16.2.2. Control in the design of algorithms

16.2.2.1. Robustness and safety

Algorithm design itself is an essential subject. Faced with the economic and commercial pressure of software development, developers tend to use "off-the-shelf" techniques, often based on AI, and to program without taking into account essential complementary expertise (e.g. in social sciences). It is necessary to ensure the conditions of robustness and security upstream of the design of algorithms. It is

---

3. "An independent European body, which contributes to the consistent application of data protection rules throughout the European Union, and promotes cooperation between the EU's data protection authorities". Available at: https://edpb.europa.eu/about-edpb/who-we-are_en [Accessed November 2021].

therefore a question of integrating technical solutions in order to deal with the ethical problems that could be caused by software that is not very robust or secure.

These issues are raised, for example, in the European Commission's "Ethical Guidelines for Trustworthy AI". Among the seven recommendations, "Technical robustness and safety [which] include resilience to attacks and security, contingency plans and general safety, accuracy, reliability and reproducibility" (Groupe d'experts indépendants de haut niveau sur l'intelligence artificielle 2019) stands out.

16.2.2.2. Risks related to opacity

When it comes to the opacity of AI systems, finding a balance may seem complicated. Indeed, the strength of current machine learning techniques is that "they do not rely on predefined rules. [...] It is possible to observe the input data [...] and the output data [...], but [...] the inner workings are poorly understood" (Villani *et al.* 2018). Nevertheless, this lack of understanding is too high a risk because if one cannot explain the decisions made by the systems, it will not be possible to identify and/or remedy identified problems, for example, discrimination. Furthermore, "the human tendency to place blind trust in automated decision-making systems" (Mantelero 2019) should be taken into account.

Recommendations related to this issue can be found in the work of the IEEE Global Initiative on Ethics of Autonomous and Intelligent Systems, which recommends:

> that the behavior of autonomous functions should be predictable to their operators, that those creating these technologies understand the implications of their work [and] that designers not only take stands to ensure meaningful human control, but be proactive about providing quality situational awareness to operators and commanders using those systems (IEEE 2017, p. 113).

This need for an approach to the ethics of ICPS at the level of technical development is also suggested, for example, in (Russell 2019): "The standard model – the AI system optimizing a fixed objective – must be replaced. It is simply bad engineering. We need to do a substantial amount of work to reshape and rebuild the foundations of AI", and (Ord 2020, p. 214):

> There are serious concerns about AI entrenching social discrimination, producing mass unemployment, supporting oppressive surveillance, and violating the norms of war. [...] What can you do? [...] Some of the most urgent work today is upstream, at the level of strategy,

coordination, and grant-making […] there will be important work in allocating resources between projects and organizations building and sustaining the community of researchers and developing strategy.

16.2.2.3. *Supervision of "high-risk AI"*

With this in mind, in its White Paper (European Commission 2020b, p. 20), the Commission proposed the introduction of specific obligations for high-risk AI applications. This qualification is based on a combination of two criteria: the AI is employed in a sector where significant risks are to be expected and the specific use of the application may lead to the occurrence of significant risks.

High-risk AI will have to meet specific requirements in terms of "training data; data and record retention; information to be provided; robustness and accuracy; human control [and] specific requirements for AI applications used for given purposes, such as remote biometric identification" (European Commission 2020b, p. 21).

The EDPB, in its opinion on the European Commission's White Paper (CEPD 2020), gave its opinion on this legal framework. The board considers that the criteria for qualifying high-risk AI systems are too restrictive due to their cumulative nature, which would not make it possible to take into account certain infringements of fundamental rights and freedoms of individuals and proposes "to model the Data Protection Impact Assessment (DPIA) regime to AI" (Crichton 2020):

> The EDPB considers […] that some AI applications (such as live facial recognition) interfere with fundamental rights and freedoms to such an extent that they could challenge the very essence of these rights and freedoms [and that] the European Commission should advocate the strict application of the precautionary principle" (CEPD 2020, recital 13)

and that "certain high-risk AI scenarios should be prohibited from the outset" (CEPD 2020, recital 38) in application of this principle.

In its resolution of last October (European Parliament 2020b), the European Parliament largely takes up the principles set out by the Commission in its White Paper.

16.2.2.4. *The need to take ethics into account from the design stage*

The guiding principles of the ethical framework for the development of AI remain centered on a risk-based approach that puts humans at the heart of the governance processes. The assessment of risks related to the development of ICPS and good understanding by the different actors of the functioning of the systems put in place in order to guarantee their control is therefore essential to their implementation.

The need to take into account ethical aspects and the protection of fundamental rights in the development of systems using innovative technologies, which has already been raised by the GDPR, will therefore take on new importance. It will truly be at the heart of the research and industry of the future.

To this end, the design of algorithms and the development of software, which are essential components of ICPS, must be supervised throughout the process by experts in both science and the social and human sciences. Moreover, early in the school curriculum, notions of ethics should be introduced, so that researchers and engineers think, as far upstream as possible, about the impact of ICPS on humans and their environment.

16.3. Liability and ICPS

Although French civil liability law is still based on five articles of the French Civil Code, dating back to 1804, liability regimes have already undergone major changes, particularly as a result of technological developments. Indeed, civil liability, in its most classical acceptation, is based on the existence of a personal fault and is activated by the combination of three conditions: a fault, a damage and a causal link between the two[4]. However, the need to compensate victims "in a maximum of hypotheses" (Marmisse 2002) has gradually taken precedence, which has led, "since [...] the industrial revolution and the appearance of new risks [...] to the development of objective liability" (Le Lamy Droit de la responsabilité 2019), i.e. no-fault liability schemes.

Today, there are liability regimes that have already been specifically designed as a result of technological developments and whose application to ICPS can be envisaged, which will be examined first (section 16.2.1). Nevertheless, certain gaps in the application of these legal regimes remain, which has led us to consider the proposals for their evolution under consideration today (section 16.2.2).

---

4. Articles 1240 and 1241 of the French Civil Code (formerly Articles 1382 and 1383).

16.3.1. *Existing liability regimes applied to ICPS*

Various existing liability regimes are intended to apply to damage caused by ICPS, either through their general scope, such as liability for property (section 16.3.2.1) and liability for defective products (section 16.3.2.2), or, on the other hand, through their sectoral approach (section 16.3.2.3).

16.3.1.1. *Liability for the action of things*

The liability regime for the action of things is objective, based on risk and not fault, i.e. a person may be held liable for damage and ordered to pay damages, for example, even though they have not committed any fault in a personal capacity. Article 1242 of the French Civil Code (formerly Article 1384) sets up this regime in its first paragraph: "One is liable not only for the harm which one causes by one's own action, but also for that which is caused by the action of persons for whom one is responsible, or of things which one has in one's keeping".

The application of this liability regime presupposes the meeting of several conditions: the existence of damage, of a thing, the demonstration of the active role of the thing, and finally the material custody of this thing. It is the custodian of the thing in question who will be considered liable for the damage caused when the conditions are met, custody being defined by case law as *the combination of use, direction and control*. The owner of the thing is presumed to be the custodian, i.e. if they contest this qualification, it will be up to them to prove that the three elements constituting custody had been transferred to a third party.

The question of the corporality of the thing, which is also the subject of doctrinal debate (Signorile 2019), does not seem to pose a problem in the context of a potential application of this regime to cyber-physical systems, since the physical part makes it possible to meet this criterion, even in the presence of a cyber part whose role is central. On the contrary, the issue of the qualification of custodian will be more difficult to decide. *Can a person really be considered to have the use, direction, and control of a thing from the point where decisions can be made autonomously?*

16.3.1.2. *Liability for defective products*

This system, contrary to the French system of product liability[5], is based on a directive of July 25, 1985[6], and is therefore unified at the European level. The text of

---

5. Although similar schemes exist in other European countries.

6. Council Directive 85/374/EEC of July 25, 1985, on the approximation of the laws, regulations, and administrative provisions of the Member States concerning liability for defective products.

the directive specifies that the Member States of the European Union do not have the right to set up another liability regime arising from defective products.

This European directive was transposed into French law in 1998[7] and is now found in Articles 1245 *et seq.* of the French Civil Code (formerly Articles 1386-1 *et seq.*). Like liability for damage to property, this is a strict liability. However, the conditions to be fulfilled in order to invoke liability are slightly different: a product, a defect in this product, its release, a person responsible (the producer, in principle), a form of damage, and a causal link between the defect and the damage.

The grounds for exemption provided for (i.e. the cases in which the producer's liability may be disregarded even though the above conditions are met) raise questions in the context of the application of the regime to industrial cyber-physical systems. These include cases in which the defect arose after the product was released and cases in which the state of scientific and technical knowledge at the time of releasing it did not allow the existence of the defect to be detected. *How should one position oneself in cases where the autonomous control system of an ICPS would have the effect of modifying the characteristics of a product after it has been put into circulation?*

Moreover, *as ICPS are complex products, with multiple actors involved in their production, how can we be sure which producer should bear the ultimate responsibility for product failure?* As the European Commission points out, in relation to the complexity of products, services and the value chain, "the demarcation between products and services is no longer as clear-cut [as it used to be, and] AI applications are often embedded in complex Internet of Things environments, in which different connected devices and services interact" (European Commission 2020b, p. 16). This complexity leads to a potential difficulty in determining the origin of a damage, tracing the person who is responsible, and consequently obtaining redress for victims.

However, as the Court of Justice of the European Union pointed out, in a decision on Sanofi Pasteur's hepatitis B vaccine, to make it:

> excessively difficult [or even] impossible to hold the producer liable [...] would disregard certain objectives pursued by that directive [...], in particular [...], *that of ensuring a fair distribution of the risks inherent in modern technical production between the victim and the producer [and] that of protecting the safety and health of consumers*

---

7. Law no. 98-389 of May 19, 1998, on liability for defective products.

(Court of Justice of the European Union CJEU 2017, recitals 31 and 32, emphasis authors' own).

Moreover, the uncertainty surrounding the qualification of the producer for complex products creates legal uncertainty for the actors in the production chain. Not being able to foresee whether, and if so, under what conditions, one can be held liable, or how this liability will be distributed between the different actors involved, can be a brake on innovation, as the risk taken in the development of certain product components cannot be precisely determined in advance.

16.3.1.3. *Sectoral liability regimes*

Technical developments and the increasing specialization of different fields of activity have led to the emergence of sector-specific liability regimes. This phenomenon of sectoral regulation limits the impact of an overall reflection on the consequences of the development of new technologies in general and of ICPS in particular. Indeed, sectoral regulations usually have the effect of excluding the application of more general regimes (notably those described above).

This is, for example, the case in the medical field, where strict regulations concerning the safety of medical devices exist and will be applied to ICPS used in this sector. Moreover, limits have already been set regarding AI applications in health, due to the reluctance of the majority of patients (Tran *et al.* 2019), such as the need for free and informed consent of the person concerned (Comité Consultatif National d'Ethique 2018).

Beyond the specificity of the sectoral regimes, proposals for the evolution of the liability regimes have emerged to globally grasp the liability issues in connection with the development of new technologies.

16.3.2. *Proposals for changes in liability regimes*

Initially, the establishment of a specific legal personality for autonomous systems and, by extension, for ICPS, was envisaged (section 16.2.3.1), but the idea has now been set aside and European institutions are now in favor of a specific liability regime (section 16.2.3.2).

16.3.2.1. *The rejected option of a legal personality*

In the early stages of reflection on the regulation of the liability of AI systems, the question of the establishment of a specific legal personality was debated. These questions are likely to be extended to cyber-physical systems, since it is the autonomy of AI that raises the question, an element that also characterizes the control system of ICPS.

Some authors have proposed, for example, the establishment of a specific status associated with a patrimony of appropriation, by comparing the situation of robots to that of slaves in Ancient Roman law (Katz 2008). Others proposed an adaptation according to the typology of the robot concerned, with a distinction between cases in which the aim would be to prevent the robot's actions, as is the case for children, and those in which the robot would have its own responsibility (Pagallo 2011).

In a resolution of February 16, 2017, the European Parliament even asked the Commission: "to examine, evaluate, and take into account [...] all possible legal solutions, such as [...] the creation, in time, of a specific legal personality for robots" (European Parliament 2017).

The idea was finally discarded. In the latest work from European institutions, it is clearly stated that there is no need to create a legal personality for autonomous systems, as the damage they might cause can and should be attributed to a pre-existing person (Expert Group on Liability and New Technologies 2019).

This is in line with the objective recalled by the European Commission in its White Paper on AI to "ensure a level of protection equal to that enjoyed by victims of damage caused by traditional technologies" (European Commission 2020b, p. 20), regardless of the origin of the damage.

The establishment of a liability specific to autonomous systems could have had the effect of limiting the possibility of victims obtaining compensation, either because of the complexity of implementing this liability or because of the absence/limited nature of the assets to be claimed.

16.3.2.2. *The choice of setting up a specific regime*

In line with the proposals in the report included in the Commission's White Paper, the European Parliament adopted a resolution containing recommendations on a civil liability regime for artificial intelligence (European Parliament 2020a). The European Commission is expected to submit a proposal for horizontal regulation, without providing a timescale for this purpose (European Commission 2021).

Following the logic of liability for defective products, the regime would apply to damage caused by an AI system throughout the European Union, whether or not a contract has been concluded. The regime thus transcends the distinction made in French law between tort and contract.

A new qualification is created, that of "operator", which designates the person who will be responsible for the AI system. The qualification is based on three criteria:

– the decision to use the AI system, which goes further than the producer concept currently prevailing in product liability;

– the exercise of control[8] over the risk arising from the use of the AI system;

– taking advantage of the use of the AI system.

A fundamental dichotomy is then established for the implementation of the regime between:

– on the one hand, high-risk AI systems, for which strict liability would apply, i.e. it would not be possible for the operator to avoid liability even in the absence of fault on their part;

– on the other hand, other intelligent systems, for which a simple presumption of liability would apply; this presumption could therefore be reversed, i.e. the operator could avoid liability if they proved that they had not committed any fault.

This system would make it possible to go beyond the product/service distinction, which may pose a problem in certain respects in the context of the application of liability for defective products at the European level or for damage to property in French law. Moreover, it would make it possible to engage the liability of certain actors who could not be qualified as producers or custodians under the current regulations.

However, while the desire for a common European regime is commendable, especially since "the risk of *law shopping* is high" (Galbois-Lehalle 2021) in this area, its scope could be limited due to the existence of sectoral regulations (see above) (James 2020).

---

8. Article 3(g) of the proposed regulation defines "control" as "any action by an operator that influences the operation of an AI system and, therefore, the extent to which the operator exposes third parties to potential risks associated with the operation and functioning of the AI system; these actions may affect the operation at any stage, determining inputs, outputs, or outcomes, or may modify specific functions or processes within the AI system; the extent to which these aspects of the operation of the AI system are determined by the action depends on the level of influence exerted by the operator on the risk associated with the operation and functioning of the AI system", Article 3(g) of the European Parliament resolution of 20 October 2020 with recommendations to the Commission on a civil liability regime for artificial intelligence (2020/2014 (INL)).

16.4. References

Casilli, A. (2020). Qu'est-ce qu'une intelligence artificielle "réellement éthique" ? In *Les Cahiers de TESaCo n°1*, Andler, D. (ed.). [Online]. Available at: https://academiesciencesmoralesetpolitiques.fr/wp-content/uploads/2021/06/Les-Cahiers-de-TESaCo-n%C2%B01.pdf.

CEPD (2020). Avis 4/2020 sur le Livre blanc de la Commission européenne. Recital 16.

Comité Consultatif National d'Ethique (2018). Avis n°129, Contribution du Comité consultatif national d'éthique à la révision de la loi de bioéthique 2018–2019.

Court of Justice of the European Union (CJEU) (2017). Judgment of the Court (Second Chamber) of 21 June 2017. N. W and Others v Sanofi Pasteur MSD SNC and Others. Case C-621/15, Recitals 31 and 32.

Crichton, C. (2020). Intelligence artificielle : avis du CEPD sur le Livre blanc de la Commission. *Dalloz actualité*, 17 July [Online]. Available at: https://www.dalloz-actualite.fr/flash/intelligence-artificielle-avis-du-cepd-sur-livre-blanc-de-commission [Accessed 12 January 2022].

Dalloz (2021). Etudes – Dictionnaire permanent Santé, bioéthique, biotechnologie.

European Commission (2018). Communication, COM (2018) 237 final, L'intelligence artificielle pour l'Europe, 25 April [Online]. Available at: https://ec.europa.eu/futurium/en/system/files/ged/ai_hleg_definition_of_ai_18_december_1.pdf.

European Commission (2020a). Rapport de la commission au parlement européen, au conseil et au comité économique et social européen. Rapport sur les conséquences de l'intelligence artificielle, de l'internet des objets et de la robotique sur la sécurité et la responsabilité, 19 February 2020.

European Commission (2020b). Livre Blanc sur l'intelligence artificielle, 19 February 2020.

European Commission (2021). Shaping Europe's digital future. Policy, Artificial Intelligence, next policy and regulatory steps on AI [Online]. Available at: https://ec.europa.eu/digital-single-market/en/artificial-intelligence.

European Parliament (2017). Résolution du 16 février 2017 contenant des recommandations à la Commission concernant des règles de droit civil sur la robotique (2015/2103(INL)), 59.

European Parliament (2020a). Résolution du 20 octobre 2020 contenant des recommandations à la Commission sur un régime de responsabilité civile pour l'intelligence artificielle (2020/2014(INL)).

European Parliament (2020b). Résolution du 20 octobre 2020 contenant des recommandations à la Commission concernant un cadre pour les aspects éthiques de l'intelligence artificielle, de la robotique et des technologies connexes (2020/2012(INL)).

Expert Group on Liability and New Technologies (2019). Liability for artificial intelligence and other emerging digital technologies. Report, Publications Office. doi: 10.2838/25362.

Forest, D. (2017). La régulation des algorithmes, entre éthique et droit. *Revue Lamy Droit de l'Immatériel (RLDI)*, 137.

Galbois-Lehalle, D. (2021). Responsabilité civile pour l'intelligence artificielle selon Bruxelles : une initiative à saluer, des dispositions à améliorer. *Recueil Dalloz*, 2(7891e).

Groupe d'experts indépendants de haut niveau sur l'intelligence artificielle (2019). Commission européenne, Direction générale des réseaux de communication, du contenu et des technologies, Lignes directrices en matière d'éthique pour une IA digne de confiance, Publications Office. doi : 10.2759/54071.

IEEE (2017). Global initiative on ethics of autonomous and intelligent systems, reframing autonomous weapons systems. Global Risk Report, World Economic Forum, Geneva.

James, T. (2020). Recommandation à la Commission sur un régime de responsabilité civile pour l'intelligence artificielle par la Commission JURI du Parlement européen. *Revue Lamy Droit de l'Immatériel (RLDI)*, 174.

Katz, A. (2008). Intelligent agents and internet commerce in Ancient Rome. SCL [Online]. Available at: https://www.scl.org/articles/1095-intelligent-agents-and-internet-commerce-in-ancient-rome [Accessed 12 January 2022].

Khargonekar, P.P. and Sampath, M. (2020). A framework for ethics in cyber-physical-human systems. *IFAC-PapersOnLine*, 53(2), 17008–17015.

Le Lamy Droit de la responsabilité (2019). 226-11 Objectivation croissante de la responsabilité civile, updated October 2019. Partie 2. Le droit commun de la responsabilité civile – Le fait personnel – Étude 226 : La faute délictuelle et quasi-délictuelle.

Mantelero, A. (2019). Intelligence artificielle et protection des données : enjeux et solutions possibles. Report, Comité consultatif de la convention pour la protection des personnes à l'égard du traitement automatisé des données à caractère personnel.

Marmisse, A. (2002). Le rôle de la doctrine dans l'élaboration et l'évolution de la responsabilité civile délictuelle au XXème siècle. LPA 188. Doctrine, PA200218901.

Ord, T. (2020). *The Precipice, Existential Risk and the Future of Humanity*. Hachette, Paris.

Pagallo, U. (2011). Killers, fridges, and slaves: A legal journey in robotics. *AI & Society*, 26, 347–354.

Russell, S. (2019). *Human Compatible, AI and the Problem of Control*. Viking, New York.

Signorile, A. (2019). Vers une responsabilité du fait des choses incorporelles à l'aune du numérique ? *Revue Lamy Droit de l'Immatériel*, 159.

Tran, V.T., Riveros, C., Ravaud, P. (2019). Patients' views of wearable devices and AI in healthcare: Findings from the ComPaRe e-cohort. *NPJ Digital Medicine*, 2(53) [Online]. Available at: https://doi.org/10.1038/s41746-019-0132-y.

Villani, C., Schoenauer, M., Bonnet, Y., Berthet, C., Cornut, A.C., Levin, F., Rondepierre, B. (2018). Donner un sens à l'intelligence artificielle : pour une stratégie nationale et européenne. Public report.

17

Teaching and Learning ICPS: Lessons Learned and Best Practices

Bilal AHMAD[1], Freeha AZMAT[1], Armando Walter COLOMBO[2] and Gerrit JAN VELTINK[2]

[1] University of Warwick, Coventry, United Kingdom
*[2] Institute for Industrial Informatics, Automation and Robotics (I2AR),
University of Applied Sciences Emden/Leer, Emden, Germany*

17.1. Introduction

Industry is in the midst of reshaping modern manufacturing by employing digital technologies. A majority of products are not solely physical entities anymore, but also have cyber equivalents (Zabasta *et al.* 2018). Therefore, a workforce with interdisciplinary skill sets covering a broad range of technologies encompassing hardware, software and systems engineering to invent, design, build and deploy industrial cyber-physical systems (ICPS) is increasingly essential (Stankovic *et al.* 2017). Although ICPS have been integrated into industrial ecosystems (Colombo *et al.* 2016, 2017), there is still much to be achieved in the domain of education, training and attracting young talents to this area (Colombo *et al.* 2015).

Building a curriculum for ICPS-oriented professionals generates teaching and learning challenges in a multidisciplinary and cultural engineering setting (Salas *et al.* 2009; Johnston 2013; Young 2015; Pechmann *et al.* 2019). The challenges to

For a color version of all figures in this book, see www.iste.co.uk/cardin/digitalization.zip.

Digitalization and Control of Industrial Cyber-Physical Systems,
coordinated by Olivier CARDIN, William DERIGENT and Damien TRENTESAUX.

understand the digital transformation migrating traditional industrial ecosystems into ICPS are hard to grasp not only for experts and practitioners, but even more so for students. This is still the case even though the concepts and standards (e.g. according to Leitão *et al.* (2020) for ICPS) have become more defined and elaborated. A wide range of skills, knowledge and competencies is required to understand, deal with and build up such ICPS. Since it is an evolving field, its knowledge base is constantly evolving and changing. As a result, lecturers in this field have to update their knowledge base constantly. Moreover, since digitalization is a cross-sectional technology, not only single subjects need to be updated; as such, the curricula of universities also need to adapt to cross-disciplinary requirements (Pechmann *et al.* 2019). At the same time, while requirements for the new cyber-physical world are defined and mature, the scope of curricula stays limited by a defined workload (EHEA 2018). More room is needed for new teaching content, and consequently, other content must vanish. When transitioning from one technology phase to the next (e.g. third to fourth industrial revolution), "old" content that is not yet completely outdated is still required, and should not be eliminated from the curricula. In addition, the basics of various engineering fields and other disciplines such as business administration and informatics are still necessary. At the same time, there is an increased need for interfacing knowledge and competencies of other disciplines as the new cyber-physical world develops further. The challenge is to find a way to integrate the changing knowledge base into the curricula and, at the same time, build up the capabilities of students (and teaching staff) to work in and with interdisciplinary teams (Filho *et al.* 2018; Colombo *et al.* 2021).

To configure an entire curriculum on industrial cyber-physical systems, it needs to be designed with its didactical, social, technological and business implications in mind (Mäkiö-Marusik *et al.* 2019a; Wermann *et al.* 2019), including the structural, functional and organizational interdependencies between the cyber and physical aspects, as well as the integration of humans in the ecosystem. This interdependence is more evident if the "digitalization process" is formally performed following a standardized industrial digitalization framework. In this context and in accordance with the background provided in Chapter 1, we describe a bachelor-level curriculum based on the recommendations from the Institute of Apprenticeships & Technical Education (UK) in section 17.2 (as shown in Figure 17.1). In section 17.3, we describe a master-level curriculum using the RAMI4.0 specifications (DIN 2016) as a formal basis for teaching and learning ICPS.

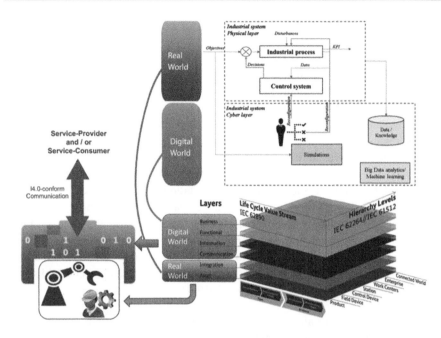

Figure 17.1. *Interdependencies between the cyber and physical aspects of an ICPS according to RAMI4.0*

17.2. University of Warwick – Bachelor-level curriculum

Aiming to bridge the gap between the realization of Industry 4.0 and educational organizations, the Warwick Manufacturing Group (WMG) at the University of Warwick developed a degree apprenticeship in Digital Technology Solutions (DTS), providing specialization in three pathways (software engineering, data analysis and network engineering) in a four-year program. The curriculum is designed in close collaboration with the industry, where all modules are developed from scratch, taking into account business requirements and adhering to: (1) the Digital & Technology Solutions Standard, published by the Institute of Apprenticeship & Technical Education, as well as benchmarks of (2) the Institute of Engineering & Technology (IET), (3) British Computer Society (BCS) and (4) Quality Assurance Agency (QAA). Students will study 12 core modules in years one and two, which sets the foundation to specialize in one of the aforementioned pathways by learning a combination of core and elective modules in years three and four.

17.2.1. ICPS education: Fusion of computer science and engineering

In this section, we discuss the knowledge, skills and behavior required by ICPS professionals, whose role lies in the domain of both engineering and computer science. There are three main facets that construct the engineering profession: (a) scientific principles, (b) mathematics and (c) realization. The scientific principles are the foundation of all engineering degrees, which are further translated to models using mathematical language. The realization aspect is very important when engineers use creative abilities to implement an invention which has social and commercial value (QAA 2019b). On the contrary, the computing discipline deals with the design and exploitation of computation and computer technology. Professionals in computing are expected to have skills in three key areas (a) computing-related cognitive skills, such as computational thinking, problem solving, design and modeling of computer-based systems, (b) computing-related practical skills, such as the ability to design and construct secure and usable computer systems, and (c) generic skills for employability, such as intellectual skills, self-management and team working (QAA 2019a).

The DTS curriculum aims to fill in the missing gap by not only including the modules related to programming, but also incorporating modules related to real-time operating systems and the IoT. Security is a major concern for most of the cyber-enabled technologies in Industry 4.0. Thus, the DTS course has a module that focuses on cybersecurity, which gives an advantage to DTS graduates over other disciplines. In fact, to make Industry 4.0 a reality, the joint aspects of all the aforementioned areas belonging to cyber-physical systems engineering should be studied together in an integrated manner, instead of in individual established fields. This interdisciplinary and joint approach helps students to develop critical competencies for future developments in Industry 4.0 compliant businesses. Consequently, the key factors in the success of these intelligent businesses are the skills and qualifications of their workforce.

However, with the fourth industrial revolution, the future workforce, who are today's students, will encounter a more globalized, automated, virtualized and networked world (Motyl et al. 2017). Graduates are exposed to industrial edge and cloud computing, which integrates communication, computation and data storage resources to deliver real-time applications (Cheng et al. 2018). For example, the increasing availability of data and the IoT (Internet of Things) helps to perform predictive maintenance using machine learning principles (Da Xu et al. 2014; Susto et al. 2014). Computer science and engineering disciplines are coming closer, but with changes in the requirements from both a functional and a non-functional perspective. For instance, the time delay to perform a computation is a performance issue in a general-purpose computer, while it may lead to incorrect control behavior in ICPS.

Hecklau *et al.* (2017) and Nafea and Toplu (2021) categorized the competencies in Industry 4.0 into four main groups: (a) technical competencies, (b) methodological competencies, (c) social competencies and (d) personal competences. Evidently, soft skills play a vital role in developing a holistic mindset for a graduate, who can think broadly and integrate interdisciplinary knowledge. We discuss the pedagogical principles of delivering DTS modules in section 17.2.3, where we cover how Industry 4.0 competencies have been mapped to each teaching phase.

17.2.2. Key enabling technologies in the ICPS curriculum

The DTS degree covers the key enabling technologies (KETs) of Industry 4.0 such as IoT, cloud networking, data analytics, artificial intelligence, vision and processing, cyber-security, real-time operating systems and control systems. This integration of the computer science and engineering discipline is providing apprentices with the minimum required knowledge of both the cyber and physical aspects of the system. For example, a specialization in the data analytics stream provides apprentices with the knowledge to understand how to collect, process and use the data generated in a digitalized industrial environment. As a result, students will be able to develop technology-enabled solutions for both internal and external customers, in a range of areas including software, business and systems analysis, data and information analysis and network infrastructure. This will enable businesses to develop new products and services and increase an organization's productivity using digital technologies. The students of the DTS course will be based predominately in their companies, attending the University of Warwick for six weeks in a year. To equip apprentices with the required soft skills, modules like personal skills for professional excellence, information business management operations and agile project management have been included in the DTS curriculum, which will prepare apprentices to understand the significance of work culture and teamwork, and acquire the skills to manage multidisciplinary projects.

17.2.3. Pedagogical principles: teaching ICPS modules

In this section, we discuss a DTS module (i.e., Internet of Things) as an example and the pedagogical principles behind its design and delivery. The main aim of the module is to introduce the concept, implementation and applications of digitally enabled objects that can transfer data over a network, without requiring human-to-human or human-to-computer interaction. This module is typically taught in the following four phases:

Research and reflection: in this phase, students are provided with videos, research papers and/or articles, so that they can get an initial idea of the forthcoming module and its applications in industry. This phase instills inquiry-based learning in individuals as they are encouraged to look around and do their research. This phase plays a role in developing Industry 4.0 required competencies, such as independent learning, research skills and motivation to learn about state-of-the-art knowledge and technologies.

Work-based learning: as our students are working in industries, they are encouraged to reflect and relate the pre-module activities to their workplace. In this way, students are able to bring their experiences into the classroom, which adds to the knowledge of their peers. This phase plays a role in developing Industry 4.0 required competencies, such as flexibility, language skills, communication skills, teamwork skills and the ability to work under pressure.

Lectures and labs: this is a didactic teaching phase that is composed of lectures and labs. Some of the lectures are delivered on campus, while others are pre-recorded. The pre-recorded lectures give students a chance to study at their own pace and instill independent learning. The lab sessions are delivered via live online session, where students are divided into groups and work on small problems, which are supervised by a tutor. This approach encourages collaboration between individuals. This phase plays a role in developing Industry 4.0 expertise, such as technical skills, process understanding, coding skills, problem-solving and analytic skills.

Project-based learning: in this phase, a group of students applies the knowledge attained from lectures, labs, independent research and reflections to a project in the workplace. This is a summative assessment and forms the part of authentic learning where students apply their theoretical knowledge to the workplace. This phase plays a role in developing negotiation skills, sustainable mindset, compliance, conflict resolution, decision-making, entrepreneurial thinking and efficiency.

17.3. University of Applied Sciences Emden/Leer – master's-level curriculum

The University of Applied Sciences Emden/Leer in Germany has been offering a master's program in Industrial Informatics since the early 2000s. In the following sections, we will describe our experiences with the redesigned ICPS-based curriculum that came into effect in 2017 (DAAD 2021).

17.3.1. *ICPS education: fusion of computer science, electrical and mechatronics engineering*

As shown in Figure 17.1, RAMI4.0 is a three-dimensional model that formally supports specifying the digitalization and Internet-based networking of any kind of industrial asset, that is, "migrating an asset into an I4.0 component" (see vertical dimension). This asset is positioned in an enterprise reference architecture specified according to the standard ISA'95 (IEC 62264) for discrete production, or ISA'88 (IEC 61512) for continuous and batch production (see transversal dimension). The business applications (vertical dimension: level 6) and associated functions (vertical dimension: level 5) of the digitalized asset will have to be positioned within the adequate phases along the value stream and lifecycle of that asset (IEC 62890). Moreover, in order to effectively design and implement RAMI4.0-compliant digitalized and networked assets, that is, cyber-physical components and systems or I4.0 components, there is a concrete set of engineering methods and technologies that must be acquired to successfully specify the asset administration shell (AAS), shown in the left part of Figure 17.1 (see also Platform-I40 2020).

Following this framework, the essential knowledge, skills and behaviors (KSBs) for ICPS engineers are closely related to:

1) learning the assets, that is, the components and systems of the whole industrial ecosystem belonging to one or more of the hierarchical levels specified by the IEC 62264 (ISA'95)/IEC 61512 (ISA'88) reference architecture. Each of these components is labeled as "Asset" by the RAMI4.0 specification. It is important to identify the position of each component, on either the operational technology (OT) or the information technology (IT) side of the technological and functional border existing within those industrial standards specifications (Givehchi *et al.* 2017);

2) learning the digitalization and networking process to migrate any asset into an "I4.0 component", a digitalized "Thing" or a "Building Block" of the architecture behind the digitalized solution. The assets are then digitalized in such a way that the physical and digital (cyber) parts are specified and implemented in six separated but integrated layers, following the vertical dimension of the RAMI4.0 specification. The assets have been digitalized in such a way that they can be put together in an Internet-based communication, control and information network;

3) learning the digitalization and networking process in such a way that physical and digital (cyber) parts, acting as one unit, expose their functions as "Services" for to be consumed by other digitalized Assets (layer 6 of the RAMI4.0-vertical dimension). Moreover, each digitalized asset can also consume "Services" exposed by other digitalized assets of the same network, along the asset lifecycle, following

the specifications of the IEC 62890. By performing this service-oriented interaction, applications and businesses based on the Internet-of-Services paradigm become a reality and the digitalized "Things" are able to achieve common business objectives that they cannot achieve as an individual component.

Figure 17.2 shows a compilation of the most essential knowledge domains supporting the basic profile of professionals dealing with the broad area of industrial cyber-physical systems.

At the University of Applied Sciences Emden/Leer in Germany, based on experience with teaching digitalization for over 10 years, different teaching methods have been developed and applied (Wermann *et al.* 2015; Zarte *et al.* 2016; Götting *et al.* 2017). The learning concept presented here is designed to quickly integrate the latest results in research and development on ICPS in the university curricula to fulfill the demands of the different stakeholder groups (e.g. students, industry), while operating on the frameset of curricula boundaries and feasibility restrictions, such as the students' and teaching staff's workload.

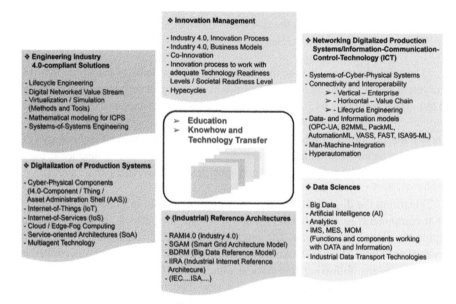

Figure 17.2. *Essential knowledge domains for industrial cyber-physical systems*

The educational approach for "ICPS Knowhow and Technology Transfer" is targeted to fulfill a set of requirements from different stakeholders with partly opposing goals. Remark: stakeholders are, for example, students as direct customers and learners, teaching staff supporting students in their learning journey and creating the right environment; education ministries and university institutions for setting the boundaries for curricula within the EHEA framework (EHEA 2018; Pechmann *et al.* 2019).

17.3.2. Key enabling technologies in the ICPS curriculum

The key enabling technologies (KETs) and key enabling features of the Master Industrial Informatics with Specialization in industrial cyber-physical systems are first a study body composed of two major graduate programs (i.e., Bachelor in Electrical Engineering and Bachelor in Computer Science) and, second, the use of a Digital Factory for learning digitalization through hands-on practical training. The Digital Factory, following the concept of the Learning Factory (Abele 2016), is characterized by, inter alia, "industrial processes that are authentic, include multiple assets, and comprise digitalized technical, as well as business and organizational aspects".

From the RAMI4.0 perspective, an engineer in Industrial Informatics (II) needs a multidisciplinary formation and has to acquire an adequate innovation capability that allows the integration of knowledge from very disjointed domains. A mapping between the essential skills to be acquired, different potential roles of the engineers and modules from the curriculum is shown in Figure 17.3.

Roles	Industrial Cyber-Physical Systems	Digitalization and Virtualization of ICPS	Robotic Systems	Industrial Data Transport Technology	Engineering ICPS	Analytics and Mathematics	Innovation Processes for ICPS	Skills
Industrial System Architect	●	●	●		●			specify logic, physical and technical architectures
Electronics & Control Engineer	●	●	●					specify control functions and interfaces
Communication Engineer	●	●		●				define communication systems
Software Engineer	●	●				●		specify AAS and algorithms
Computer Engineer		●		●				design computer systems
Information Engineer	●	●		●	●	●		design information systems
Technical Management Engineer	●	●	●		●		●	manage business applications
Business Specialist		●					●	manage IP strategies
Mechatronics Engineer	●	●	●		●			design digitalized assets

Figure 17.3. *Potential roles and skills mapped onto modules of the II curriculum*

Figure 17.4 shows the set of knowledge domains that has been proposed by the authors in order to create a new curriculum for a master's degree in Industrial Informatics, with a special focus on industrial cyber-physical systems and Industry 4.0 solutions (DAAD 2021). In this sense, the DIN Specification 91345 RAMI4.0 has been selected as a blueprint for building the curriculum for the master's degree. Essentially, there is a concrete mapping of core modules of that three-semester master's program into the three dimensions of 3D RAMI4.0. The curricular activities are organized into at least four levels as follows:

Mandatory courses: compulsory courses required for the master's degree in industrial cyber-physical systems, distributed in two consecutive semesters.

Optional courses: optional courses of which a minimum amount of credits must be met, also distributed in two consecutive semesters, as shown in Figure 17.4. The list of compulsory optional courses aims to be a starting point, which can be extended, maintaining the rigorous requirements and academic excellence established, both in terms of content and academic responsibility.

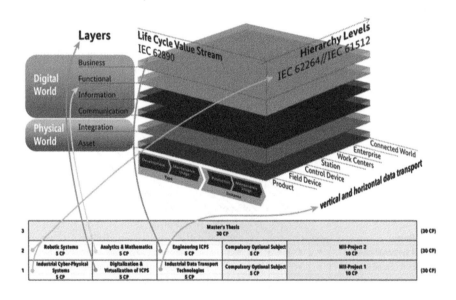

Figure 17.4. *The curriculum and its relation to RAMI4.0*

Project: the aspirant to the master's degree has to carry out one project per semester in the first two semesters, in an industrial environment or in the laboratories of a university under the teachers' and industrialists' supervision, allowing students to apply the acquired knowledge in a real industrial environment. Within a project, the candidates for the master's degree carry out research (30%) and development (70%) that allows them to (1) make a first familiarization with the practical aspects related to the understanding, development, implementation and/or operation of CPS, (2) implement research and innovation methodologies and (3) proceed to write scientific and technical reports.

Accredited mentoring and research activities: the aspirants to the master's degree, with the guidance of their directors, should choose to deepen their knowledge of the theoretical and practical topics that will give sustenance to their work that they will do in their thesis, which will be carried out in the third and last semester of the curriculum.

17.3.3. Pedagogical principles: teaching ICPS modules

The following principles are based on experiences and a set of considerable lessons learned by teaching digitalization of industrial systems (Colombo *et al.* 2020; DAAD 2021). Different teaching and learning methods have been developed further and applied, focusing particularly on four major steps: (i) linking theory learned in the classroom with the analysis of published research results, screening of industrial patent applications complemented with acquisition and analysis of requirements of the manufacturing industry, done by the students, (ii) transferring this acquired knowledge to prototype innovations and implementations in a digital factory model of the university, performed by teams of two to three students, (iii) transferring some of the prototypes and acquired foreground know-how to the industry and (iv) disseminating the research and innovation results performed by the students of the master's in Industrial Informatics, in an international context (see, for example, Haskamp *et al.* 2017; Porrmann *et al.* 2017; Mäkiö-Marusik *et al.* 2018; Mäkiö-Marusik *et al.* 2019b).

As an example, and following these pedagogical principles, the qualification goals of the module industrial cyber-physical systems are: *to understand and work with standardized industrial frameworks covering the "digitalization" of industrial systems based on the ICPS technologies.* Moreover, since the same industrial trend is also evident in other domains, for example energy, healthcare, transportation, robotics and smart cities, ICPS are the backbone, the enabler of digitalization, connectivity, composability and interoperability between those seemingly disparate domains and application sectors.

The content of the ICPS module conduces to learn a set of technologies and architectural patterns to enable the specification, implementation and operation of industrial cyber-physical systems under the DIN Specification 91345 (RAMI4.0) and the Industrial Internet-Reference Architecture (IIRA) standards. In this context, the major specifications of the (i) enterprise standard architectures PERA, ISA'88, ISA'95 (IEC 62264, IEC 61512), (ii) Lifecycle and Value Stream (IEC 62890) and (iii) Asset Administration Shell (AAS) technology have to be learned; complemented with studies and analysis (technology and trend screening) of currently implemented industrial solutions for ICPS.

Based on the technological concepts of ICPS and IoTS (Internet of Things and Services), the students studying the ICPS modules can understand the characteristics of the assets and learn the engineering steps required to digitalize the hardware and software components of an industrial enterprise. Students will be able to analyze those components ("digitalized things" or "I4.0 components") under various perspectives, such as data maps, functional descriptions, communications behavior, hardware/assets or business processes. Furthermore, students will be able to create a digital copy (digital twin) of industrial components and systems, focusing on data and value streams, and virtualize it, completing their formation with theoretical and practical knowledge of prototyping, specifying, developing, implementing and operating asset administration shells in a digitalized industrial ecosystem.

17.4. Conclusion

Industrial cyber-physical systems (ICPS) forge the core of real-world digitalized and networked industrial infrastructures. Although the concepts behind the engineering methods, tools and technologies for ICPS have become more defined, elaborated and mature, the challenges for learning, teaching, applying, working and living with them, that is, living in an Industry 4.0 environment, are hard to grasp, for experts, industrialists and practitioners, but even more so for students.

In this chapter, inspired by the experience and lessons learned by the authors, a set of essential requirements to configure and implement a curriculum on ICPS, for both graduate and postgraduate study programs, has been introduced to the reader. In this context, we then described a bachelor-level curriculum offered at the University of Warwick (UK) and a masters-level curriculum implemented at the University of Applied Sciences Emden/Leer (Germany). In both cases, a recommendable teaching best practice is to have didactical and pedagogical, social, technological and business implications in mind, including a deep understanding of the structural, functional and organizational interdependencies between the cyber and physical aspects, as well as the integration of the human in the ecosystem, when foundational and expert knowledge has to be transferred to the future workforce through the integration of multidisciplinary subjects. Finally, we confirm that this interdependence, as well as the adequate human integration in the ICPS, is more evident if the curriculum is formally mapped into a standardized industrial digitalization framework, such as the DIN Specification 91345 (RAMI4.0).

Digitalization and networking technologies are continuously evolving, as well as the engineering methods for dealing with the continuously increasing amount of ICPS, which is adding the requirement for a continuous actualization of the ICPS curriculum.

17.5. References

Abele, E. (2016). Learning factory. In *CIRP Encyclopedia of Production Engineering*, Produ, T.I.A., Laperrière, L., Reinhart, G. (eds). Springer, Berlin, Heidelberg.

Cheng, B., Zhang, J., Hancke, G.P., Karnouskos, S., Colombo, A.W. (2018). Industrial cyberphysical systems: Realizing cloud-based big data infrastructures. *IEEE Industrial Electronics Magazine*, 12(1), 25–35.

Colombo, A.W., Schleuter, D., Kircher, M. (2015). An approach to qualify human resources supporting the migration of SMEs into an Industrie4.0-compliant company infrastructure. *IECON 2015 – 41st Annual Conference of the IEEE Industrial Electronics Society*, 003761–003766.

Colombo, A.W., Karnouskos, S., Shi, Y., Yin, S., Kaynak, O. (2016). Industrial cyber–physical systems [scanning the issue]. *Proceedings of the IEEE*, 104(5), 899–903.

Colombo, A.W., Karnouskos, S., Kaynak, O., Shi, Y., Yin, S. (2017). Industrial cyberphysical systems: A backbone of the fourth industrial revolution. *IEEE Industrial Electronics Magazine*, 11(1), 6–16.

Colombo, A.W., Veltink, G.J., Roa, J., Caliusco, M.L. (2020). Learning industrial cyber-physical systems and industry 4.0-compliant solutions. *IEEE Conference on Industrial Cyberphysical Systems (ICPS)*, 384–390.

Colombo, A.W., Karnouskos, S., Hanisch, C. (2021). Engineering human-focused industrial cyber-physical systems in Industry 4.0 context. *Royal Academy, Philosophical Transactions A*, 16 August.

Da Xu, L., He, W., Li, S. (2014). Internet of Things in industries: A survey. *IEEE Transactions on Industrial Informatics*, 10(4), 2233–2243.

DAAD (2021). Master in Industrial Informatics – Specialisation Industrial Cyber-Physical Systems. DAAD German Academic Exchange Service [Online]. Available at: https://www2. daad.de/deutschland/studienangebote/international-programmes/en/detail/4775/ [Accessed 22 February 2021].

DIN (2016). DIN SPEC 91345: Reference Architecture Model Industrie 4.0 (RAMI4.0). DIN Std. DIN SPEC, 91(345), 04 [Online]. Available at: https://www.din.de/en/ wdc-beuth:din21:250940128 [Accessed 21 February 2021].

EHEA (2018). Appendix III: Overarching framework of qualifications of the European higher education area (revised 2018) [Online]. Available at: http://www.ehea.info/Upload/document/ministerial_declarations/EHEAParis2018_Communique_AppendixIII_952778.pdf [Accessed 22 February 2021].

Filho, W.L., Raath, S., Lazzarini, B., Vargas, V.R., de Souza, L., Anholon, R., Quelhas, O.L.G., Haddad, R., Klavins, M., Orlovic, V.L. (2018). The role of transformation in learning and education for sustainability. *Journal of Cleaner Production*, 199, 286–295 [Online]. Available at: https://www.sciencedirect.com/science/article/pii/S0959652618319834X.

Givehchi, O., Landsdorf, K., Simoens, P., Colombo, A.W. (2017). Interoperability for industrial cyber-physical systems: An approach for legacy systems. *IEEE Transactions on Industrial Informatics*, 13(6), 3370–3378.

Götting, M., Gosewehr, F., Müller, M., Wermann, J., Zarte, M., Colombo, A.W., Pechmann, A., Wings, E. (2017). Methodology and case study for investigating curricula of study programs in regard to teaching industry 4.0. *IEEE 15th International Conference on Industrial Informatics (INDIN)*, 533–538.

Haskamp, H., Meyer, M., Möllmann, R., Orth, F., Colombo, A.W. (2017). Benchmarking of existing OPC UA implementations for Industrie 4.0-compliant digitalization solutions. *IEEE 15th International Conference on Industrial Informatics (INDIN)*, 589–594.

Hecklau, F., Orth, R., Kidschun, F., Kohl, H. (2017). Human resources management: Meta-study-analysis of future competences in Industry 4.0. *Proceedings of the International Conference on Intellectual Capital, Knowledge Management & Organizational Learning*, 163–174.

Johnston, L.F. (2013). *Higher Education for Sustainability: Cases, Challenges, and Opportunities from Across the Curriculum*. Routledge, New York.

Leitão, P., Pires, F., Karnouskos, S., Colombo, A.W. (2020). Quo Vadis Industry 4.0? Position, trends, and challenges. *IEEE Open Journal of the Industrial Electronics Society*, 1, 298–310.

Mäkiö-Marusik, E., Ahmad, B., Harrison, R., Mäkiö, J., Colombo, A.W. (2018). Competences of cyber physical systems engineers – Survey results. *IEEE Industrial Cyber-Physical Systems (ICPS)*, 491–496.

Mäkiö-Marusik, E., Colombo, A.W., Mäkiö, J., Pechmann, A. (2019a). Concept and case study for teaching and learning industrial digitalization. *Procedia Manufacturing*, 31, 97–102 [Online]. Available at: https://www.sciencedirect.com/science/article/pii/S2351978919303798.

Mäkiö-Marusik, E., Azmat, F., Ahmad, B., Harrison, R., Colombo, A.W. (2019b). Evaluation instrument for engineering modules and courses. *IEEE 17th International Conference on Industrial Informatics (INDIN)*, 1139–1144.

Motyl, B., Baronio, G., Uberti, S., Speranza, D., Filippi, S. (2017). How will change the future engineers' skills in the Industry 4.0 framework? A questionnaire survey. *Procedia Manufacturing*, 11, 1501–1509.

Nafea, R.M.E.D. and Toplu, E.K. (2021). Future of education in industry 4.0: Educational digitization – A Canadian case study. *Research Anthology on Digital Transformation, Organizational Change, and the Impact of Remote Work*, 1977–1997.

Pechmann, A., Wermann, J., Colombo, A.W., Zarte, M. (2019). Using a semi-automated job-shop production system model to prepare students for the challenges of Industrial Cyber-Physical Systems. *Procedia Manufacturing*, 31, 377–383.

Platform-I40 (2020). Details of the asset administration shell part 1 – The exchange of information between partners in the value chain of Industrie 4.0 [Online]. Available at: https://www.plattform-i40.de/PI40/Redaktion/DE/Downloads/Publikation/Details_of_the_ Asset_Administration_Shell_Part1_V3.html.

Porrmann, T., Essmann, R., Colombo, A.W. (2017). Development of an event-oriented, cloud-based SCADA system using a microservice architecture under the RAMI4.0 specification: Lessons learned. *IECON 2017 – 43rd Annual Conference of the IEEE Industrial Electronics Society*, 3441–3448.

QAA (2019a). Subject benchmark statement: Computing [Online]. Available at: https:// www.qaa.ac.uk/docs/qaa/subject-benchmark-statements/subject-benchmark-statement-computing.pdf?sfvrsn=ef2c881_10 [Accessed 24 February 2021].

QAA (2019b). Subject benchmark statement: Engineering [Online]. Available at: https:// www.qaa.ac.uk/docs/qaa/subject-benchmark-statements/subject-benchmark-statement-engineering.pdf?sfvrsn=1f2c881_16 [Accessed 24 February 2021].

Salas, E., Goodwin, G.F., Burke, C.S. (2009). *Team Effectiveness in Complex Organizations: Cross-Disciplinary Perspectives and Approaches*. Routledge, New York.

Stankovic, J.A., Sturges, J.W., Eisenberg, J. (2017). A 21st century cyber-physical systems education. *Computer*, 50(12), 82–85.

Susto, G.A., Schirru, A., Pampuri, S., McLoone, S., Beghi, A. (2014). Machine learning for predictive maintenance: A multiple classifier approach. *IEEE Transactions on Industrial Informatics*, 11(3), 812–820.

Wermann, J., Kliesing, N., Colombo, A.W., Moraes, E.C. (2015). Impact of new ICT trends for the educational curriculum in the area of Industrial Automation and engineering. *IECON 2015 – 41st Annual Conference of the IEEE Industrial Electronics Society*, 003643–003648.

Wermann, J., Colombo, A.W., Pechmann, A., Zarte, M. (2019). Using an interdisciplinary demonstration platform for teaching Industry 4.0. *Procedia Manufacturing*, 31, 302–308 [Online]. Available at: https://www.sciencedirect.com/science/article/pii/S2351978919304123.

Young, A.T. (2015). Multidisciplinary research teams: A quantitative analysis of interventions and barriers to their success. PhD Thesis, Texas Tech University, Lubbock, TX.

Zabasta, A., Peuteman, J., Kunicina, N., Fedotov, A.K., Prylutskyy, Y., Fedotov, A.S. (2018). Development of industry oriented curricular on cyber physical systems for Belarusian and Ukrainian universities. *IEEE 6th Workshop on Advances in Information, Electronic and Electrical Engineering (AIEEE)*, 1–6.

Zarte, M., Pechmann, A., Wermann, J., Gosewehr, F., Colombo, A.W. (2016). Building an Industry 4.0-compliant lab environment to demonstrate connectivity between shop floor and IT levels of an enterprise. *IECON 2016 – 42nd Annual Conference of the IEEE Industrial Electronics Society*, 6590–6595.

Conclusion

Conclusion and Outlook

William Derigent[1], Olivier Cardin[2], and Damien Trentesaux[3]

[1] CRAN CNRS UMR 7039, University of Lorraine, Nancy, France
[2] LS2N UMR CNRS 6004, Nantes University, IUT de Nantes, France
[3] LAMIH UMR CNRS 8201, Université Polytechnique Hauts-de-France,
Valenciennes, France

C.1. An initiative of the French and international IMS community

This book is the first book around which the intelligent manufacturing systems (IMS) community, in particular its French laboratories, has come together to collaboratively produce a body of knowledge around industrial cyber-physical systems (ICPS). Long before the present book, many researchers had expressed their wish to be able to coordinate themselves in order to produce a common work, the essence of the work carried out by the community over the last 30 years. Indeed, as the Foreword expresses so well, industrial engineering has been progressing ever since the First Industrial Revolution, always being influenced by the technologies that support industrial systems. The introduction of infotronic technologies into workshops, from the first RFID chips to the Industrial Internet of Things, has led to a profound change in our vision of industrial systems, leading to ICPS and, consequently, to the conceptualization of new forms of control adapted to these systems. Even though it has accelerated in recent years, this evolution has nevertheless been slow, driven, on the one hand, by the evolution of technologies and, on the other hand, by the evolution of our economies, the two being ultimately closely linked.

This could certainly explain why the idea of writing a summary book has been in the minds of researchers for a long time, but has finally taken shape only now, in the

Digitalization and Control of Industrial Cyber-Physical Systems,
coordinated by Olivier Cardin, William Derigent and Damien Trentesaux.
© ISTE Ltd 2022.

form of this collection written by many hands; this is the time it takes to reach maturity. Following a general solicitation sent throughout France and abroad, numerous contributors of this book naturally came forward, conscious of the interest and the urgency that there was to devote a complete work to the digitalization and the control of the ICPS. We would like to thank all the authors who participated in this adventure, both for the time they have devoted to it and for the quality of their chapters.

C.2. A work designed as a bedside book

The primary objective of this book was to produce a reference for Master's or PhD students who wish to familiarize themselves with the notions related to ICPS, for teachers and researchers who wish to widen their knowledge of the concepts, for industrialists who wish to discover the applicative potential of the ICPS concept, or simply for people who are curious about what an ICPS is. The construction of this book has been deliberately broad, dealing horizontally with all aspects of an ICPS as well as with examples of applications, so that it can be approached in different ways.

Part 1 is indeed a good entry point for all those looking for general concepts related to ICPS and their potential impacts on sustainable transition. PhD students might read it for example to clarify/understand the concepts. Captivated by this reading, students who wish to better understand the functions of ICPS will then dive into the following more specialized, parts, that deal with complementary issues (Parts 2–5). Depending on the problem they are dealing with, students will have reduced their reading to just those sections of interest. The industrialist interested in ICPS will most likely have had a completely different reading experience. They have most probably started by learning about the impact that these systems could have on their field or even on their application case before having gone deeper into the concepts. In this sense, they most likely started with Part 7. Thus, the division of this book into almost independent parts simplifies the reading and makes it a bedside book as well as a reference book where the search for information will be quick and relevant.

C.3. Towards the future of ICPS: people, training and ethics

For the first time in its evolution, humankind is massively implementing so-called "intelligent" systems, equipped with more advanced learning and reaction capabilities. The design approach of these systems is necessarily multidisciplinary, by questioning the designer not only on the environmental aspect but also on the safety and regulatory aspects. This design must therefore be addressed in new dedicated training courses. Moreover, these intelligent systems question human beings on their own cognitive capacities as well as on the consequences that this could have on their freedom and security. Mechanization has deprived them of their physical strength, automation of part of their memory, and this latest revolution could even take away their decision-making power, leading them to question their usefulness in the end. Rabelais said long ago that "science without conscience is but the ruin of the soul". It is therefore essential to design the future of ICPS by developing ethical concepts in industrial systems, where human beings must be put back at the center of the loop. For these systems are first and foremost there to serve humans and not the other way around.

List of Authors

Bilal AHMAD
University of Warwick
Coventry
United Kingdom

Freeha AZMAT
University of Warwick
Coventry
United Kingdom

Eric BALLOT
Physical Internet Chair
MINES ParisTech
PSL Research University
Centre de gestion scientifique
i3 UMR CNRS 9217
Paris
France

Thierry BERGER
LAMIH UMR CNRS 8201
Université Polytechnique
Hauts-de-France
Valenciennes
France

Theodor BORANGIU
University Politehnica of Bucharest
Romania

Olivier CARDIN
LS2N UMR CNRS 6004
Nantes University
IUT de Nantes
France

Armando Walter COLOMBO
Institute for Industrial Informatics,
Automation and Robotics (I2AR)
University of Applied Sciences Emden/Leer
Emden
Germany

Catherine DA CUNHA
LS2N UMR CNRS 6004
Ecole Centrale de Nantes
France

William DERIGENT
CRAN CNRS UMR 7039
University of Lorraine
Nancy
France

Maria DI MASCOLO
Université Grenoble Alpes
CNRS
Grenoble INP, G-SCOP
France

Yasamin ESLAMI
LS2N UMR CNRS 6004
Ecole Centrale de Nantes
France

Frank FLEMISCH
Institute of Industrial Engineering
and Ergonomics
RWTH Aachen University
and
Fraunhofer Institute for Communication
Information Processing and Ergonomics
Wachtberg
Germany

Franck FONTANILI
Université de Toulouse – IMT Mines Albi
Industrial Engineering Department (CGI)
Albi
France

Antoine GALLAIS
LAMIH UMR CNRS 8201
Université Polytechnique
Hauts-de-France
Valenciennes
France

Youcef IMINE
LAMIH UMR CNRS 8201
Université Polytechnique
Hauts-de-France
Valenciennes
France

Gerrit JAN VELTINK
Institute for Industrial Informatics,
Automation and Robotics (I2AR)
University of Applied Sciences Emden/Leer
Emden
Germany

Laurent JOBLOT
Arts et Metiers Institute of Technology
LISPEN
HESAM University
UBFC
Chalon-Sur-Saône
France

Sylvie JONAS
Partner Cabinet AGIL'IT
Paris
France

Stamatis KARNOUSKOS
SAP
Walldorf
Germany

Nathalie KLEMENT
Arts et Métiers Institute of Technology
LISPEN
HESAM University
Lille
France

Mariam LAFKIHI
Physical Internet Chair
MINES ParisTech
PSL Research University
Centre de gestion scientifique
i3 UMR CNRS 9217
Paris
France

Françoise LAMNABHI-LAGARRIGUE
CNRS Emeritus Research Director
Signals and Systems Laboratory
CentraleSupelec
Université Paris-Saclay
France

Paulo LEITÃO
Research Centre in Digitalization and
Intelligent Robotics (CeDRI)
Instituto Politécnico de Bragança
Portugal

Mario LEZOCHE
CRAN CNRS UMR 7039
University of Lorraine
Nancy
France

Patrick MARTIN
Arts et Métiers Institute of Technology
University of Lorraine
HESAM University
LCFC
Metz
France

John MBULI
Bombardier Transport France
Alstom Group
Saint-Ouen
France

Octavian MORARIU
Centre of Research in Robotics and CIM
Bucharest
Romania

Maroua NOUIRI
LS2N UMR CNRS 6004
Nantes University
IUT de Nantes
France

Marie-Pierre PACAUX-LEMOINE
LAMIH UMR CNRS 8201
Université Polytechnique
Hauts-de-France
Valenciennes
France

Shenle PAN
Physical Internet Chair
MINES ParisTech
PSL Research University
Centre de gestion scientifique
i3 UMR CNRS 9217
Paris
France

Silviu RĂILEANU
University Politehnica of Bucharest
Romania

Yves SALLEZ
LAMIH UMR CNRS 8201
Université Polytechnique
Hauts-de-France
Valenciennes
France

Ali SIADAT
Arts et Métiers Institute of Technology
University of Lorraine
HESAM University
LCFC
Metz
France

André THOMAS
Retired

Philippe THOMAS
CRAN CNRS UMR 7039
University of Lorraine
Nancy
France

Damien TRENTESAUX
LAMIH UMR CNRS 8201
Université Polytechnique
Hauts-de-France
Valenciennes
France

Index

Printed and bound by CPI Group (UK) Ltd, Croydon, CR0 4YY

27/10/2024

14580238-0004